BEYOND FUNDAMENTALISM

BEYOND
FUNDAMENTALISM

Daniel B. Stevick

JOHN KNOX PRESS ■ Richmond, Virginia

Library of Congress Catalog Card Number: 64-10645

Except where otherwise indicated, Scripture quotations are from the Revised Standard Version, copyright 1946 and 1952 by the Division of Christian Education of the National Council of Churches of Christ in the United States of America.

Printed in the United States of America

8281

CONTENTS

*Let every man praise the bridge
that carries him over.*

English Proverb

INTRODUCTION

This is an essay in friendly polemic.

The book grows out of a series of letters written to friends over a period of five years or so. The letters are part of a conversation going on within a group of people who are trying by discussion to examine, defend, oppose, alter, understand, or, in some cases, escape from Fundamentalism. A contact with the Fundamentalist movement and a willingness to inquire are the points in common among the participants. Some members of the discussion would be proud to be known as Fundamentalists; many others are critical of the movement in one degree or another; and some are outside it altogether. But all, for one reason or another, find it a subject of personal interest. These letters were a contribution to this amicable but lively exchange of ideas.

The letters, with some of their informal, personal, occasional aspect retained, are now put together. In taking or changing an attitude toward Fundamentalism, personal rather than academic considerations are usually determinative—hence this somewhat personal rather than purely academic book.

A well-informed friend—a student of social history—hearing that I was preparing something on Fundamentalism, asked if that were not a long-dead subject. As a matter of public notice, it is. The classic Fundamentalist-Modernist controversy is no longer the ultimate—nor even the penultimate—chapter in the history of American religious thought. The original, colorful leaders are gone, and Mencken is no longer here to report on them. But when they stopped making national headlines, the Fundamentalists did not expire. And for the hundreds of thousands of us whose religious life has been influenced by the institutions and personalities of the still vigorous Fundamentalist movement and for whom this influence has been (with whatever qualifications) a means of grace, this subject remains as contemporary and as absorbing as any could be.

In fact, the topic of Fundamentalism is under more general discussion now than it has been for decades. The conversation represented by these letters is being occasioned very largely by the emergence within Fundamentalism of a new stirring of scholarship and self-criticism. This movement is unorganized. Its representatives try to avoid giving themselves any party label. They represent a significant troubling of the waters, and these letters have tried to give them due recognition. The issue of Fundamentalism was, after all, a pretty tired dispute until they began to give it new and altered interest.

A word about the *dramatis personae* of this epistolary conversation:

The participants other than the writer and Theophilus will be recognized as names from St. Paul's catalog of friends in Romans 16.

The "Theophilus" of these letters is something of an amalgam of several of my original correspondents—most of them quite critical of Fundamentalism, but most of them still much closer to it than I am. The name "Theophilus" is not intended merely as a literary echo of St. Luke; I can assume on the part of the readers whom I have in mind a personal interest in the Fundamentalist version of Christianity, a willingness and an ability to think, and a paramount concern for the Christian Gospel. They are lovers of God, "theophiloi," and my argument is addressed to them as such.

"Spermologos" may not have so much to recommend him. This name is the contemptuous term used of St. Paul by the sophisticated Athenians. It is translated "babbler" in the Authorized Version, but it is, literally, "seed-picker," one who gathers and purveys odd scraps of information—"an ignorant plagiarist," says Souter; others suggest "gossip," "chatterer," "parasite," "hanger-on," "literary idler," "a man with a smattering of secondhand ideas." Perhaps this is as much authority as I can properly claim for the judgments offered here. Little in this book is original with me, and yet I can speak for no one but myself. Nonetheless, it is some small comfort to think that of the titles of the greatest of the Apostles there is at least one that I can share.

It is my hope that no more than these assumptions about the writer and the reader is necessary to provide the material for a bridge across a chasm of misunderstanding. It is a bridge across which I have traveled. I hope I have not yet forgotten the landmarks on both sides, or the way they look from the opposite side, or the way they look from part way across.

I

THE
HISTORICAL
SITUATION

Historical-mindedness is so much a preconception of modern thought that we can identify a particular thing only by pointing to the various things it successively was before it became that particular thing which it presently will cease to be.

CARL BECKER

THE
INTERNAL DIALOGUE

O Theophilus,

You remarked in your last letter about the rash of articles and books which seems in one way or another to indicate a Fundamentalist "renascence" and an awareness of this new show of life by the theological world outside Fundamentalism. I guess the thing you have in mind is pretty widely observable. Fundamentalism had become only a fading memory in many quarters. Now, unexpectedly, writers and speakers of the "conservative" wing are saying things of significance which are creditably presented and obviously addressed to an outside audience. They are more aware than they were of opinion beyond their own circles, and they often show some appreciation for the thinking of those they oppose. On the other hand, respectful notice is occasionally being taken of Fundamentalism by the non-Fundamentalist press. You noticed that Carnell, Ramm, and Jewett have written for the *Christian Century*. How long has it been since anything like that has happened? I think I sent you Chad Walsh's appreciative editorial on youth work methods written some time ago after a visit to a Young Life Camp. The work of the I.V.C.F. has provoked Fr. Hebert to try an irenic polemic, *Fundamentalism and the Church*. This in turn has elicited one full-scale reply already, *"Fundamentalism" and the Word of God*, by J. I. Packer. Yes, I thought Sherman Roddy's article was good.[1]

The list of such notices could be extended. A real conversation struggles to begin where there has been only silence and suspicion for many years.

You asked what I thought was behind all this.

I don't suppose there is any one simple cause. Many things—personalities, occasions, thought currents—are involved. But if I were to try to trace what I think are the reasons, I would say that conversation is now possible and apparently under way because two sides are in a position to listen more appreciatively and to speak more understandably to each other than they could a decade or two ago. The dynamics of Fundamentalism and the dynamics of Liberalism have moved both of the groups into phases which change the issues that once defined their separateness. Two groups formerly so widely apart that conversation was impossible are now close enough together for at least an occasional "halloo." There seems to be some uncertainty on both sides as to whether these should be in a friendly tone or not—previous communications between the groups have been pretty hostile. But the possibility of continued conversation seems to be present and likely to remain present. And we can hope for the best in its future course.

But I go too rapidly. Though your question was about the present, an answer must start with the past. We must look into some history. In the past, few Fundamentalists have had a vantage from which to view their own religious position. They have not realized that it has an inner history—a short one. Neither have they seen their own movement as a part of the flow of social, religious, and intellectual currents. They have not recognized its historical conditioning. Instead, they have equated it uncritically with "New Testament Christianity" (in which they also fail to see any inner history or outer conditioning). Knowing it only from within, they have accepted the form of their religion as the absolute pattern into which all that is really Christian must fit. It is surely noteworthy that the only two histories of the Fundamentalist movement—by Cole and Furniss—have been written from quite unsympathetic points of view. Defenders of Fundamentalism have not written of it historically. However, Carl F. H. Henry's recent lectures *Fifty Years of Protestant Theology* and *Evangelical Responsibility in Contemporary Theology*,[2] and a few similar studies, seem to show a new critical attempt by Fundamentalists to see Fundamentalism in context. So we may find a brief sketch of history useful.

I. THE RISE OF AN ORGANIZED MOVEMENT

Around the turn of the century the conventional form of the Christian faith was seriously challenged. Let me summarize this familiar story. The challenge came from several sources almost simultaneously. The new geology vastly extended the known age of the earth. The application of scientific principles to the investigation of the Bible was upsetting cherished notions of its composition and distinctiveness. The evolutionary hypothesis seemed to invalidate the Genesis stories and to destroy the uniqueness and dignity of man—it defined man by his relation to the animal level rather than by his relation to the divine. Anthropological discoveries made it seem that the teachings of the Bible, rather than being uniquely God's Word, were a part of a rather generally diffused human wisdom. The idealism of the prevalent philosophies blurred the particularity of the Gospel record and made its proclamation of a radical redemption seem unnecessary and rather crude. These new conceptions seemed to arise together and to sweep all before them. At the same time, radical social thought was gaining a following. Further, from many quarters the long-accepted ethical standards which had been derived in great measure from the Christian faith were attacked as dated, unnatural, and oppressive. With the rise of Darwin, Huxley, Spencer, Marx, Nietzsche, and Freud, it seemed that all the pieties were on the defensive. The ax was laid unto the root of the trees.

For some reason, the violent form of the reaction to this challenge came late in this country. Both here and abroad some Christian thinkers had been living with the new ideas for quite a while on more or less peaceful terms. They had found it possible to reconcile their faith with the new scientific discoveries. There were loose ends, to be sure. Some unnecessary compromises were made; some compartmentalizing devices saved the day for unsettled minds; and with the rapid opening of new fields of knowledge, some people, not necessarily lacking in courage, remained wisely and selectively agnostic. The immediate shock seemed to be taken up. But, just after the turn of the century, two groups in America seemed to agree, in their different ways, that reconciliation was impossible. One had to choose the old religion or modern thought.

To one group of religious thinkers, the new learning was simply overwhelming; it reduced much of the old faith to superstition. If Christianity were to be salvaged at all, its content would have to be determined by the "modern mind." So a "Modernist" version of Christianity emerged which retained many of the inherited categories and terms but with their distinctive meanings deeply compromised. To its critics, this all seemed a hasty capitulation. "Modernism" seemed to them to be an answer to the illegitimate question "How little of the traditional beliefs can we retain and still call ourselves Christians?" This is probably unfair to the motives of the Modernists. The times were difficult. And the new, "reduced" Christianity was undoubtedly adopted after struggle by many people as the only way in which they could retain a religious attitude toward life and duty in a world in which science and positivism were calling the dance.

But extremes beget extremes. Other religious thinkers chose to meet the threat by a tactic of "massive resistance." They attempted to preserve the familiar orthodoxies at every point. All of the old was right; all of the new was wrong.

Some of those whose conservative instincts led them to this way of responding discovered enough common ground to enable them to form a readily identifiable movement in American church life —the movement which came in time to be called "Fundamentalism."

The latest authoritative survey of the subject traces the origin of the World Christian Fundamentals Association to a conference held in 1916. From that meeting came a call to the movement— a call whose tone was an eloquent indication of the mood of the time. The conference announced, "The time has come for a correlation of the orthodox conservative forces yet found in the Churches."[3] This wording implies that the situation is already far gone, and the few remaining orthodox Christians must stand together.

The World Christian Fundamentals Association, which came into being in 1919 in answer to this call, became the leading co-ordinating organization of the movement. Some of the leaders of the movement were W. B. Riley, R. A. Torrey, Charles G. Trumbull, James M. Gray, J. C. Massee, L. W. Munhall, J. Frank Norris, Harold Roach Stratton, Gerald Winrod, T. T. Shields, Paul Rader, and Bob Shuler (still names to conjure with in sections of Fundamentalism). The popular lay leader and national spokesman for the movement was William Jennings Bryan. Such organizations as *The Sunday School Times,* the Bible Institute of Los Angeles, and the Moody Bible Institute participated. Many Bible conferences, large and small, were organized. One of the earliest and best known was at Billy Sunday's summer home in Winona Lake, Indiana. Scores of periodicals were begun (many of them short-lived). And hundreds of books were written to popularize the convictions of the group and to attack its enemies.

The movement seems to have gotten the name "Fundamentalism" from the series of booklets entitled *The Fundamentals: A Testimony to the Truth,* printed in twelve paperbound volumes between 1909 and 1915, and given wide distribution throughout the English-speaking world. The essays in this collection are, on the whole, well written, well argued, and quite responsible. They make their case for "the fundamentals," as their writers saw them, with a sense of urgency but without shrillness and abuse of opposing ideas. They discuss a wide range of apologetic, theological, and biblical topics, such as the virgin birth, religion and science, and the new cults. Carl Henry notices that among the contributors to *The Fundamentals* there was no insistence on complete agreement.[4] He further judges that present-day Fundamentalism shows a decline from the standard represented by these booklets, into a reactionary mood in which the gift for scholarly apologetic has been largely lost. Perhaps the freedom and breadth of the thinking of the contributors might be attributed to the nurturing of many of them—for example, Warfield, Orr, Griffith Thomas, Kyle, Moorehead, Morgan, Moule— in the great traditions of theology. But when the Fundamentalist leadership rejected continuity with the great traditions, the movement became inevitably narrowed and defensive.

The "fundamentals" were generally designated as: the inerrancy of the Bible; the virgin birth and the physical resurrection of Jesus Christ; a substitutionary theory of the atonement; and the imminent, physical second coming of Christ. These "five points" were critical points at this turn in thought. A strict biblical literalism could admit no compromise or redefinition at these places, and the new immanentistic Liberalism sought its redefinition on just these doctrines.

These "fundamentals" do not define Christianity. They were

not the points at issue during the era of the Fathers when the Trinity and the incarnation were disputed as the church sought to interpret to itself its own Gospel. These were not the points raised by the Reformers either—in fact, as Carnell has pointed out, justification by faith does not appear among the "fundamentals," and all five of them are also held by the Church of Rome.[5] The line of defense was chosen in the early 1900's just at the strategic places where the new thinking was challenging the literalist interpretations. In defining itself on these points, a given theology declares what, in its eyes, seems to be the true relation between God and the world. So Fundamentalism defined itself over against the rising Modernism rather than in relation to the central Christian affirmations. Its stance was essentially negative—to oppose Modernism. The security of an accepted way of thinking and believing was threatened, and a defense line along the points of attack seemed all-important.

From its early days, another mark of the Fundamentalist movement was its interest in eschatology. The apocalyptic element in the Bible—the visions of the end, the day of judgment, Christ's coming in the clouds, the saints on their thrones—was particularly uncongenial to the new Idealism. Yet it was so inescapably biblical that the biblicists championed it. In fact, they found this dramatic picture of cosmic struggle taking on new significance in the light of their situation. They saw themselves as champions of light in a climactic struggle with "apostasy." While a premillennial eschatology was not shared by all of the groups related to Fundamentalism, it did characterize the movement to a marked degree. The feeling that "these are the last days" that the "signs of the times" can be discerned was prevalent. The Niagara Prophecy Conferences, dating back into the late 1800's, were among the first of the organized movements that led into Fundamentalism. And the "dispensational" scheme of the Plymouth Brethren, popularized by the Schofield Bible of 1909, with its Christendom-denying, world-denying, "losing-team" eschatology, became almost everywhere a distinctive mark of the movement.

The conservative vs. liberal bifurcation which we have been tracing is a normal human reaction whenever established ways are challenged. Perhaps the remarkable thing about the Fundamentalist-Modernist controversy is that in most respects, and in a relatively short time, the conservatives lost! The more usual thing (especially in religion) in such conflicts is for the safe, conservative pressures to be the stronger and for groups representing "the newer thinking," regardless of the merits of their case, to be forced into schism. The statesmanship on both sides in 1900-1930 led to a different outcome.

II. TWO PHASES: THE FIRST GENERATION, 1900-1930

A kind of "anatomy of revolution" can be traced in the organized life of Fundamentalism—the first-generation phase and the second-generation phase. We must look first at the first generation.

The earliest leaders of Fundamentalism were, for the most part, active members of one of the larger established denominations. Riley, Shields, and Norris were Baptists; Machen, Erdman, R. D. Wilson, and Bryan were Presbyterians; Shuler was a Methodist; Gray, a Reformed Episcopalian; Torrey, a Congregationalist. In many cases they were pastors of influential churches or teachers in seminaries. They felt the threat of "Modernism" in terms of loyalty to their churches, so this became a period of intradenominational discord. The Fundamentalist program then was to resist what seemed to be the calculated infiltration of seminary faculties, mission boards, or denominational offices by persons with dangerous leanings.

It was a time of freewheeling crusades and grandiose claims. As Furniss puts it:

> The leaders of the movement often used martial symbols to describe the controversy, but in their minds it was not a skirmish on the periphery of theology, a duel between a crusader and an infidel. Rather it was a momentous engagement between two great armies for a victory of eternal significance.[6]

Wide-open controversy was at its height. The teaching of evolution in the public schools was energetically protested throughout this period. This aspect of the controversy reached its climax in the widely-reported Scopes trial of 1925. Impassioned efforts were made to block the election of certain officials or to oppose the actions of denominations. The period was marred by a violent, intemperate spirit.[7] And since animus of this kind is hard to confine, more than one leader of "conservative" religious forces in those years discredited his cause by associating it with anti-Semitic, anti-Catholic, nativist, or extreme right causes. The cleavage was well defined. Fundamentalism was something one had to be radically for or radically against.

You and I can just remember the last years of this period of intensity and severity, of acrimony and narrowness, of unchristian bitterness, division, passion, and fanaticism. It is characterized in my memory by extreme seriousness, hard-driving Gospel songs, inflamed speakers, and the messianic sense of a beleaguered remnant which was trying to keep an awful calamity from befalling the church and the nation. This was the time when Fundamentalists sought publicly to change the direction of things in church and society.

By about 1930, the situation was changing distinctly but gradually. The intradenominational battle had largely been lost. The Fundamentalist movement had captured not one major denominational body. Its agitations had led to schism in several churches (Baptist independent splinters came in the 20's and early 30's; the Presbyterian crisis led to schism in the years between 1926 and 1935), and the independent bodies formed in separation were living on their own. (The Independent Fundamental Churches of America, for example, began in 1930.) New seminaries had been formed, and the chain of Bible institutes had grown considerably. The new leadership was, for the most part, no longer affiliated with the larger denominations but with some independent body or with none at all. Thus the center of gravity in Fundamentalism shifted to its own institutions and into isolation from the affairs of the church at large. The Fundamentalist-Modernist issue came to be regarded as a regrettable past chapter for most denominational bodies.

And perhaps it would not be entirely frivolous to observe that the national "headquarters" (unofficial, of course) of Fundamentalism shifted from Philadelphia to Chicago.

III.   TWO PHASES: THE SECOND GENERATION, 1930-1960

By contrast, Fundamentalists of the second generation, of whom we now must speak, assume a situation of nondenominational (almost antidenominational) independency. (And whatever denominationally affiliated leaders do remain find their loyalty to their group deeply qualified.) Their problem is no longer that of crusading for the establishment of a church or a school in which biblical inerrancy can be freely taught. Rather, they work within institutions where "the fundamentals" have been the accepted standards for as long as they can remember. Their problem is one not of "coming out" and impressing others with the need for doing so but of conserving the convictions preserved by earlier separations. Their concern is not to establish a position over against its opposite; it is to nurture the people who have only known religious life within a Fundamentalist context. The new situation has produced internal changes.

This second-generation situation is partly responsible for making modern Fundamentalism become so "youthy." Since its task is to conserve a religious life brought up within its own institutions, its problem is pointed up most critically at the teen-age and college years, and its characteristic expressions have therefore changed from bitter doctrinal polemic to trombones, accordions, and entertainment. The songs are now choruses and appealing rhythmic, chromaticized Gospel songs. The smoothly led youth movements, with their calculated "cult of personality," that are now so characteristic of Fundamentalism are an attempt to deal on one level with this second-generation need. The present goal is not to separate but to attract and to hold.

Another aspect of the second-generation problem is the new search for status. The first generation scorned academic standards and "worldly" insignia of status. The anti-intellectualism of the movement was aggressive and unashamed.[8] Much learning was thought to lead to skepticism and atheism. The Fundamentalists of the first generation were content with the most unadorned worship and the starkest, prosiest publications. They seemed to hold that culture was a subtle evil. But the new generation is not content with this austere standard. (An atmosphere of "perpetual revolution" is impossible to sustain.) It wants what the first generation could only have regarded as compromises. The first generation saw itself over against the world; the second generation wants more acceptance by the world than the first generation would have thought healthy for the life of the spirit. Bible Schools that once scorned accreditation are now becoming "Bible colleges" and adding courses leading to recognized degrees. Churches that only a few years ago would have nothing of a robed choir are now gowning their choirs and seeking some beauty, order, and dignity in worship. Cinder-block "tabernacles" are being replaced by brick and stone churches of permanence and some distinction.

In recent years Fundamentalists have been appealing to history for their side. Whereas a few years ago it was enough to say, "The Bible says . . ." now it is more common to hear, "Historic Christianity says . . ." This slight change, so generally observable, indicates a search for the support of a tradition and the preemption of some kind of theological middle position for Fundamentalist doctrines. The new phrase seems to imply a greater breadth of argumentative base. The works of older generations of conservatives, nurtured within the great theological traditions, are being reprinted to supply the largeness and richness lacking in the isolated Fundamentalist movement. Its spokesmen no longer want to represent a position on the extreme right; they want to be central and normative. Concern is being shown for the production by "evangelicals" of the kind of scholarly work that commands recognition. Just recently two journals have appeared—*Christianity Today* and the *Gordon Review;* these seem to be symptoms of a need to articulate the "conservative" position on a respectable level.

I think of *The Sunday School Times* as a representative popular journal of the first generation and *Christian Life* as representative of the second generation. Can you imagine serious reviews of "Gospel recordings" (country style and Western) appearing in the former? And would not the "Why I Left My Denomination" series that the *Times* ran many years ago seem irrelevant and contentious in the latter?

Quite obviously both emphases, the first-generation and the second-generation types of Fundamentalism, now coexist. There are still those who agitate the first-generation issues. The vitriolic attacks on the Revised Standard Version of the Bible and its translators, the pillorying of Billy Graham by his own exclusive right wing, the disruptive activities of the "apostles of discord," are a carry-over of issues of the type that stirred the first generation.[9] But the second-generation interests are certainly ascendant. The attempt to consolidate already-established institutions is everywhere to be noticed. The rate of new internal divisions has lessened. The new leadership is addressing itself to the new questions.

Perhaps I might observe here that, for the most part, the search for status has not led to participation in the institutions and organized life of non-Fundamentalist society so much as it has led to imitation of them by distinct movements. Fundamentalism has its own press, its own entertainment personalities, its own schools and accrediting associations, its own councils of churches.

IV. THE CRISIS IN THE SECOND GENERATION

The first generation of a protest movement is inevitably conversion- or decision-centered. In a sense it is evangelistic; it has a message on which it wants people to act. The contrast between the former and the latter states is its main religious emphasis. The second generation, led by those who have always known and accepted the Fundamentalist outlook, has a less dramatic and more long-term attitude. It is concerned not so much with conversion as with sanctification and conservation.

It is these second-generation interests that are stirring the waters in Fundamentalism now. For they are pointing up, I believe, significant deficiencies in the movement as it was inherited from the older generation. The shape of Fundamentalism has been so evangelistic, activistic, or revivalistic that it has given little attention to the means of sanctification. Worship, the sacraments, a sense of the Christian fellowship, continuity with the Christian heritage, counseling for troubled spirits, devotional depth, guidance for man in a bewildering social context, intellectual contact with culture—all these necessities for the nurture of the whole Christian have been missing. The great emphasis in Fundamentalism is on being "saved" and on being associated with others who are also "saved." The second generation is rightly wondering now, "Very well, I am, by our common definition, saved. Where do I go from here?" If the reply is, "Go and save others," the question might then be, "Yes, but what do we do with them or tell them to do?" I once heard Canon Raven remark that it is a great error to isolate the ministry of conversion from the total, varied life of the historic Christian community. To do so may frustrate the great stores of spiritual energy and commitment in new converts by providing too little to sustain them in responsible Christian living. It is an impoverished lot of converts, for example, whose spiritual life is to be nourished only on Gospel songs and choruses because their spiritual mentors had scrapped the great heritage of a profound hymnody, leaving it "behind in their denominational hymnals at the time they became independent."[10]

In isolating itself from the larger ecumenical church bodies, Fundamentalism isolated itself as well from the larger worldwide issues of our time. The movement became preoccupied with religion, and religion became trivialized by removal from a responsible social role.

I think that this general lack of the means for the sustenance of the long-term Christian life is being felt by many in Fundamentalism. They sense a need to recover the values lost in the first generation's radical break. They are realizing that the structure of society that has set standards and shaped status is not altogether arbitrary. They are seeing that the humanities and the sciences contain truth that is essential to Christian maturity. They are not only seeking status and intellectual depth, but to avoid a split in the conscience they are also working out a rationale to justify the status and the Christian intellectualism they seek. I sometimes think I detect among them a feeling that the Fundamentalist founders were not so much "conservatives" as "revolutionaries."

Among certain people who would not have questioned it a generation ago, "Fundamentalism" has become a bad word— "conservative" or "evangelical" (though I think neither is properly applicable) is much preferred. Groups which once enforced the Fundamentalist taboos now admit some criticism of them. Thoughtful spokesmen are rising who do not quote Harry Rimmer except to belittle his apologetic methods. Conservative groups in the Reformed traditions have had a point of view from which many of the vagaries of Fundamentalism have long been apparent, and criticism from this quarter is not a new thing. Those who have studied and read widely outside the Fundamentalist index realize that there are new problems in the world and an altered opposite party in theology. They are concerned that this realignment be heeded among "conservatives."

Perhaps it would not be far wrong to adapt the widely used phrase of two decades ago—"repentant Liberals"—and speak of a group of "repentant Fundamentalists." In 1934 W. M. Horton reported:

A teacher in a well-known liberal seminary said to me recently that hardly a sermon had been preached or a lecture delivered within its walls for a year which did not at some point go out of its way to take a crack at liberalism—and that in spite of the fact that most of these sermons and lectures were thoroughly liberal in all their presuppositions![11]

The situation has progressed far with respect to Liberalism since Horton made this observation. But perhaps now something like that might be said about at least a group of articulate leaders of "evangelicalism." When one reads Carnell's entry on "Fundamentalism" in the recent Living Age series, *A Handbook of Christian Theology,* or his critical sections in *The Case for Orthodox Theology,* or Carl Henry's second and fourth chapters in *Evangelical Responsibility in Contemporary Theology,* or much of the writing of A. W. Tozer, or Ramm's *The Christian View of Science and Scripture,* or when one observes much of the work from such centers as the Inter-Varsity Christian Fellowship, Fuller Seminary, Calvin and Gordon colleges, one becomes aware that there is a group of spokesmen who go out of their way to take a crack at Fundamentalism—and that in spite of the fact that most of their sermons, books, articles, and lectures are thoroughly Fundamentalist in all their presuppositions!

In 1950, just before I leaped over the wall, a discriminating member of the I.V.C.F. group in Madison, Wisconsin, told me something like this, "Our last four talks have all been largely critical of some aspect or other of Fundamentalism." I did not realize then how nearly he echoed the teacher who had spoken to W. M. Horton in another context fifteen years earlier.

I think the first evidence of self-criticism on the part of Fundamentalism that came to my attention was when, in the fall of 1946, an informal report was given a clandestine circulation from a small conference held that summer on the campus of Wheaton College. The conference had no official connection with the college and was quite hush-hush. It was called the "Christian Problems Conference," and it sought to evaluate honestly the impact (or lack of it) of Fundamentalism on the most vital areas of our society. The members of the conference were largely younger, thoughtful men, pretty much in what I am calling the second-generation position—with a background in Fundamentalism but with enough dissatisfaction with it to be

willing to look at it critically. The report listed internal divisions, anti-intellectualism, departmentalization of life, and social
irrelevance as points of weakness, and it indicated a spirit of surprisingly free and penetrating inquiry. I keep in my files a shabby
old carbon copy of this report, and I well remember my excitement when I first read it. For I saw so many of my half-formed
critical impressions articulated intelligently in the thinking of
this group. I was glad that someone had said these things out
loud—even if in this unpublicized way. Most of what is in the
report has been said better since, and the destructive diagnosis is
notably better than the constructive prescription. But I remember how these ideas all put together in one document came to me
as a veritable apocalypse in 1946.

In June of 1947 a strong article, "Can Fundamentalism Win
America?" was contributed to *Christian Life* by Harold John
Ockenga.[12] At that same time the *Christian Century* had run a
fine series on "Can Catholicism Win America?" "Can Secularism
Win America?" and "Can Protestantism Win America?"
Ockenga answers the question in his title by saying, "Categorically, no!" He scores the divisive spirit of the movement—"Frag-
mentation, segregation, separation, criticism, censoriousness,
suspicion, solecism, is the order of the day for fundamentalism."
He writes forcefully of the negative aloofness from social problems of worldwide urgency. And he cites some unethical practices,
"self-advertising," and irresponsibility that had brought disrepute
on the movement. His only hope lay in the work of the (then
rather new) National Association of Evangelicals. Ockenga's
pungent remarks, coming from within the Fundamentalist leadership, caused a stir at the time.

This flurry of self-criticism was further marked in 1947 by the
appearance of Carl Henry's slender book *The Uneasy Conscience
of Modern Fundamentalism*. The book is perceptive, and again
it had the grace and significance of coming from within the
respected leadership of the movement it criticizes. Unfortunately,
Henry's weighty style and erudition made such demands on the
readers that the book never was as popular as its substance
merited. In it Henry mainly inveighs against the withdrawal of
Fundamentalism from the redemptive relation to urgent social
ills which he finds to be properly native to the biblical and
evangelical outlook. He complains that the denunciation of

merely individual sins and the offer of a merely individual redemption is largely irrelevant to modern man. And he speaks
hopefully of "the evangelical uneasiness" which "is one of the
most promising signs of the times."

There have been events since these that are of at least equal
importance, for example, nationwide associations of conservatives
in the fields of science and theology were begun in the late 40's.
But these were a few of the indications that I was closest to, and
they suggest the stir of self-criticism.

I think that the willingness on the part of at least a few
leaders to use the term "Fundamentalist" in a pejorative sense
dates from about this time. Many younger leaders will now grant
the justice of some of the accusations made against Fundamentalism, but they dissociate themselves from this term and say,
"But you see, I am not a Fundamentalist." There is a curious
ambivalence in their sense of loyalty. One would think that as
soon as a person had been able to use the term "Fundamentalism"
with enough objectivity to give it an uncomplimentary overtone,
the power of the term (or movement) to command his allegiance
would be broken. But the position of these "repentant Fundamentalists" is such that they feel obliged to defend many aspects
of the movement with real vigor. They are in it and yet not in it;
they are critical of it, but they are still identified with it; they
regard it as terribly wrong, but they think of it as finely right.

V. PRESENT STRESSES

When I think of the present stresses within Fundamentalism,
I tend to see within the group several distinguishable subspecies.
Elements from at least four strains of American religion were
drawn into a unity by a common tactical sense of the best way in
which to meet a new threat. (1) *Evangelicalism*, the spiritual
descendent of the Wesleyan revivals, contributed an attitude, a
piety, a form of assumptions about what was normal in Christianity. It was warm, simple, biblical, experience-centered, and
individualistic. Surely this was the most immediate and important
of the ingredients of Fundamentalism. At its best, evangelicalism
was capable of vast earnestness and reality, of individual- and
society-transforming effectiveness. But its weakness was in an
inclination toward "sweetness," "preciousness"—toward what
Samuel Butler once called "brimstone and treacle." (2) *Puri-*

tanism from the beginning contributed the heritage on which most of the scholarly Fundamentalists drew. Its best representatives showed Reformed theology to be thorough, learned, and realistic. However, in decline, it became a sterile, rigid orthodoxy. (3) *Revivalism* colored much of Fundamentalism from the start—in fact, some of the important churches of the movement were gathered around once-itinerant evangelists who had settled into pastorates. Its activism, dash, individualism, simplified moral perspective, impatience with learning, conspicuous choristers, mass methods of evangelism, vigorous Gospel songs, and mercurial experience patterns were contributed directly to the rising Fundamentalist movement. (4) The *Plymouth Brethren* made a contribution out of all proportion to their numbers. Their style of disciplined devotion—broadly of the pietistic type, the creation of self-conscious cells of Christians—was much admired. And the dispensationalist eschatological scheme of the Darbyites was adopted with little alteration throughout much of Fundamentalism.

This alliance was never entirely peaceful. The Calvinist Puritans and the Arminian Wesleyans never reconciled their differences. The Reformed theologians, for the most part, rejected the eschatological views of the Plymouth Brethren. But both the Reformed tradition and the Plymouth Brethren joined in distrust of the professional "Hollywood" revivalists. Thus the multiple ancestry of Fundamentalism is evident in its family rifts.

However, these differences could go ignored and unresolved for the period of the first generation. As long as Fundamentalism was largely an action group, there could be the "intentional moratorium on discussing doctrinal differences" that Henry observed.[13]

But now this alliance is under stress. The crisis from within caused by the second generation is raising substantive questions and bringing into self-consciousness the differences among the groups. It would be safe to guess that the present situation cannot be permanent. The emphases that combined to make up the Fundamentalist movement are going in divergent directions. The unity among the groups has been of a largely pragmatic sort. It was never defined in what could be called a "theology" of the church or of the movement. The next few years should decide how much unity, if any, still remains.

I do not want to seem to say that Fundamentalism is dying. Most parts of it are in a vigorous state of health, and numerically it is growing steadily. I only want to say that its character is changing. It is losing one sense of identity and struggling to gain another.

This process is fascinating to watch. I enjoy speculating on how far the change has gone and in which direction it is heading. Through some venturesome leaders, certain sections of Fundamentalism are gaining a measure of freedom and are reaching out for a reestablished contact with Christendom at large. Some greater cordiality toward science and evolution seems to be permissible now. A cautiously liberal social outlook is increasingly common. All in all, significant currents are stirring where critics had expected only stagnation. I do not mean that the great bulk of the constituency of Fundamentalism is changing its ways; I am quite sure it is not. One must always distinguish between popular Fundamentalism, which is seldom scholarly, and scholarly Fundamentalism, which is seldom popular. What is true of one is likely to be untrue of the other. Yet they are parts of a complex of groups which still recognize and fraternize with one another. Thus far the self-criticism of which I speak has been confined to the scholars. And their slightest move in the direction of freedom is opposed by their own friends from the farther right. So I only mean to say that on the part of some persons there is now the desire for intelligent, cordial conversation as there has not been for some time past. Moreover, the outside notice which Fundamentalism has been receiving lately suggests the reawakening of a dialogue where formerly people were talking only to themselves.

Our friend Epaenetus writes, "There is in Fundamentalism today, as there was not twenty years ago, a humility, a desire for *rapprochement,* a readiness to acknowledge error and to change . . ." Insofar as what he says is true (and he is in a position to know), interesting and creative times lie ahead for many earnest Christians.

Cordially,
Spermologos

THE
EXTERNAL DIALOGUE

O Theophilus,

Of course. The fear you express at the end of your letter might come true. The new readiness to converse on the part of Fundamentalism might meet with no response. But, as I hinted before, I do not think that will happen. Let me indicate why I think that from the non-Fundamentalist side, too, there may be a possibility for genuine dialogue.

Until recently the apologists for Fundamentalism were so intent on keeping the old, familiar, simple issues alive that they were years behind in observing one of the great turns in the history of Christian thought. (You will recall that even in the late 40's it was hard to find any of our teachers who had read, firsthand, Barth, Niebuhr, or Tillich, so we finally had to read them for ourselves.) If you want to look into contemporary theology, you must dismiss preconceptions, do your own investigating, and judge for yourself. Learning about the modern theological world has for many of us been accompanied by some equally crucial unlearning.

I. THE RISE AND DECLINE OF LIBERALISM

The challenge presented by the new ideas of the second half of the 19th century was felt throughout Western Christendom. The Fundamentalists were not wrong in taking it seriously. They understandably looked for some "fundamentals" to which to cling. But in the face of "the new thinking," the Fundamentalist tactic of massive resistance was not the only choice open. Some Christians were ready to concede a great deal to the new sciences and to reformulate Christian doctrine along Hegelian and Darwinian lines. In its more "advanced" expressions the redefined Christianity of "Modernism" gave up many of the elements that keep the Christian Gospel in touch with the ultimate reaches of moral reality and in recognizable continuity with its classic meaning.

Its God was an immanent principle that worked toward goodness. Jesus was the most admirable embodiment so far of this divine principle. Its view of human nature was optimistic and its view of society utopian. It felt that man, being related essentially to God, was indefinitely perfectible. His obvious present injustice to his brother man was a bit of bestiality left over from his long ascent from the jungle. But since it was due largely to a faulty environment, the furtherance—in the spirit of Jesus—of educational, sanitary, social, and humanitarian work would reduce this lag—eventually, in fact, remove it. And we would have brought in the Kingdom of God. The Bible was the record of some of the more noteworthy of man's experiences thus far in quest of the divine. I hope that H. R. Niebuhr's classic sentence is not too threadbare yet: "A God without wrath brought men without sin into a kingdom without judgment through the ministrations of a Christ without a cross."[1]

This Liberal version of Christianity rose, first in Europe, then in England, and later in the United States during the last half of the 19th century. It never went unprotested, but it was undoubtedly in the ascendant in this country in the early 1900's. It was appealing to many of the best of the younger thinkers. Its greatest days were just before and just after World War I.

Between 1918 and 1930 new forces were stirring (again reaching this country from England and Germany, with modifications en route). By 1937, when Niebuhr wrote his famous epigram, he used past tenses. He was describing a waning epoch in Christian thought.

The story has been told many times of how and why the prevailing theological mood changed entirely between 1930 and 1940. Let me sketch some aspects of it here in the way in which you and I must learn about it—by titles, authors, and dates.

We may look first at a handful of volumes representing the recovery of Christian realism—signposts of an exciting turn in Christian thought.

In my mental calendar I have marked 1934 as a significant year. Three critiques of Liberalism appeared in that year. One of these, Walter Marshall Horton's *Realistic Theology,* is doubly interesting because it is a secondary work. That is, it describes the progress of a critical movement already well under way. The book is addressed to a question raised in an article by John Bennett in the preceding year: "After Liberalism—What?" Horton remarks:

> Professor John Bennett is right, I believe, when he says that "The most important fact about contemporary American theology is the disintegration of Liberalism." Disintegration is not too strong a word. The defeat of the liberals is becoming a rout.[2]

Horton develops a penetrating analysis of the "human predicament." And he sets the radical power to heal in the message of traditional Christianity over against the disease of humanity.

Also in 1934 Edwin Lewis shook Methodism and Protestantism at large with his *Christian Manifesto*—still an eloquent book long after the battle tide has turned. It was an indictment of facile, this-worldly, utopian piety and a plea for the recovery of a lost dimension. He wrote:

> We cannot recover it [the New Testament faith] unless we can also recover the sense of sin, the sense of a great tragedy hanging over every human soul, the sense of an inward need that only God can meet, the sense of his incomprehensible grace in having provided for that need.[3]

In that same year, Reinhold Niebuhr wrote his *Reflections on the End of an Era.* This book announced the death—from constitutional defects—of a superficial Liberalism, and it pleaded for a more conservative and unsentimental theological outlook and at the same time a more progressive and uncomplacent social outlook. By the time of *Beyond Tragedy* in 1937, Niebuhr's own remaining idols had shown their feet of clay, and the religious dimension of evil was clearly evident. In *The Nature and Destiny of Man,* 1941, the doctrine of man's sin—in its individual and corporate, religious and social, implications—was completely rehabilitated as a vastly relevant part of theology. Niebuhr is probably the leading figure in this movement of thought. He is perhaps as near as we have ever gotten to a Christian with no illusions.

In England, D. R. Davies, much influenced by Niebuhr, wrote his powerful *On to Orthodoxy* in 1939. His book of ruthless analysis of the political aspects of the disease of sin, *The Two Humanities,* came out in 1940. His great little commentary on the General Confession, *Down Peacock's Feathers,* carries the story to 1942.

Like a refrain, "two world wars and a major depression in one generation" keeps ringing through the writings of this movement. The rising lines on the social graphs had not continued as plotted. The events of history had uncovered depths of human twistedness and self-deception that the Idealists had ignored. The notion of inevitable progress had been given a blow by world events of 1914-1945 from which it does not seem likely to recover under world conditions of atomic terror, 1945 to date.

Of course, Continental thought had been shaken as we had not been by World War I. Brunner's searching book on sin, *Man in Revolt,* was written in 1937 and translated in 1939. Berdyaev, with his Dostoievsky-like awareness of human lostness, wrote *The Destiny of Man* in 1937. And perhaps the most important landmark of all, Barth's *Romans,* written in 1918, was translated by Hoskyns in 1933. It was a trumpet call of the Word of God, an affirmation of his beyondness, his "otherness," and his summons to judgment and salvation.

The mention of Hoskyns suggests another line of thought fully as important as the recovery of realism—biblical theology. For it was Hoskyns and Davies' great book *The Riddle of the New Testament,* 1931, which showed the English world that, press the critical methods as you will, you always in the New Testament get back to an interpreted Christ, a theological affirmation, and a call to faith. Thus the ultimacy and determinative position of scientific criticism was denied, and the elucidation of the essential biblical message took its place as the paramount concern of biblical studies.

The reasons for the decline of Liberalism lie fully as much inside the churches as they do outside them. A change was not forced on reluctant theologians by the course of world events. It was a case of Christian thought looking to its own origins and recovering from the source its always-relevant good news.

Just listing a few early works here may suggest the men and the movement: C. H. Dodd, *The Apostolic Preaching,* 1936, and *History and the Gospel,* 1938; Newton Flew, *Jesus and His*

Church, 1938; T. W. Manson, *The Teaching of Jesus,* 1931; Vincent Taylor, *Jesus and His Sacrifice,* 1937; J. S. Stewart, *A Man in Christ,* 1935. The list could be extended into the 40's and 50's to include the later work of C. H. Dodd and Vincent Taylor, the writings of Oscar Cullmann, A. G. Hebert, Alan Richardson, H. H. Rowley, and William Neil among English and European biblical theologians. And it might include Americans like John Wick Bowman, Floyd Filson, G. Ernest Wright, A. N. Wilder, John Bright, John Knox, Paul Minear, Bernhard Anderson, and Frederick Grant. All of these men give unreserved assent to the central biblical message of redemption in Christ, but at the same time they are fully at home with the critical views of the biblical documents. This combination is bewildering to Fundamentalists—it isn't supposed to be able to happen. But it has happened, and it has maintained itself for a longer period of time than any mere compromise could manage. This combination of faith and criticism is observable in *The Interpreter's Bible,* in which the exegetical and critical work on some of the books is "advanced" while at the same time the exposition may be a fine evangelical statement of the theological and religious message of the book under discussion.

Much of this whole turn of thought found its voice through the rediscovery of Søren Kierkegaard. His exposure of the complexity, the perversity, the exquisite disguises, the defiance, the elusiveness, and the utter need of grace of the human soul spoke with profound urgency to those who were finding Liberal idealism unrealistic. Behind much of recovered realism and recovered biblicism lies a Christian existential stance—which, in its demand for life and decision above understanding and system, only restates as a philosophically respectable position what vital religion has always said, without philosophical recognition. Theistic existentialism has reminded us that the need of the self, just because it is a self and not a thing, is a need beyond the reach of all biological, social, cultural, or psychological curatives. At a time when Liberalism was trying to worship abstractions spelled with capital letters, the prophetic insight of Kierkegaard, of Martin Buber, and of others (usually dependent on these two) helped rediscover the living God who—because he is an "I," a subject, and never an "it," an object—can never be enclosed in our schemes and systems.

It should be observed here, too, that even in its most heady days of popularity the effects of Liberalism were uneven. In 1907 Gore and Forsyth were replying to the "New Theology" in terms fully as trenchant as those used by the "repentant Liberals" of our generation. Scots like Denney and Mackintosh never lost their sense of sin and redemption. And in 1931 Bishop Temple was telling the students at Oxford that human nature is at heart not right, but wrong:

> The worst things that happen do not happen because a few people are monstrously wicked, but because most people are like us. When we grasp that, we begin to realize that our need is not merely for moving quietly on in the way we are going; our need is for radical change, to find a power that is going to turn us into somebody else. That is what the Gospel offers to do.[4]

Perhaps it need not be labored longer that the old optimism about human nature is shattered. Man's tragic lostness, the necessity of a divine intervention if he is to be saved, and the good news of his renewal through the life, death, and resurrection of Jesus Christ are affirmed by those who represent the best and most influential forces in today's theological thought. Breaks between periods of thought are never sharp, but original sin is now completely reestablished in creative theology—not by rote, nor by fashion, but by fire. For man's lostness, the most modern scheme of Christian thought offers nothing more, but nothing less, than the old message of redemption through Christ. It would be a remarkable person who could be equally enthusiastic about every aspect of modern theology. It is varied and free and has no single "party line." But original sin and divine redemption are no longer less-than-respectable doctrines. The life has been gone from Liberalism for at least twice the number of years that you and I have been theologizing.

This "resurgence of the Gospel"[5] seems to provide a common ground on the part of non-Fundamentalist theology for conversation with Fundamentalists. The old Modernism, with its uncomprehending grasp of the central message, could see nothing but the crudities in Fundamentalism. The early Fundamentalists, with their hostility to new thought and their resistance to accommodation, could see nothing but the heresy of Modernism. But times have changed—because people make history, and people are never static.

This point was well summarized by William Hordern:

The present situation may not prove stable. With non-fundamentalists coming to a new appreciation of orthodoxy and a new group of conservatives arising, there are evidences that the groups are once more approaching a position where they may at least have enough in common to engage once more in an exchange of ideas. Furthermore, a new theological generation is arising that no longer has conditioned responses to members of the other group.[6]

These are exciting days for those who are touched by this trend. The Spirit has much to say to the churches. A new conversation has such vast, unknown possibilities within it that it can be seen as a threat by the insecure as well as an opportunity by the mature. It seems to me that there is a readiness now that bodes rather well.

II. A CHRISTIAN CONVERSATION

Very well, a conversation is now possible. How is it going to be conducted? No one can say. I would like to think it can be a Christian conversation. But if so, it must be determined by the Gospel rather than by the wish to score against an opponent.

The best thing in Fundamentalism is its hold on the essential Gospel. It was wrong in thinking that some of the unfortunate institutional features of its ethos were necessarily linked to the preservation of the Gospel; it seemed intent on preserving too much. It was wrong in rejecting new insights from science and modern thought. But the movement was surely right in seeing the Gospel in peril—and in moving to defend and preserve it. If the fathers of Fundamentalism warned of a new paganism coming and of difficult times for faith and of calamities for the world, events have certainly proved them far more right than those who foresaw only a better world just ahead. Their message, unhappily, was not related creatively to the moral, political, and cultural human context, and their prophetic witness became irrelevant. But even in unbiblical escape from involvement, Fundamentalism was faithful to the biblical statement of the Gospel. The stress on evangelism and the unwearying missionary work are reminders of the importance to Fundamentalism of the redemptive message and vocation. The Fundamentalist may be admired for his insistence on personal Christian experience, for his dedication, and for his willingness to be courageously different from his society because of his faith. These qualities have sometimes been accompanied by spiritual bullying and articulated in a belligerent spirit. But at its best the religion of Fundamentalism has ministered a deep personal devotion in which saintliness is not uncommon and the paramount demands of the biblical Gospel are humbly recognized.

The best thing about the renewed life of the ecumenical church is its recovery of the Gospel. Even in their days of greatest domination by secular beliefs, Liberals retained a profound loyalty to Jesus. Jesus was to them the disclosure of God; he was critic of the Bible, of the Christian, and of Christendom. The Liberals kept the "Jesus only" emphasis learned from Evangelicalism, and their devotion to it was creditable. Whatever may have been the state of their creedal orthodoxy, they never committed the ultimate heresy of presenting a Jesus who was uninteresting, unappealing, unlovely. The same could not always be said for their opposite numbers. The Liberals were always close to the Synoptic Gospels. But in the modern, repentant epoch the larger theological message of salvation has been recovered. The Gospels have been reunited with the Epistles. If the fathers of Liberalism warned that an individualistic, pietistic message, unrelated to the great political, social, and ideological issues of the day, was as good as no message at all, events have certainly proved them far more right than those who assumed that the impassioned proclamation of an individual salvation would solve racial, economic, and international tensions. Despite its doctrinal thinness, we are indebted to Liberalism for bringing Christian thinking into relevant and creative relation with the exciting horizons of modern thought and sensibility. This relation—as Liberalism rightly saw—is one in which Christianity has much to learn as well as much to contribute. Modernism may have conceded too much to the modern mind, but at least the Liberal emphases saw the forces shaping the modern mind as opportunities for Christian thought—and not merely as threats.

There may have been a kind of naïveté about some Liberal efforts to come to terms with secular thought, and a more profound grappling with the modern predicament may have been left to post-Liberal realism. But the very admission of the legitimacy of the task of matching positive Christian answers with deeply analyzed human questions is a Liberal contribution. To its everlasting credit, the Liberal movement broke down the exclusively religious and biblical preoccupation of evangelical thought and raised the problem of relevance. Post-Liberal realism, in reacting against the naïveté of preceding decades, may have fallen into perils of its own. It seems so afraid of a false optimism that its message is often more of sin than of salvation. Perhaps in its concern to avoid utopianism and sentimentalism, this realism has too easily made peace with an ethic of power. In its admirable concern for a message with social and political relevance (any other kind of message in our day being self-defeated), realism risks making the Gospel over into a program, and it regards too lightly the simplicity of life-changing personal religion. But it is the authentic biblical Gospel, and not less than the Gospel, that is its animating spirit. There are weakness and confusion and dissipated effort, but there is less uncertainty about the message than there has been for many years.

So, any conversation between the two groups can be, and should be, under this common biblical Gospel. It must be a conversation that listens and talks to the other party only after both have listened to God.

I find it hard to condemn or to approve either classic Fundamentalism or classic Modernism categorically. The effort would be largely academic anyway, for neither is present in its classic form of a generation ago. Both have "repented" in some measure. Each has learned something—not from the other, but from what the other represented. The issues in theology today have deep ties with both the liberal and the conservative emphases but are exactly determined by neither. In many ways, the best in modern theology has gone beyond Fundamentalism-Modernism.

It should be possible, then, for both parties—now chastened—to forget dated stereotypes and to engage creatively as fellow Christians in conversation in which issues are considered on their merits alone.

Fundamentalism has been largely ignored by the rest of the theological world. It is usually dismissed with a superior air as one of the opinions which of course no one really takes seriously nowadays. As a matter of fact, some form of Fundamentalism is still the faith of hundreds of thousands of Christians in this country and elsewhere. It cannot be ignored by any discussion intended to be fair and comprehensive. As Roddy put it, "The nature of the ecumenical responsibility does not allow this.

Rather, it demands that channels of communication be sought."[7] Furthermore, increasing numbers of Fundamentalists hold their convictions intelligently, and they are prepared to think. Thought must be answered with thought. The Fundamentalist arguments deserve more detailed examination than they are usually given—partly because of their merit as arguments and partly because of the new humility, sincerity, and intelligence with which they are being presented. Those who would be opponents of Fundamentalism must encounter the real thinkers of the movement rather than the "sitting ducks" of 1915—and they may find a disarming amount of agreement.

As for the other side, the Liberalism that is opposed by the Fundamentalist apologists is too often a kind of thought that was being discredited in its own circles twenty-five years ago. Popularly, the controversial remarks of the Fosdick of 1920 are still assailed from Fundamentalist pulpits. So here, too, conversation must be with real people and with their actual opinions, not with caricatures. Fundamentalism still has some important things to urge against its detractors. Some of the questions it has been raising about the Bible and theology are the right questions, and they are coming into their own. But the issue does not lie just where the Fundamentalists suppose it does. They have been out of the conversation for so long that they misconstrue what others are saying, and they often miss out on opportunities to make their own best points. They, too, might be pleasantly surprised to know what their opposite numbers are really saying these days.

Fundamentalists of the original generation seem never to have understood what the Liberals were all excited about. They never recognized as theologically significant the revelations from geology, psychology, anthropology, biology, criticism, and the like. But conservatives of the newer generation have encountered the world. They are beginning to deal with the questions of truth and relevance that have long seemed important to others. Liberals of the original generation seem never to have understood what was so important to the Fundamentalists about the classic biblical message. Its realities of creation, fallenness, atonement, and the like could be defined away with no sense of having lost the radical redemption which gave strength and grandeur to the ethics they wished to retain. But the newer generation has encountered the Bible. It is now reckoning with the issues of sin and salvation. Each can understand what the other saw as important. Conversation should now be possible—but for those conditioned responses of which Hordern spoke.

Blame for the breakdown of communication between the two groups lies on both sides. And so does responsibility for its resumption. Carl Henry wrote some articles a few years ago under the menacing title "Shall We Renew the Conflict?"; I would like to think that it is possible to be less pugnacious. Differences still exist between the two sides—whatever changes may have taken place—so one cannot well belong to both parties. Nevertheless, it does seem to me that the changes of recent decades have exposed an area of common consent which is more fundamental than the areas of dispute. All Christians' oneness in Christ is a given element inherent in being a Christian at all. Our partisan manyness is relatively superficial. Thus I cannot but think that there could be an adequate polemic which would stress the strongest things both sides hold in common rather than the weakest points of each. In submitting to the common Gospel which has apprehended both parties, Christians can approach each other through Christ, the Truth. Ultimately, there is no other ground of unity. In a discussion among Christians, it should be possible to dwell more on the positive faith toward which all our little faiths and allegiances point in some degree than on the pettiness and perversity which we all share.

A renewed conversation has already begun. It is not very far advanced. I devoutly hope it can be creative and Christian.

Cordially,
Spermologos

II

THE
CRUCIAL
ISSUE

. . . the well-known fact that every theological problem seems ultimately to involve every other.

CLAUDE WELCH

THE
DIAGNOSIS: LAW

O Theophilus,

Your complaint that "we are all talking about something which we know exists, but which no one defines" has all my sympathy. Your efforts toward an acceptable definition are, I agree, inconclusive. My last letter was not much help, I am afraid. I wrote descriptively and historically. And though historically and sociologically there has been a reasonably identifiable movement called "Fundamentalism," I am sure you are right in seeking a definition that penetrates beneath appearances.

I once offered a definition of Fundamentalism on the analogy of such groups as the Presbyterian Alliance, the Anglican Communion, and the Lutheran World Federation. The definition was this: "all those churches or persons in communion with the Moody Bible Institute." I was half serious, for there is an exchange of good offices and a mutual recognition among a number of rather different institutions (most of which have a cordial contact with the Moody Bible Institute) and almost no commerce between these and the outside. But on the whole, insofar as this was one of my attempts to be half unserious, it fell flat.

We have all encountered the problem you describe. The best labels nearly always oversimplify. Certainly the term "Fundamentalist" has become, as you said, "a term of opprobrium." No one seems to want it attached to him. The existence of a new and partially reconstructed "saving remnant" in Fundamentalism has complicated the business of definition. This group is and is not Fundamentalist. We do not know whether to make the old term

"Fundamentalist" stretch to include new meaning or to say that
we have a new thing rather than an old thing revised, and so
look for a new label. I regard the terms the group itself prefers
—"evangelical" and "conservative"—as strictly inapplicable. The
"revisionists" have largely dissociated themselves from the term
"Fundamentalist." Yet both Hebert and Packer had to use it in
their titles; no substitute has established itself. So objections may
be made to any name or definition.

The bothersome thing, as you say, is that we are trying to
define something that is undeniably there. Without expecting
to come up with a tidy definition, I might share with you a line
of thinking that I have followed. I set out to look for an underlying spirit in the movement as it was and is. Fundamentalism,
as I see it, is not just a group of organizations, not just a way of
using the Bible, nor just a taboo on tobacco, nor a style of religious experience, nor a distinctive body of teachings. You and
I know that Fundamentalism is not a grab bag of separable doctrines and practices, each of which is open to discussion or question in isolation. It is a religious, intellectual, social, and psychological fabric of remarkable cohesiveness. And it grips a person as
a whole. So I think common factors can be found that define
the inside of Fundamentalism as a state of mind.

I. THE SPIRIT OF LEGALISM

There is a way of maintaining certain ideas or taboos that
gives them a flavor in the context of Fundamentalism that these
same ideas or practices do not have when they appear, as many
of them do, among conservatively inclined Christians elsewhere.
The distinguishing factor in this attitude I cannot but think
of as *legalism.*

Legalism is always a pitfall for vital religion—intensified for
Christians by the biblical stress on inward grace. Legalism is the
easy way out. The ethic of love is a terrifying standard. So
we look for a way that gives us cause for more frequent self-
congratulation. We substitute artificial rules for the divine imperative, and we score ourselves by our own scheme of do's and
don't's.

Legalism is by no means restricted to any one group of people
or any one time in history, and it appears under many forms.
It is the persistent plague of the spiritual life. The prophets

opposed it in Israel. Jesus opposed it in the Judaism of his time. St. Paul opposed it in the early church. I must oppose it in my own church and parish. And, worst of all, I confess it in myself.

But at least two groups in modern Christendom have given legalism an institutional sanction within which it cannot be recognized for what it is. They are Roman Catholicism and Fundamentalism. Both claim that their legal structures derive from an infallible divine authority. One is a church-legalism. The other is a Bible-legalism.

Neither set out to be a legalism.

Rome's distortion of the Christian spirit began as a states-manlike expression of the Latin genius for government. In the disintegration of the Roman Empire, leadership passed from the Greek East to the Latin West, and the church suffered a conse-quent change of character. The Latin church asserted its leader-ship by seeking *uniformity*—the separated, half-barbarian ele-ments of Christendom could be held together by a uniform language, a uniform rite, and obedience to a single leader. Once this Roman ideal emerged, the history of the Western church became the story of the attempt to achieve governmental uniformity in spite of upsetting bursts of new life within the church and political and cultural changes outside it.

It would be a mistake to suggest that the attempt has been more successful than is actually the case. A living community will always reject complete standardization. Agreement at some fundamental points gave to the culture of the Middle Ages (even with all its diversity) a homogeneity that looks impressive, and to some people quite appealing, beside our contemporary frag-mentation. But both then and now the Roman tradition has produced and encouraged life, scholarship, sainthood, and ex-periment in a remarkable profusion of type. Its variety is at least as impressive as its unity. The disfiguring legalism lies at the point of the initial assent to ecclesiastical authority that the Roman system requires. The first matter to be settled is that of obedience to an external authority. God, Christ, creed, salvation, and guidance depend on the church. The legalistic aspect is heightened inasmuch as this authority is placed beyond the pos-sibility of error, criticism, or reform. So, while the Roman com-munion is not the monolith it often appears to be from the out-side, it is, in the greatest of all issues—the issue of authority—a rigid system, hardened in post-Tridentine Romanism by the challenge of Protestantism.

In the case of Fundamentalism, too, legalism was an understandable defense measure—rigidity of response, I suspect, is always defensive. In the face of the breakup of the Victorian certainties, the leaders of Fundamentalism decided (in something like an atmosphere of panic) to freeze thought and practice where they were, to oppose all that was new, to preserve all that was familiar.

Here, too, the result did not crush all spontaneity and differences. Within a rather narrow spectrum, some basic issues are still open, and refreshing variations of the spiritual life are found. "The Holy Ghost" still "over the bent world broods." But here again, the legalism lies at the point of the requirement of an initial assent to an external authority. God, Christ, creed, salvation, and guidance depend on the Bible. And again the legalistic aspect of the matter is heightened in that the authority is dogmatically said to be infallible. So, while differences of opinion and variations of practice are allowable within Fundamentalism, they are only the differences within a group which has answered the first question in the same way—unquestioning submission to an inerrant, objective authority. At this point, Fundamentalism, too, has become a rigid system—hardened by the challenge of modern thought.

Thus it might be almost equally true to say that Fundamentalism is a perpetuation in Protestantism of a Roman error, or to say that Romanism is a Fundamentalist perversion of the spirit of Catholicism. Neither sacramental Catholicism nor evangelical Protestantism has to be legalistic—though each can be made so.

Symptoms of the legalist infection in Fundamentalism can be observed quite readily. Some bits from letters on my desk may illustrate.

Andronicus complained recently that the glaring inconsistencies in rule-making were the "real problem" of Fundamentalism. He thought it incongruous, for example, that movies were categorically disallowed, radio approved, and television (which combines radio and movies) permitted with little hesitancy and hardly a dissent. Now, such inconsistency shows the inevitable shortcomings of a legalistic approach to behavior. For laws are not flexible enough to judge the inner nuances of personalities.

Laws are fixed; people change. Laws are only able to judge one's external conduct, not his interior life and motives. Laws cannot be cleverly enough arranged to anticipate every circumstance—hence, the science of casuistry. So human life, under a legalist system, will necessarily have its inconsistencies; it will have areas which cannot be reduced to conformity. The laws may fit each other, but they cannot fit people.

Another clue to the pervasiveness of legalism is in Amplias' report of the "Christian Progress Conference." Did you notice his observation that "the effort to find quick and ready answers to all problems is a Fundamentalist trait that must be discarded in any serious search for the truth"? This effort is a symptom of a mental legalism no less artificial than the ethical legalism. Fundamentalists look for "the answer" to every question. Apologists offer "the refutation" for every objection. The Bible is a handbook of proof texts, so there is no call to open prior methodological questions. Books like Torrey's *What the Bible Teaches* have organized the Bible's statements into a kind of "Home Doctrinal Adviser." This faith in the existence of "quick and ready answers" is the result of a legalist outlook which, in the intellectual realm no less than in the moral, is the easy way out.

On a later page the same report is again helpful. In speaking of a discussion which included a preponderance of Fundamentalist participants, it mentions that the question of biblical authority was "perhaps the most supercharged issue presented." This touchiness on the subject of the Bible is evident to all who have dealings with Fundamentalists. I suspect the reason for it is that right there, at the presumed point of the voice of God in revelation, Fundamentalism seems to find divine sanction for its legalist state of mind. Hence, to call into question a Fundamentalist's attitude toward the Bible is to question his whole structure just where it seems to him to be rooted in the mind of God.

This attitude toward the Bible is utterly crucial, for *methodology is not one thing and content and experience another.* Fundamentalism cannot well maintain Christian faith and life, working all the while with a sub-Christian (really a Moslem) conception of revelation. In religion, no less than in science or logic, the way questions are asked has a great deal to do with the answers that are received. This is what Tillich calls

"the doctrine of the theological circle." Petty inconsistencies
of behavior or legalistic attitudes in general cannot be cured
if the legalist infection is also present in the approach to the
source (i.e., revelation) whence Christianity must always seek
renewal. Once you admit a mechanical way of finding religious
truth as your methodology, mechanical attitudes will become
all-pervasive.

II. THE PRACTICE OF LEGALISM

Let me suggest five areas in which the legalistic character of
Fundamentalism is evident: Beginning with a *legalist methodology*, Fundamentalism forms a *legalist theology*, which leads to
a *legalist ethos*, practicing a *legalist ethic*, and seeking to follow
the Christian life according to a pattern of *legalist piety*.

In its *legalist methodology*, Fundamentalism seems to take
the Bible to be a statement of the mind of God. In Fundamentalism, a point is commonly established by providing a catena of
apposite biblical citations and heading the list with "God says
so." I am sure that, for most Fundamentalists, "It is taught in
the Bible" is equivalent to "God says so." Packer says as much:
"To learn the mind of God, one must consult His written Word.
What Scripture says, God says."[1] This equivalence of the Word
and the words is assumed to be true of the entire Bible. (Of
course, this can only be maintained by the occasional resort to
such dodges as allegorizing, typologizing, dispensationalizing, or
downright evasion of difficulties.) Thus the Bible is significant
in that it is a group of sentences, many of them embodying
otherwise unknowable truths, each of them being free from error
—historical or religious—and the whole being free from omission
of necessary truth.

Even a man who has so refined away the crudities of the
usual Fundamentalist understanding of revelation as has Carl
Henry holds a position like this. He writes, "The rationality
of the self-revealed God and His intellectual attributes provide
evangelical Christianity a framework which makes possible both
the conceptual knowledge of God and an inscripturated propositional revelation."[2] Here you have it: The Scriptures are a
"propositional revelation," giving to the concepts of man's mind
a correspondence to the mind of God.

Observe that dreadful word "inscripturated." You have complained about its sudden ubiquity in Fundamentalist theology. It is, as you say, objectionable both as theology and as an ugly piece of jargon. But apparently its users shrink neither from its aesthetic offensiveness nor from its theological implications. It is deliberately intended to signify the objectification of revelation. Revelation is turned into a thing, an object, a thing-in-itself; it is packaged, externalized—"inscripturated." As such, it can be shuffled, dissected, compared, cross-referenced, divided; the letters can be counted, and Daniel and Revelation can be dovetailed.

Religiously, the authority of the Book is ultimate. The more sensitive minds in Fundamentalism dislike the accusation of having set up a "paper Pope." But Fundamentalism is, as few religious expressions—Christian or otherwise—have ever been, a religion of the Book. The first and final test of doctrine or practice is, "Is it 'scriptural'?" Personal Bible reading is the most highly rated means of grace and the best route to spiritual maturity. Christian education is largely a matter of learning Bible content. Personal evangelism that is to be effective is a technique of knowing the apt "salvation texts." Preaching is so exclusively expository as to be sometimes almost Bible lessons.

Behind this view of the Bible and this manner of using it is an implied view of God and his way with man. Fundamentalists apparently assume that if God is really going to reveal himself to men his revealing work must be errorless. Somewhere, in the midst of our imperfection and uncertainty, there must be an objective, perfect something.

But every presumption is against this view that in one place —the Bible—God has declared himself unambiguously and infallibly. No one, to my knowledge, has put it better than John Oman:

> God does not conduct His rivers, like arrows, to the sea. The ruler and compass are only for finite mortals who labor, by taking thought, to overcome their limitations, and are not for the Infinite mind. The expedition demanded by man's small power and short day produces the canal, but nature, with a beneficent and picturesque circumambulancy, the work of a more spacious and less precipitate mind, produces the river. Why should we assume that, in all the rest of His ways, He rejoices in the river, but, in religion, can use no adequate method save the canal? The defence of the

infallible is the defence of the canal against the river, of the
channel blasted through the rock against the basin dug by an
element which swerves at a pebble or a firmer clay. And the question is whether God ever does override the human spirit in that
direct way, and whether we ought to conceive either of His spirit
or of ours after a fashion that could make it possible. Would such
irresistible might as would save us from all error and compel us
into right action be in accord with God's personality or with ours?[3]

Yet it is felt in Fundamentalist circles that the Bible is just
such an infallible thing and that to question anything in it
—the historicity of any event, the validity of any teaching—
plunges one into a shoreless sea of uncertainty and subjective
judgments. In short, Fundamentalism is committed to the ultimacy of an infallible Bible and to the methodology of "It's in
the Book."

In its *legalist theology*, Fundamentalism presents a brittle
pattern of ideas and insists on conformity to them.

The first question about an unknown speaker, book, or organization is: "Is he (or it) 'sound'? Does he conform to just our
pattern of theological statement?" Certain of the ingredients in
the pattern may be gathered from the rather similar doctrinal
statements which most Fundamentalist institutions have. They
usually begin: "We believe in the Scripture of Old and New
Testaments as verbally inspired of God, and inerrant in the original writings." Some affirmation of the divinity (sometimes the
divinity and the humanity) of Jesus Christ is included; this is
invariably coupled with the virgin birth. Some terms indicating
a penal, substitutionary theory of the atonement are sure to be
found. A statement of the literal, bodily resurrection of Christ
and his literal, imminent (often explicitly premillennial) return is usual. Whatever is said about the church is certain to be
about an invisible church. Such lists vary in details, but this
will suggest important elements which in one degree of elaboration and refinement or another make up the theological content
of Fundamentalism. From such a defined position it is easy to
evaluate other thinkers as slightly to the right or to the left.
I often heard among Fundamentalists certain theologians
solemnly appraised as "All right, but 'off' on the second coming."
A book under review is criticized "more for what it leaves out
than for what it says"—that is, because it fails to duplicate completely the standard pattern.

It is, however, not the content but the structure of theology that concerns me. For it is in the shape of the whole that the legalism inheres. That is, it is quite possible to affirm a statement of justification by grace through faith but hold it in a system which by its structure says "justification by correct statement." The record of evangelicalism within the Christian family is such as to suggest that it believes not so much in salvation by the Cross of Christ as in salvation by a particular theory of the efficacy of the Cross. In other words, the sub-Christian manner of the theologizing may contradict the quite biblical and Christian proposition of the content.

"The Task and Method of Systematic Theology" were defined in staunchly conservative fashion once by the great Princeton theologian B. B. Warfield. His exposition, written in the days when Fundamentalism was rising, would, I expect, still be entirely acceptable throughout that movement. Warfield's lucid phrases are worth citing. All theology begins with Holy Scripture, which Warfield refers to as bearing objective authority "as the documented revelation of God." In the Scriptures, through "exegetical theology," then, we find the data we seek—that is, the knowledge of God, but "in its *disjecta membra*." This disordered material does not become theology of a systematic sort until the mind has been used "to set forth in systematic formulation the results of the investigations of exegetical theology." Following this method, theology is "thus, the systematized knowledge of God." "At last, in systematic theology, it [the knowledge of God] stands before our eyes in complete formulation." "It is systematic theology which . . . makes it [the knowledge of God] our assured possession that we may thoroughly understand and utilize."[4]

Assumptions and procedures in the theological use of the Bible very like those outlined in Warfield's article underlie Fundamentalist theologizing. But the task, thus defined, takes two distinguishable directions in practice. One is the popular or "Bible School" theology. The other is the less influential, much smaller, but vastly deeper and more learned tradition of Reformed theology. The two result in different formulations, idioms, and literatures; and between them there seems to be some mistrust.

In the Bible Schools of Fundamentalism the proper business of theology has been taken to be the codification of Bible texts.

Appropriately, Bible School courses are often called "Bible Doctrines" rather than "Systematic Theology."

This popular Fundamentalist theology tends to be atomistic; its parts can be discussed without reference to one another; it has no inherent unity. (This may be one way of saying that it is hardly theology at all. Warfield, of course, would be critical of this.) Oddly, despite its purported dependence on the Scriptures, Bible School theology has failed to tap the inner, unifying currents of biblical theology—a strangely neglected discipline in most "conservative" schools. The structure of "Bible Doctrines" is externally imposed. Biblical texts are extracted and artifically organized under traditional headings—headings which owe as much to Peter Lombard as to the Bible itself. This suggests some divorce between the Bible and the theological categories with which Fundamentalism operates. Its announced biblical method is inductive, but its theological practice is deductive. It looks into the Bible knowing ahead of time what it is going to find. It maintains an inherited body of doctrinal teachings which it insists on reading back into the Bible itself. In a recent, striking sermon, C. W. J. Bowles notes that the distinctive teachings of Fundamentalism

> are part of a traditional interpretation of Scripture which is regarded as being as essential as the authority of Scripture itself. This corpus of traditional interpretation is the test of admission, not to union with Christ, because repentance and the commitment of personal faith in Him are demanded for that, but to the undefined but very real and close-knit brotherhood of those who are held to be "sound" and "spiritual."[5]

Being even superficially biblical, the teachings of Fundamentalism do contain many ideas that are centrally Christian. But they are more than a little selective in their use of the Bible. They lack a sense of history in treating the biblical record itself. Further, some profoundly Christian ideas such as the Trinity, the humanity of Christ, the meaning of the church, and the sacraments are given at best perfunctory acknowledgment.

But Warfield's essential method has been used, too, by the Reformed theologians of the more scholarly traditions in Fundamentalism. The work in this tradition, as is characteristic of Calvinism, shows real strength and completeness. A system of sturdy fiber is worked through from first principles.

Here, too, despite the learning and the subtlety, the end product is the sort of thing I could not but call, in the wide sense in which I am using the term, "legalistic." It perpetuates the theological legalism often called "Protestant Scholasticism." This, like the medieval variety, is an authoritarian thought-scheme. For it, the content of revelation is given in a single, infallible, unquestioned body of propositions—for conservative Protestants, the Bible; for Roman Catholics, the Bible plus church dogma. These authoritative sources are held to be consistent from end to end. So the work of theology is simply to organize the propositions into a full and orderly scheme and to reconcile apparent discrepancies by subtle distinctions. This is the method of "secondary thinking" or scholasticism wherever it appears. For scholasticism, theology is not a task to be pursued; it is a deposit, already settled, to be maintained, refined, and applied without addition or diminution.

This trust in a final system has again reduced "the truth" to a thing—a doctrinal statement external to me with which I must bring myself into alignment, a perfect knowledge of God which I may "possess" and "utilize." This objectification of truth is characteristic of legalism. (Where the same process is carried out in more gross, material forms, it is called "idolatry.") On certain assumptions a logical superstructure is reared. But, as in the case of mathematics, the question then is: "This is a fine arrangement of symbols, but does it refer to anything?" The living, deciding, questioning Christian thinker, confronted by a living, loving God has been so completely left out of the theological method that the resulting theology is academic and sterile. Some comments that D. W. Soper made on Louis Berkhof might have been made about almost any of the more conservative theologians. He remarks:

> He mentions that God is immanent as well as transcendent, but never refers to immanence again. The world, the historic process, does not appear in the book from first page to last. Berkhof's Bible, like his universe, is static. The treatment follows his usual distribution of the great themes—God, Man, Christ, Salvation, Church and Last Things. You do not begin, as Tillich does, with man the question, nor with God the answer; Berkhof begins, continues and ends with the Bible. It is his only epistemology; it is not a dialogue with man, but a divine monologue.[6]

So true is this that most conservative theologians, I think, would be puzzled to realize that Soper's characterization was meant to criticize, not to compliment, such theology.

In its *legalist ethos* Fundamentalism gives institutional embodiment to its state of mind. By "ethos" I mean a body of attitudes or a conscious "group mind" which does one's thinking for him. A way of talking, a way of acting, a body of predictable responses, have grown up within Fundamentalism, and conformity with these is the criterion of acceptance. One must applaud, laugh, and weep at the right stimuli. A quite specific group of catchphrases mark a Fundamentalist. Some of them, such as "infallible Word," "second coming," "Jesus saves," "accepting Christ," and "personal Savior," are not strictly biblical. Yet these shibboleths are made the basis for inclusion or exclusion by a group which claims sole and supreme loyalty to the Bible. Certain "big name" personalities, certain musical styles and types, mannerisms, phrases, and devices in the conduct of public meetings serve to define the movement. Terms such as "Christian" or "God's people" are applied exclusively to one's own group. Persons from the constituency of approved institutions, books from approved writers or publishers, are looked upon with immediate favor; others are met with suspicion. In fact a good index of the isolation and distrust in which Fundamentalism lives could be observed (to take only a tiny, but perhaps not misleading, symptom) in the bookstores of the movement. If you visit the stores of its schools, institutions, or crusades, I venture that you will find the same situation everywhere—at least in my own incomplete survey I have found no suggestion of an exception. On the shelves you will find only the literature of the Fundamentalist movement. (An occasional dictionary or cookbook might qualify this statement.) You will look in vain, for example, for anything by either of the Niebuhrs or Tillich; by Barth, Brunner, Buttrick, or Bennett. One would not expect that the school or anyone in it should agree with anything or everything in these writers; their opinions are openly disputed at Union, Yale, and Harvard; in fact these writers at times try to set each other straight. But for a movement and its institutions to profess a paramount interest in religion and then to insulate its followers against firsthand contact with the more powerful minds grappling with the religious dimension of today's bewildering world—and to do so in the name of education—points up the retreat of the movement into a life of its own.

Any ethos, if it is to have cohesiveness and holding power, tends to define itself on an emotional level in ritual actions and incantatory words. Fundamentalism has done this. No premium is put on originality; the Fundamentalist idiom has preserved the sound of an era for which one otherwise must look in the pages of a chronicler like Frederick Lewis Allen. Further, the shape of this cult has so altered the religion of the New Testament and Christian tradition that the chief communal action is no longer the Lord's Supper, but the invitation.[7] The real presence of Christ in active, grace-giving, miraculous power which is quite generally ruled out of the sacraments by Fundamentalists is shifted instead to this evangelistic device. The great ritual of death, rebirth, and communion which the church, at her Lord's direction, has found in baptism and the eucharist is now re-located by Fundamentalists in their (altarless) "altar call." Here, as in a kind of racial memory, the rural community, living close to the soil, to seedtime and harvest, has the twice-yearly visi-tation of the revivalist—the priest of this sacred rite. Through repetition, a kind of liturgy has developed around this rite—less dramatic than the rhythm of the Christian year, less exalted than the poetry of the anaphora, but similarly meant to fix a sacred moment in the death and rebirth drama in appropriate form. This Fundamentalist litany allows little freedom except in length—it may be indefinitely repeated. But its terms follow rather set lines. The rubric reads: *Organ (full tremolo), up and under.*

> And now while every head is bowed,
> And every eye is closed,
> Is there one who will raise his hand
> And say, "Pastor, pray for me"?
> On my left,
> On my right,
> Down here in front,
> Man or woman,
> Boy or girl,
> Is there one? Is there one?
> (I see you, Brother ... Sister ... Oh, thank God!)

And now, while the choir sings softly,
　　And while Christians are praying,
You who raised your hands, won't you leave your seats and come
　　forward here—someone will come with you—and accept the
　　Lord Jesus Christ as your own personal Savior?
　　　　　On my left,
　　　　　　On my right,
　　　　　　　Down here in front,
　　　　　　　　Is there one?
　　　　　　　　　Come to Jesus.

Much might be observed about this device. But for the moment
let me ask: Where in the Bible or the early church is there
precedent for carrying on evangelistic appeals as a part—the
most climactic and sacred part—of a service of Christian worship?[8] Yet this nonbiblical pattern of corporate life is made the
criterion of who is and who is not "evangelical" or "Bible-
believing." This liturgical novelty is made the criterion of who
is the real "conservative."

I suspect that, more than anything else about Fundamentalism, the church outside resents this confusion of primary and
secondary matters. It is on the basis of quite petty issues that
"evangelicalism" has carried the blight of divisiveness wherever
it has appeared in Christendom.

In its *legalist ethic* Fundamentalism has made over Christian
life and obedience into a handy list of "do's" and "don't's." Our
world is faced by staggering problems affecting every person,
family, and community—atomic power, world Communism, the
chain-reaction population explosion, the problem of hunger in
two-thirds of the world and the equally acute problem of abundance in the other third, the rise of the nonwhite races through
nationalism abroad and the aggressive protest against injustice
at home. Yet, large and difficult as they are, these are our problems; responsible ethics must deal with them. Further, we may
add to them such problems as the impact on personal and family
life of our urban-industrial society—dehumanization, the organization man, planned obsolescence, the loss of the dignity of work
in mass production, the deterioration of our inner cities and
their abandonment by the churches. Yet in the face of the claim
of a broken world—a world whose brokenness is ours—the Fundamentalist ethic still concentrates on marking out the moral
universe into black and white areas and avoiding contamination.

It is principally concerned with its own purity. There is a long heritage in Fundamentalism of inflamed attacks on the theater, John Barleycorn, tobacco, dancing, cardplaying, and other sinful indulgences—in other words, a long heritage of fiddling while Rome burns. Fundamentalists are, I discover, becoming increasingly aware that this preoccupation with the external and the trivial misses the whole heart of the Christian ethic. Much I.V.C.F. literature and the recent book *Christian Personal Ethics*, by Carl Henry, are quite perceptive on this. Such influences are emancipating; they put ethical decisions in larger, more thoughtful settings. But Fundamentalist emphasis is still largely on individual questions of conscience and conduct. One cannot but wonder if such preoccupations are not escapist, irresponsible, out of touch with the great elemental moral realities of our time. Does not the Fundamentalist move to define itself by prohibitions have the net effect of isolating the group from the world where it ought to be ministering? Is it not a "passing by on the other side"?

In its *legalist piety* Fundamentalism has pressed Christian experience into a pattern. The schematized experience has two crises: conversion and the "dedication of one's life to the Lord." Being "saved" is regarded as a definite, datable, conscious event. Then, at some time subsequent to conversion, if one is to be a "fully consecrated" Christian, there is another, also definite, datable, conscious crisis of dedication—often to a specific mission or calling. The emotional effort of Fundamentalism is directed toward eliciting these responses.

It is difficult to say much that is critical of a style of piety without appearing to call into question the sincerity or value of someone else's innermost life. This I do not mean to do. But perhaps it is within the competence of an observer to remark that devotion in the Fundamentalist pattern seems to gain in intensity by withdrawal from the world. The crises of conversion and dedication as well as the means of grace for the sustenance of Christian life tend to be isolated from all else; they draw in upon themselves. The sense of struggle and victory in the inner life in the Fundamentalist community tends to be articulated in exclusively religious terms. It stays out of touch with the inner anguish of the life of our time except insofar as it provides escape. This religious preoccupation lends to Fundamentalist piety an attractive sense of certainty and holiness. It is a witness to the beyondness of Christian trust; it is a contact with a sure stronghold in an uncertain world. Part of the appeal of Fundamentalism in our time is, I am sure, on the grounds of this apparent religious certainty. Archbishop Ramsay commented, "It offers authority and security, quick and sure, to a generation restless and insecure."[9] On my last visit with Appeles, he told me that despite his agonizing awareness of the shortcomings of Fundamentalism he was going to stay on with his group because it was only there that he saw results—only there that he was sure of the reality of God, doing things in human life. Of course, the recognizable and measurable results were due to the reduction of God's activities to conversions and dedications. Where these were present, God's power was manifest—one could verify it statistically. This is the only "fruit of the Spirit" that even so sensitive a person as he was willing to recognize as such. I gather from his remarks that other critical young leaders of Fundamentalist institutions have felt similarly. They see the weaknesses in Fundamentalism, but only there can they be sure God is active. This definiteness in the style of piety is, for these persons at least, a great advantage. But the gain is at a tremendous cost—a cost which is not just a tactical loss, but also a loss in reality and authenticity. A Christian's religious experience dare not be out of touch with his basic humanity. His religious language, symbols, struggles, and hopes are part of a unified vocation involving his total life in the world. His piety cannot be deep but irrelevant. The task of relating the practice of sanctity to our highly articulate and self-conscious world is difficult and subtle. It quickly shows up the inadequacy of narrow, individualistic, schematized forms of piety.

This explanation of five symptoms—methodological, theological, cultic, ethical, and devotional—may indicate what I mean by diagnosing the innermost problem of Fundamentalism as legalism. It may be a grim diagnosis, but only an adequate analysis of the problem can point to an adequate cure. I observe that another diagnostician, C. W. J. Bowles, in the sermon cited earlier, also relates these various aspects of a common spirit:

> The distinguishing marks of Fundamentalism of every kind are the same: an alleged, absolute certainty, an exclusive claim and a sectarian policy. The basic assertion is identical in form: We have the truth of God, you have not; we are the Church of God, you

are not; we have the grace of God, you have not; I have the guidance of God, you have not.[10]

I have been trying to define the interior of Fundamentalism —to give you my idea of its spirit. Any attempt to find unity in diversity risks oversimplification. Despite the bypaths taken to avoid too much generalization, I am sure I have oversimplified. Many persons related to the institutions of Fundamentalism might read my remarks and say, with some justice, "Yes, but all or at least part of this does not apply to me." I cannot but hope they would be right—the fewer people to whom all of this applies, the better. Nonetheless, despite the range of differences now present in the Fundamentalist constituency, I venture that most of what is said here applies to most characteristically conservative work. Fundamentalism has exhibited a unifying spirit, and if this description has not precisely defined it, I do not think it has missed entirely. I accept in advance whatever qualifications you or your friends may want to make of this case. In anything moving as rapidly as is the inner life of Fundamentalism, exceptions will be increasingly numerous. I hope they may someday be so numerous that these generalizations of mine become altogether false. Meanwhile this is an exploratory essay, trying to isolate for purposes of analysis the common spirit in an admittedly complex movement. I look forward to your comments.

Cordially,
Spermologos

THE
PRESCRIPTION: GRACE

O Theophilus,

I appreciate the qualities of your mind more all the time. Without you to push, prod, needle, exhort, lecture, exasperate (or whatever it is you do; I never know what to call your methods), I am sure I would always drop a topic just short of the point at which something constructive might be said. You are surely right. It is not enough to diagnose. Prescription is also necessary. That last letter was indeed too negative. So let me pick up where it left off.

Perhaps a positive line of thought such as you seek is implied in the diagnosis itself. Despite your qualifications and exceptions, you seemed to accept, at least as a working hypothesis, my analysis of the innermost problem of Fundamentalism as legalism. If this analysis is anywhere near the truth, we might hope that a cure addressed to the basic malady might relieve the symptoms.

I. THE SPIRIT OF GRACE

You will feel at home, I am sure, if for a really thoroughgoing corrective we turn to the categories of Christendom's leading expert on legalism, St. Paul. He drew a contrast between *law* on the one hand and its opposite, *grace*.

Law, he observed, is valuable; it can announce a standard of duty, and it can condemn for failure to meet that standard. It gives moral order to life. But it leaves man his own savior. It is ego-centered—I must learn the law; I must perform it; if I do, I am good; if I fail, I am sinful. Law cannot effect an inner renewal. It cannot give power for the demands of the present; it cannot deliver from the failure of the past. It cannot remove the inner contradiction between the I who knows to do right, and the I who continues to fail, so it leads at last to despair.

But grace communicates just these inward necessities. It works inwardly because it is not impersonal, as law is. It is the acceptance of the sinner, not the righteous. It is on the level of a loving personal relationship. "For what the law could not do . . . God did."

We know God in grace through his own self-disclosure, Jesus Christ. In Christ he has met us graciously. His method was a historic act. God reveals and redeems through history—not above it or outside it. His act, while thoroughly divine, is within the conditions of history. He does not violate the nature of manhood in order to reach men; rather, the incarnation means that he accepted and submitted to the law of that nature.

Of several incipient heresies in Fundamentalism, the most noticeable is Docetism—the turning of Jesus' humanity into a mere appearance. Fundamentalist piety and preaching insist so vehemently on the diety of Jesus Christ that his manhood is made unreal. The incarnation becomes like one of the appearances of the gods in Greek mythology—the god masquerades as a man. In popular Fundamentalism one detects a widespread feeling that Jesus was really omniscient in his earthly life—his indications to the contrary were accommodations to avoid offending the audience. But the formula of Chalcedon indicated clearly that to deny or to qualify Christ's humanity is as heretical as to deny or to qualify his Godhead. Fundamentalists cannot seem to divest themselves of post-Nicene insights and enter the world of the Synoptic Gospels. They are out of touch with that startling figure who so haunted the minds of the Liberals. They do not recognize the Jesus who grew and learned and matured as you and I do, "yet without sin." He was tempted. He grew weary. He asked questions because he wanted information. He prayed because he needed the Father. He used the thought-forms of his day because he knew no others; his sense of mission only grew on him with time and experience. He was a particular man in a particular time and place, reacting to particular circumstances. Of course, he was God, working out man's redemption through the terms of that particular human life—but not a person in his own day understood what was happening. This way of grace—to work through the weakness of the condition of the one to be helped—is the way of the God of the Bible and Christian faith.

Perhaps my whole case might be summarized when I say that the shape of Fundamentalism—its view of the Bible, of theology, and of life—is gravely Docetic in tendency.[1] It tends to violate or destroy the integrity of the human in its concern for the claims of the divine.

II. THE VISIBLE SIGNS OF GRACE

So with this insight into the way of grace, and again recalling that methodology is not one thing and content another, let me try to sketch a *methodology of grace,* a *theology of grace,* an *ethos of grace,* an *ethic of grace,* and a *piety of grace.*

As for a *methodology of grace*: There is a certain congruity between a Docetic Christology and the theory of the verbal infallibility of the Scriptures. Dear old Dr. Thiessen used to support his case for an infallible Bible by relating the revelation in the Bible to the "perfection of the divine character."[2] He assumed that an imperfect Bible could not worthily represent a perfect God. Now, his phrase "the perfection of the divine character" is more Aristotelian than biblical. When Jesus demanded that the citizens of the Kingdom be perfect as the Father in heaven is perfect, he did not mean his term as Thiessen did his. Jesus meant equality in love for all without discrimination—the term was personal, purposive, moral, and defined in the interrelationship of God and men. (Compare the parallel in St. Luke, where the idea is "mercy," not "perfection.") He did not mean the perfection of an isolated, static being. We do not know God through his formal qualities or his abstract character; we know him through his self-revealing actions. The pattern for our understanding of him is not to be some quasi-Aristotelian speculation about qualities of pure being or absolute perfection of form; rather, the pattern is his act of grace in Christ. We conclude what we can of God's nature from his own acts of self-disclosure; we do not decide beforehand what his acts must be like to accord with some previously determined general idea of his qualities. The pattern of grace does not suggest formal perfection or inerrancy—instead it leads us to expect the divine at work through the human. The way of God in the Bible is not unlike the way of God elsewhere. The human qualities of the Bible are not unreal; the Bible is not magical. What a priori consideration would lead us to entertain "the conception that in the Bible God precipitates a solid block of inerrant matter into the world of otherwise imperfect things"?[3] Everywhere God does his work through human weakness, perversity, and blundering. He is chary of miracle, for he appeals to faith, not demonstration. God's normal way seems to be "strength made perfect in weakness," "treasure in earthen vessels." Faith must rest only in God; perfection is not in man or his works—else we would worship them. Yet by the Holy Spirit a true meeting with God can be mediated through imperfect witnesses.

Packer tries to turn the edge of this Christological analogy.[4] He goes so far as to claim that the Christological parallel actually supports verbal inspiration. I must say that his discussion leaves me unpersuaded. His logic would seem to approach an idea of two incarnations of the Word—one in a person, one in a book; the Word made flesh, and the Word made words. He speaks, in fact, of "the divine Word incarnate" and "the divine Word written" as equal. To be sure, the Christological analogy must be used discriminatingly. As John Baillie has pointed out, the overenthusiastic use of any parallel with Jesus, who represented the divine acting in perfect humanity, will break down, for the other line of the parallel will involve the divine acting in imperfect humanity.[5] But in general, the point of the analogy seems intact even after it has been disputed and qualified. The whole conception of incarnation (as distinct from mere appearance or deception) implies divine self-limitation. The biblical record tells of a Jesus whose divinity was not self-evident:

> The New Testament makes it entirely clear that Jesus could be, and was, mistaken for any one of a variety of ordinary or extraordinary human beings. There was (and there is) *no* externally compelling evidence of divine glory. Every claim by him or for him, everything in the way of a proof, appears as ambiguous and problematical, both for Jesus' chronological contemporaries and for us.[6]

In the general sense that reticence and self-emptying are characteristic of the manner of divine grace, there seems to me to remain a valid parallel between inspiration and incarnation.

To regard the Bible as God's Word need not involve its infallibility. The Fundamentalist notion that revelation and inerrancy must go together needs to be criticized in the light of grace. Who said that they must go together? Suppose the Bible were inerrant; would that prove it to be divine revelation? Suppose the Manhattan telephone directory were to come out without error or omission of necessary truth; would it for that reason be the Word of God? Much slovenly thinking goes unchallenged on this point. Two things may be said emphatically: (1) Inerrancy, even if it could be proved, need not imply divinity; and (2) divinity, if we are to use the clue of the manner of grace, need not imply inerrancy.

This realization cuts away the "all or nothing" alternative with which Fundamentalists approach the Bible. The alternative is deadly. P. T. Forsyth once said:

> "The whole Bible or none," it was said. "Take but a stone away and the edifice subsides." This came from the Bible having been reduced to a fabric instead of an organism. And how many skeptics that course has made! How many Pharisees! How many spiritual tragedies! If I were a Secularist I would not touch by assault the doctrine of plenary verbal inspiration and inerrancy. I should let it work as one of my best adjutants.[7]

He goes on to cite the "One Hoss Shay"—that admirable vehicle which held together for a hundred years without repair and then fell apart all at once.

Taking our clue from the way of grace, we can allow for flexibility and discrimination in the use of the Bible. We can frankly accept its humanness. Our methodology can recognize that "its Word is a Revelation which speaks the language of experience but with the voice of Eternal God."[8] (Forsyth again, and a great phrase.) The Bible's message evokes faith, commands obedience, and mediates the saving message of God's love in Christ—but it does so through the history of an insignificant and self-willed tribe and finally through the ignominy of a Cross.

This story is reported through the imprecise methods of transmission in antiquity by men who believed in the midst of their unbelief, who both battled and compromised with the nature-religions, who understood much and misunderstood much —men in the full exercise of their human freedom and under the same judgment as ourselves. Such a view of the Bible is the implicate of an incarnational religion. It is our methodology of grace.

As for a *theology of grace*: Again I would like to consider theology as a whole, its pattern and approach, rather than its specific content. For beyond the legalism often apparent in conservatives' definition of God in his ways (their fondness for such categories as the divine decrees, a penal substitution theory of atonement), legalism shows in the scholasticism by which the whole theological enterprise is carried out. The claim to a final system is the point at issue and the point at which we would like to see grace supplant law.

It would be an impressive step toward the establishment of a final theology if we could say (as deductive theologies imply), "We begin with God." Unfortunately, we cannot be that impressive; only God can begin with God. Theology is never even properly "the study of God," for God is never an object that can be investigated or manipulated, or defined by our categories; rather, he is God, who is always a subject. He addresses himself to men. We do not study him; we listen.

So we do not begin with God; we begin with revelation. However, this will not mislead us if it is really revelation. If it is God's own act of self-disclosure with which we are in touch, God will truly be given to us in revelation. He speaks to be heard.

But we cannot properly begin with revelation in itself. Revelation is incomplete until it is consummated in human faith. God's revealing acts surely stand whether anyone believes them or not—I am not preaching subjectivism, for the revealing events are part of the givenness of history. But until there is belief, the acts are not known to be revealing. (The invasion of Judah by Sennacherib, for example, meant something different to Assyrian chroniclers from what it meant to Isaiah, we can be sure.) For man, as he is addressed by God in revelation, is not an object or a thing any more than God is. Man, in the relationship established by revelation and faith, is never passive. God summons him to the exercise of his truest freedom. The relationship is personal —like a meeting or an encounter. It is the kind of relationship that (like all really interpersonal relationships) moves above the subject-object antithesis; it is biblical faith. Two subjects are in mutual address. God in the Bible is always God as known to

man by revelation, and man in the Bible is always man as confronted by God in Christ for judgment and salvation.[9] In Buber's
now familiar terms, revelation involves the relation not of I-it
but of I-Thou. "Reveal" as a biblical term has little to do
with communicating information or true propositions; its more
characteristic thrust is suggested by St. Paul's phrase "to reveal
his Son within me." God, not information about God, is what is
given in revelation. So we cannot begin with revelation in itself;
we must begin with revelation as believed by a person—until it
has reached that point, nothing has been revealed. But again, we
need not be disheartened, for this will only be misleading if
Christian experience is invalid. If Christian experience is actually
a work of God—and the prophets, apostles, saints, and martyrs
have not been deluded—God will actually be given to us in our
believing response to revelation. As the great Roman Catholic
theologian Karl Adam has said:

> ... if it be genuine divine faith, the faith of a Christian is in very
> truth a "showing of the spirit and of the power" of the Holy
> Ghost. It is not we who believe, but the Holy Ghost within us.
> The experience of Pentecost is continually repeated, and our faith
> is in its essence nothing else than the pentecostal faith of the
> apostles.[10]

The soul is the ultimate place where authority becomes authoritative and where revelation becomes revelatory. The earliest Christian confession was not in the form of a catechetical definition of
God; rather, it was the affirmation "Jesus Christ is Lord."

But even this is not a complete point of departure for
theology, for Christian experience of God is never solitary. It
is always the result of witness. It is always mediated by the
Spirit-bearing fellowship. "What hast thou which thou didst not
receive?" Becoming a Christian is always an entry into family
life. The Gospel is communicated within the believing community.

So, if we are to locate the point of origin for Christian
theology, it will be this: the revelation of God in his redemptive
actions in history as these events have become creative of the
faith of the church.

If this is the actual starting place for theologizing, at least
two implications are apparent.

(1) Faith precedes theology. Theology is a process of reflection upon this starting place. Theology is a Christian person's thinking. One always theologizes from within faith; one is always part of his own data. Standing within faith, one must think. Faith, in a rational person, will reach toward self-consciousness, toward rational articulation. Theology is an attempt to define and explain what is already true in the religious realm of faith —and to explain it in such a way as to preserve its redemptive significance. However, one may define and explain very badly. He may bring too little of his biblical and dogmatic heritage to the task of thinking about the questions raised by his world. Or, with equally bad results, he may isolate his religious heritage from his world. In either case he cannot but understand his faith in an inadequate fashion. Thus a distinction is possible between faith and the understanding of one's faith. It is quite possible for one's faith to be genuine in spite of some wrong-headed theology. It is equally possible for an impeccable orthodoxy to disguise (alas, even to oneself) the defectiveness of one's faith.

(2) There is no final theology. Theology is not a fixed orthodoxy to be amplified, refined, defended, and handed on. It is a task which never ends. It is conversation between dramatic, presystematic biblical faith on the one hand and systematic, reasoned formulation on the other. It is living religion in creative tension with the culture with reference to which it must explain itself. It is faith, returning to its own sources to rediscover its own meaning. The whole of this process is within historical conditioning—the philosophical commonplaces of one age with which its theological task must reckon are in the scrap basket of the next age. Theology relates the Word of God to the varied, ever-changing flow of human thought. To fix it is to kill it. Christian theology is always theology *in via*. The theologian, like all other Christians, is a pilgrim. H. R. Mackintosh put it this way:

> In systematic thought there is no final form. Theologies from the first have perished; they wax old as doth a garment; as a vesture Time folds them up, and lays them by. Nothing save the Gospel is abiding, and its years shall not fail.[11]

The scholastic method assumes a revealed system of doctrine permanent for all people and all places. It further fixes the system so irreformably that there is little discrimination between what is primary and what is secondary. The whole web moves when a strand is broken. So, perhaps as a corollary to this point, I might observe that the theological process carries within itself its own criteria for self-criticism. Theology must remain flexible enough to alter itself in nonessentials in the light of its own essentials. Jesus' criticism of the legal scrupulosity of the Pharisees was that the inner spirit of the Old Testament religion had been obscured by minor regulations. He called for a new, creative perspective. He wanted the center once more located at the center. Theology must always be doing this. It grows by returning over and over again to its sources. It dares to raise for each emergent challenge its own fundamental questions.

As for an *ethos of grace*: The scandalous wall of suspicion that Fundamentalism erects around itself must come down if grace, not law, is to rule. The fellowship of grace, says John Oman, recognizes "no frontiers except those it exists to remove."[12]

If grace is the shaping force, the impact of the Christian community will be redemptive. Fundamentalists, of course, formally agree with this. In fact, they maintain their very separateness in the interest of their redemptive mission. They feel that being misunderstood by the world and by worldly churchmen is a part of the offense of the Cross and an inevitable part of the redemptive role.

Now I have no wish to minimize the scandal of the Cross. I only wish to insist that the offense in Christianity should be the Cross, and it alone—not the arbitrary offensiveness of Christians. It is possible, in the name of principle, to surround the Christian message with sub-Christian features which repel men for reasons that have nothing whatever to do with a response to Jesus Christ.

Some Fundamentalists, of course, reject the charge that they have a restricted conception of the Holy Spirit's work; they think of themselves as liberal-minded and catholic in their sympathies. But I read not long ago a remark by J. E. Fison (himself a former Fundamentalist) which effectively challenges any easy presumptions of liberality. Canon Fison says:

> Regardless of the warning of the scripture about "the sin against the Holy Ghost," the biblical fundamentalist is often obliged by

his dogmas to deny the self-evidencing work of the Holy Spirit except where that work is being demonstrated among his fellow-fundamentalists. . . . And if a fundamentalist replies that he does not so confine the work of the Holy Spirit, let him . . . produce relevant evidence of effective and wholehearted co-operation in matters of faith with non-fundamentalists and I will gladly believe him.[13]

He is surely right. If doctrinaire exclusiveness is to be broken down, it must show in something more than a grudging acknowledgment of some uncovenanted mercies here and there beyond the limits of one's own group. Any recognition of Christian graces is the discovery of a brother.

Ethos is a matter of attitudes, of the "intangibles" of one's religious loyalties. If I am right that the ethos of Fundamentalism has, in legal fashion, drawn its circles so as to shut out brothers of unquestionable Christian faith and devotion, the attitudes need reconstructing. But the behavioral sciences have provided valuable insights about the changing of attitudes. The power of information or study in itself to alter deeply rooted attitudes is apparently highly questionable. No secondhand or paper acquaintance with non-Fundamentalists on the part of Fundamentalists will remove the estranging prejudgments half as well as would firsthand personal contacts. Mutual understanding and trust among believing people of different names can only flourish where there is the possibility of a shared life of discussion, prayer, growth, and engagement in common service for Christ. Where these active steps are taken, appreciation of the manifold gifts of the Spirit follows; sympathy for varying doctrines, presuppositions, and practices grows; narrowness is modified. A closed body of doctrines can begin to open to new light when a Christian's experience of fellowship extends beyond his familiar landmarks. Thus, if Fundamentalism is to overcome an ethos that is legalistic in basis, more is involved than re-thinking or restudying documents. It is an exercise in Christian love, an enlargement of the sympathies, and a wider sense of communion and mission that is called for. If we are planning to wait for complete doctrinal accord before we review our attitudes toward others, we are bad psychologists as well as poor Christians —and in for an indefinitely long wait as well.

As for an *ethic of grace*: Here, too, what derives from grace will be redemptive. The Christian society is related to the wider human society as its redemptive instrument—it shares the priestliness of Christ. But before the Christian community can be redemptively related to the hurt in human life it must be responsibly related. That is, separateness is not the most urgent among the Gospel's demands. The ethic of withdrawal was not learned from the Friend of sinners. The Puritan denunciations and fastidious taboos in Fundamentalism have no redemptive meaning. They only serve to make self-righteous people more contented with themselves. They are in the spirit of "Lord, I thank thee that I am not as other men." Any redemptive effectiveness presupposes not withdrawal but responsible participation. This means that the isolation of Fundamentalism is a serious liability. God calls us to work within our urbanized, industrial, ethnically varied, highly organized, rapidly moving, technical, deeply interrelated society. We must start where we are—with a commitment to our own particular world. Christians ought to live in responsible involvement with the complex, morally muddied world of which God has made them part.

If responsible relations are established, how can they become redemptive? The legal approach is futile. Only an impotent moralism stands above and lectures the groundlings. Much that is done as "helping others" is similarly egoistic and patronizing. The longer and more costly way of creative love, listening, sacrifice, patience, mutual forgiveness, and understanding is the mark of grace. When the tortured complexity of the moral world is accepted, oversimple blacks and whites can be forgotten. Flexibility and the recognition of differing standards are not a false casuistry; they are the humbling lessons taught by grace. And they open the way for interpersonal relationships which convey, rather than contradict, the Christian message. A formalistic ethical stance provides no way into the human need. In the light of a message of forgiveness of sin, proclaimed to sinners and by sinners, ethical absolutism needs rethinking. It stands in the way of the Christian mission.

As to a *piety of grace*: The problem here is the "perfectionism" of Fundamentalist piety—the presumption that the "saved" and the "dedicated" and the "real Christians" are known, that living "at the center of God's will" is a simple possibility, and that the moral ambiguity of life can safely be overlooked in the case of Christians. If grace is our clue, the harm of judging—of separating, by anticipation, the sheep from the goats—is incalculable.

Perhaps the necessary first step in rethinking the pattern of piety into a form based on grace would be to question the "saved" and "unsaved" division which looms so large in the Fundamentalist outlook. What, after all, are the supposed determinants? How well do they stand scrutiny? Are they, as they would have to be if they are to be used at all, final and infallible? Are the "saved" identified with the sin of the world, or are they exempt? What, if any, is the ultimate difference between the sins and the virtues of a Christian and the sins and the virtues of a non-Christian? Is it legitimate to think of becoming a Christian as a process rather than an event, or has the invention of the sawdust trail made that an unnecessary complication?

And perhaps time would not be ill-spent in examining critically the "consecrated" vs. the "unconsecrated" Christian division which looms nearly as large. If the sixth chapter of Romans says anything, it says that Christian life, at its very birth in baptism, is consecrated, bound over into the life of Christ. An unconsecrated Christian is in the New Testament a contradiction in terms. Any decision we may make—and hopefully we will make many—is made on this basis; we are already consecrated persons.

Grace cannot move with pat formulas and ready-made answers which are distributed to all alike. Grace cannot be schematized. "The wind bloweth where it listeth." Grace puts us in touch with ourselves—perhaps for the first time. It does not ask us to play a role or adopt a pose. If it is really grace, it opens the possibilities of individuality and spontaneity. Variety in a community is a mark of authenticity and of life. The Holy Spirit in every case, through all of the variety, means to take over weak, sinful human lives and re-create them in the image of Jesus Christ. But there is no single scheme of how he goes about it. He has as many ways of working as there are people to be reached. He never forces his way on anyone, for he, too, is love. He always respects man's freedom—his freedom to say "no" even to God. In some cases sudden tactics may be employed, but they need not be normative. There is great mischief in trying to reproduce in others the pattern of Christian experience that is right for one.

The Spirit, we can be sure, claims us in the fullness of our humanity. He seeks us as fully functioning human beings. Piety is thus not separable from all that has made us human—all that has made us ourselves. True piety is not a withdrawal; we do not reach God by retreating from man. For true godliness, nothing is secular. We learn of our humanity from the arts and sciences and their knowledge of the depths of life. We learn from poets, dramatists, painters, psychologists, sociologists. Through them we are sensitized to ourselves and to our world; we face the ambiguities in our humanness; we see the meaninglessness that haunts our generation (and we see it with some terror, for it has had its effect on each of us). Without this acceptance of our humanity as members of our generation, identified with its anguish, we are offering to the disposal of the Spirit of God only partial, incomplete persons. Without this recognition of our involvement in humanity, our acts of dedication, our use of prayer and Bible study, are escapist. With an acceptance and conse-cration of our humanity, our piety is turned outward, not in-ward. It is unlikely to sour. It will resist all efforts to schematize it. The Spirit is bigger than any channels he customarily uses and into which we seek to confine him. He shows his divinity in the sovereign way in which he sets aside, and works outside, the schemes with which we have become preoccupied.

III. THE PROBLEM IN PERSPECTIVE

You have had my diagnosis of the basic problem of Funda-mentalism. Now you have my prescription.

I am persuaded that a thorough analysis must include at least this full a picture of the movement. For all of these areas are related. It has been interesting to observe that the second gener-ation Fundamentalists who detach themselves from the move-ment begin their criticism at different points. The taboos, evolu-tion, biblical criticism, the arts—any of these may be important as a starting place for defection. Eventually, however, the whole complex is interrelated, and criticism that stops partway and does not come to terms with the whole remains edgy and ambiv-alent. This is the state just now of some of the Fundamentalist critics of Fundamentalism. Men like Harold John Ockenga, Carl Henry, or Bernard Ramm seem to say, "We reject a belligerent attitude and a 'know nothing' apologetics. But we are concerned that our orthodox theology which has really been right all along be given a chance to vindicate itself without some of the disgraceful associations it has had." I am reasonably well aware of how far their self-criticisms have gone—much farther than I had realized until I made it my business to find out, on your suggestion. Much that Soper said about Berkhof's theological posture, for example, would hardly be true of the most recent work of Carnell. But in spite of their redefining, the work of these able men is still carried out with reference to a movement which remains pretty much as I have described it. Their criticisms, penetrating as they often are, are still not thorough enough. Henry has called for a rethinking effort among conservatives no less rigorous than that which has been going on in Liberalism.[14] But, so far, the self-criticism within the movement has not dealt searchingly enough with the institutionalized legalism of which I have been speaking. The spokesmen for the newer conservativism remain unwilling to review their own complete theological stance. At the vital center of thinking, they cling to the absolute of the "inscripturated" revelation and a finally formulated orthodoxy. They fall quite readily into an "elder brother" pose, saying, in effect, "We never left home." Sometimes they seem to want "repentant" representatives of other theological strains to come up and apologize. In a review article in the *Christian Century*, Martin Marty once remarked: "The latter-day evangelicalism, unlike most post-modernism, does not say 'we were wrong' but only 'we had bad manners.' "[15] I contend that ethos and doctrine, method and substance, theology and ethic, are all of a piece. The bad manners were related to the mistaken ideas.

Carnell has proposed a distinction between two varieties of orthodoxy.[16] He distinguishes "cultic" orthodoxy—separatist, rigid, vain, which he declares bad, from "classical" orthodoxy—historically oriented, enlightened, but traditional, which he declares good. He says that though the two had been united in the Fundamentalist movement they are different in nature and have now become distinguishable. He urges that the former be regarded with some patience and understanding, but he thinks it has forfeited its right to a serious hearing. The latter, on the other hand, he thinks is deserving of an invitation "to the tables of theological discussion." He wants orthodoxy (classical version, of course) invited largely on the basis of its moral realism—a realism preserved by its loyalty to the doctrine of justification by faith as found in Galatians and Romans. Since this issue is being rediscovered in the church at large, Carnell reasons, the relevance of orthodoxy should be recognized in ecumenical conversation. This distinction and this plea of Carnell's seem to me to be significant and promising, but inadequate. The same doctrine of justification which judges the "cultic thinking," censoriousness, and lovelessness of the groups that Carnell criticizes judges also the traditional scholasticism of those whom he defends. We cannot sit down together showing the "mutual signs of humility" that Carnell desires if one party to the conversation wants it understood from the outset that it represents a "classic" normative truth which is that of the Bible and the church throughout the ages. If this diagnosis and this prescription have hit anywhere near the "real problem" of Fundamentalism as it has been known in the history of the past two generations, those who would like to restate a conservative position for a new day must be more thoroughgoing in their criticism of what they have inherited than any have yet dared to be.

These pages may have suggested to you as well my notion of why the fine old term "Evangelical" is wrongly expropriated by the Fundamentalists. The primary reference of the term is not to a religious pose or to a formulation of doctrine—though in the 19th century it became both of these. Its primary reference is not to the finality of the Bible, though this is nearer the truth. The primary reference is to the biblical message, the evangel, the Living Word, Christ himself. This is the informing spirit of the Evangelicalism of the great tradition. If the new-Evangelicals want to claim the title, they must be willing to abide by its innermost meaning. I share C. C. Morrison's indignation:

> That term "evangelical" has been adopted avowedly to offset the prejudice which the term "fundamentalism" had acquired in its earlier, intensely controversial period. Thus the noblest word in the vocabulary of Christian evangelism has been raped by its association with this unevangelical deviation from New Testament Christianity.[17]

The Gospel—not laws, not external propositions, not narrow loyalties—must be the shaping force of the whole religious, social, psychological, and intellectual fabric if a group wants clear title to this name.

Fundamentalism, however, fails to take its own Gospel seriously enough to venture a life of thinking and doing on grace. The legal spirit errs in objectifying religion. It makes God (the knowledge of, and obedience to, him), revelation, faith, and community into things that can be defined, manipulated, and controlled. Law tends inevitably to treat persons as things; it depersonalizes whatever it touches. It seeks a God who is more predictable and manageable than the God of biblical faith. This externalization of grace and faith is the root of the error of legalism. And this interior flaw leads to the exterior brittleness.

The more vital approach suggested here as corrective would place living, deciding Christians as participants in redemptive life rather than as observers of it. No one stands outside life, looking on with a true map in his hand. Rather, there is an outreach of holy love from God which has met us in the midst of life and which becomes real as it does something within us and we act upon it. Those who begin to live with this divine act as their determinative center begin the grand Christian venture. Into their struggle for truth has come the Word of God; they can think with all truth as their province and the Spirit of truth as their Lord. Into their quest for purpose has come God's claim and promise; they can live to the full, for the Creator has reclaimed his lost world and has called them to fill a responsible place in the fulfillment of his creative and redemptive work. Here is no system of rigid laws for the mind or externally imposed regulations for life. There is no deliverance from the difficulty and the paradox of our humanity. Christians still must think and choose and risk. But the God who deals with men by grace is liberating, not confining. He wants sons, not slaves. A religion centered in grace is on the offensive, not the defensive. I suppose this can be a little frightening—it certainly is risky. But is anything less than this really Christian?

Cordially,
Spermologos

III

THE
BIBLE

When someone is honestly 55% right, that's very good and there's no use wrangling. And if someone is 60% right, it's wonderful, it's great luck, and let him thank God. But what's to be said about 75% right? Wise people say this is suspicious. Well, and what about 100% right? Whoever says he's 100% right is a fanatic, a thug, and the worst kind of rascal.

AN OLD JEW OF GALICIA
(Used as the epigraph of
The Captive Mind, by
Czeslaw Milosz)

IN DEFENSE
OF THE CRITICS

O Theophilus,

So you showed my last letter to your friend, and now he calls me "Screwtape"! Well, do tell him that "your affectionate uncle" has placed your eternal weal in jeopardy by writing again.

Your last letter to me was as perceptive as usual, and it stirred me to some thinking—as usual.

You are surely right in saying that the theory of verbal inspiration is "the electric fence around the Fundamentalist pasture." William Hordern has said that "the heart of Fundamentalism is in its concern for salvation. The only really important question is, 'Have you been saved?' "[1] He feels that Fundamentalists maintained their view of the Bible as a first line of defense. They felt that the God who saves could not be a religious reality long if uncertainty about the Bible arose.

> If one began by doubting any statement of the Bible, he had started down the slippery slope that, the fundamentalist believed, would lead to the denial of God and the divinity of Jesus, the loss of certainty of salvation, and finally the loss of ethics.[2]

This is probably a correct account of the initial motives for the emphasis on verbal inspiration and for the passion with which the doctrine is still defended. But in the course of time the teaching that may have been championed as a means to the preservation of the saving Gospel has been so identified with the Gospel that it is the constitutive thing in the movement. The qualifying term "Bible-believing" has for two decades or more been added to "Christian" among Fundamentalists, to indicate their conscious differentia. There is no real acceptance of others who may believe the classic Christian Gospel and creed if they do not also believe the Fundamentalist theory of the Scriptures. On the other hand, latitude is allowed on material issues within Fundamentalism, and acceptance is not withheld as long as the right conception of inspiration is affirmed. More than any other single factor, verbal inspiration is the movement's criterion for acceptance or rejection.[3]

This being so, the struggle over verbal inspiration is usually the most anguished part of any Fundamentalist's religious misgivings. He has been led to suppose that defection here, no matter how conscientious, must in principle involve defection from Christ. You have certainly hit the critical point.

Prompted by your remarks, I would like to devote a letter or two to the inspiration and the authority of the Bible.

The terms of this issue are not just where the conservative group sets them. The matter has progressed in recent decades beyond the point at which the dispute was drawn when conversation was broken off. New questions, altered in form, have grown out of the old questions. The ideas of "verbal inspiration" and "inerrancy" remain with us, like the marsupial mammals, survivors from an era otherwise quite extinct. However, the issues of that past era still live in the thinking of the Fundamentalist constituency, and one must enter into them in order to bridge out of them.

I. VERBAL INSPIRATION RECONSIDERED

In the dispute over biblical criticism, the case for verbal inspiration and inerrancy assumed fairly set form. This defense is so familiar that anyone who today wants to see his way out of the Fundamentalist form of thought must in some sense relive the old disputes. He must look at the traditional case with new eyes. I would like to examine it critically point by point. One philosophical issue demands first attention. Then we may look at the various bases on which the case is made to rest.

Is the Affirmation Possible?

Initially I propose that even to make the affirmation of biblical inerrancy is philosophically perilous.

To rigorous thinking, anyone affirming categorically that

something within history is inerrant is beyond his proper depth. He assumes his own omniscience. He claims to know as God knows.

To stress the absence of error throws the emphasis in the dispute on the factual element in the biblical documents. Fundamentalist apologists ransack archaeology and other sciences for facts and artifacts to support the Bible's statements. But to maintain that a body of historical literature is inerrant—that it cannot be mistaken—implies a knowledge of all facts. Any argument about the presence of errors lies in the scientific arena where any categorical statement of infallibility is out of place. There is a dialectical leap from any cumulative body of evidence in favor of the general reliability of a historical document to a categorical statement that it cannot be in error. The two matters are on different levels. On the scientific plane where facts are considered, all general statements must be provisional. God's usual avoidance of the perfect or the infallible throws the burden of proof on the contender for inerrancy; every presumption is against him. He dare not, in his position, affirm categorically the inerrancy of the Bible unless he lay claim to omniscience. For it is possible that, if there were only one fact still unknown to him, that might be the one fact that would show the Bible mistaken in some particular. As R. H. Strachan put it, "Infallibility is simply a category which men cannot use; we are entirely without the data in experience from which such a notion can be constructed."[4]

It is possible to raise the level of the issue. After all, what is involved is not only a body of factual statements but a principle of religious authority. So, if the inerrancy of Bible cannot be "proved" by induction out of the data in experience, possibly it can be affirmed as a religious absolute on the a priori basis of attestation by some qualified authority. This, of course, makes these authorities of the utmost importance. Unless that which attests the infallibility of something else is itself without error, it might be misleading us in this crucial matter of biblical accuracy. Then, if it is infallible, we have two infallibles, not one—the Bible and the thing which says it is infallible. But this multiplication of infallibles is not an attractive position for a Fundamentalist or for anyone else. However, if this second authority, which attests the Bible, is not completely trustworthy, we are still left in uncertainty. Frequently, despite this disquieting general consideration, conservative argument has recourse, in some sense, to the attestation of authorities which supply the Bible with its credentials.

The Credentials: Christian Experience

The authority of Christian experience is not as much used as might be expected of as "experimental" a religious expression as Fundamentalism. Perhaps it is feared that to use this argument to support inerrancy would be a plunge into the very subjectivism the conservative seeks to escape.

However, one sort of appeal to experience is involved by the belief in the internal testimony of the Holy Spirit. This line of argument is only "subjectivism" if we are not Trinitarians. And it has a distinguished lineage in Christian thought. But just what can this argument do?

In some sense the principle of a self-authenticating, inward, divine witness is a part of any adequate statement of religious authority. This inward witness can establish the authority and the divinity of the Bible's message. In fact, no quantity of external testimony can persuade a person that he is confronted by God in revelation. The final verification of the Word of God must be by God in the soul. One of the great early Bible critics in the English-speaking world, W. Robertson Smith, put it effectively:

> If I am asked why I receive the Scripture as the word of God, and as the only perfect rule of faith and life, I answer with all the fathers of the Protestant Church, *Because the Bible is the only record of the redeeming love of God, because in the Bible alone I find God drawing near to man in Christ Jesus, and declaring to us in Him His will for our salvation. And this record I know to be true by the witness of His Spirit in my heart, whereby I am assured that none other than God Himself is able to speak such words to my soul.*[5]

But Robertson Smith's positive understanding of the witness of the Spirit was matched by an equally lucid understanding of what this inward testimony cannot properly be expected to do. The inner witness cannot establish matters of fact; these have their own proper verification. Smith wrote:

> Our general views of the Bible history, our way of looking, not merely at passages, but at whole books, are coloured by things

which we have learned from men, and which have no claim to rest on the self-evidencing divine Word. This we forget, and so, taking God's witness to His Word to be a witness to our whole conception of the Word, we claim a divine certainty for opinions which lie within the sphere of ordinary reason, and which can be proved or disproved by the ordinary laws of historical evidence. We assume that, because our reading of Scripture is sufficiently correct to allow us to find in it the God of redemption speaking words of grace to our soul, those who seek some other view of the historical aspects of Scripture are trying to eliminate the God of grace from His own book.[6]

"Truth" is a multi-leveled word. The inward testimony of God which is necessary to establish the "truth" of one's ultimate convictions is not the proper means whereby to establish the "truth" of the authorship of a disputed book or the date or the actuality of a particular event. One does not consult the inner witness of the Spirit to establish the exact distance from the earth to the sun. So, while the internal testimony of the Holy Spirit is necessary to the finality and the authority of the biblical revelation, it cannot establish such things as the factual accuracy of the text or the conservative conclusions on criticism. The Spirit can say, "Here is the voice of God speaking savingly to you, calling for your complete trust and commitment." But the Spirit does not say, "You may abandon all investigation of the evidence, for I verify the inerrancy of this document and certify some introductory matters about it." So the appeal to the attestation in experience is valid only if it is carefully qualified. We must remember what it can attest and what it cannot.

The Credentials: The Church and Tradition

What about the witness of the church?

This forms the base for the Roman Catholic argument for verbal inspiration. And Rome is not afraid of her own logic: We know the Bible is infallible on the authority of the church, and we have the infallibility of the church on very good authority—she claims it for herself! Thus the Roman Church emerges with two infallibles—the church and the Bible. (This will illustrate the principle stated earlier, i.e., once it is said that the Bible is infallible on some authority, a regression is started which is hard to stop, for the question is then, "What infallible thing said so?" And infallibles multiply like rabbits.)

But Fundamentalists, too, use the argument from church tradition. Gaussen's classic work defending verbal inspiration cites the witness of antiquity thus:

> With the single exception of Theodore of Mopsuestia . . . it has been found impossible to produce, in the long course of the first eight centuries of Christianity, a single doctor who has disowned the plenary inspiration of the Scriptures, unless it be in the bosom of the most violent heresies that have tormented the Christian Church.[7]

This verdict, as amplified by more recent conservative writers, is in a sense true. While the Fathers, scholastics, and Reformers were not all equally literal in their way of treating the Bible nor explicit in their doctrine of it, their statements or inferences certainly favor the unquestioned authority and reliability of the Bible. The "higher critics" were always present but were few in number.

However, this is not to say that any traditional view was precisely that of the present-day Fundamentalists or that the Fathers would maintain today the same positions they did in antiquity. For between their time and ours has come a new factor in thinking, the importance of which perhaps exceeds that of the Renaissance—the rise of scientific thought. And this new factor has influenced biblical studies immeasurably. Antiquity was generally uncritical of documents. If the Donation of Constantine or the epics of Homer were advertised as by a historical Constantine or a historical Homer, the matter was not questioned. The issue of "inerrancy" was never raised in a scientific manner until the modern era.

Insofar as the Fathers recognized problems and discrepancies in the text of Holy Scripture (as many of them did), they seemed able to accept some ingenious reconciling explanation or to shift to allegorical exegesis. That is, they would observe the problem passage and then say that the apparent difficulty concealed a mystery: This number stood for one thing; this river was a symbol of something else; and this person was a type of still another thing. Put them together as an allegory, and the problem passage becomes a revelation of great truth. This method, it should be said, was not an irresponsible dodge. In the intellectual climate of antiquity the unseen tended to be more real than the seen, the thing symbolized to be more true than the mere appearance. The Scriptures had a manifold meaning because the world did. In such a philosophical atmosphere this form of exegesis (practiced in one degree of elaboration or another by all of the Fathers) was a genuine way of getting at the real meaning of a religious text—a way open to serious (but, one hopes, gentle) criticism from the modern point of view, but a way which in its own time did not lack integrity. However, since at least the seventeenth century, our minds have become increasingly dominated by a one-level, positivistic way of looking at the world and at religious documents. Only as the logic of this trend gathered force was the explicit question of error in the Bible raised as crucial. Only in modern times were the explicit theory of verbal inspiration and the literalistic canons of interpretation clearly articulated.[8]

Since the issue was never raised in modern terms in antiquity, tradition does not speak on this specific matter at all. If we are to assume from the writings of the Fathers before the scientific period that they would agree with the Fundamentalists today, now that the terms of the problem are altered, we must be prepared to assume as well that if the Fathers were writing today they would reject the sphericity of the earth and would retain their naïve cosmology in defiance of the evidence of science. We must also assume that they would repeat ancient psychology and biology. For all these matters (like biblical studies) have undergone dramatic change since the rise of modern science. What the Fathers said in their day on matters in which science is competent to inform us cannot, it seems to me, be taken to be the judgment they would make today in full awareness of the way in which the terms of the question have changed.

The Credentials: The Authority of Jesus

The authority of Jesus is often cited in support of verbal inspiration. He is even cited in defense of conservative judgments on the dating and the authorship of such Psalms as 110, 69, and 16; on the Mosaic authorship of the Pentateuch; on the literal historicity of the Jonah story; and on the Isaianic authorship of material classed by competent scholars as having been written by the unknown "second Isaiah."[9] However, at least one authority of quite conservative opinions who is held in high esteem among Fundamentalists has spoken well on this line of argument:

> We have not in this argument sought unduly to press our Lord's testimony [on literary matters of Old Testament criticism], for we allow that His words may fairly be in part explained by His acceptance of current views of authorship, which it was no part of His mission to pronounce upon. We do not, by quoting Homer or Shakespeare under these names, pronounce a judgment on the literary questions involved in the ascription of certain poems or plays to these persons as their authors. Our Lord naturally referred to the books He was citing as "Moses" or "David," or "Isaiah," and no more thought of giving an authoritative judgment on the history or mode of origin of these books, than He had it in view to settle questions of modern science as to the motions of the heavenly bodies, the age of the earth, or the evolution of species.[10]

Some conservative writers use Jesus' statements ". . . I have come not to abolish . . . but to fulfil . . ." (Matt. 5:17) and ". . . scripture cannot be broken . . ." (John 10:35) to support their claim. But these remarks must not be taken to mean more than they intend. These texts do indicate Jesus' reverence for the Old Testament revelation. But the citation from Matthew appears in a passage in which Jesus himself undertakes a radical transcending of Old Testament morality. In other words, his confident use of the Old Testament was mixed with its own kind of higher criticism. If we are going to appeal to the way Jesus drew on the Old Testament, we must also appeal to the way in which he set it aside. In using the text from John, we at once face the problem of how the words of Jesus in the Fourth Gospel (so unlike the Synoptics) relate to the mind of the historic Jesus. Further, the parenthetic nature of the remark on Scripture, the strained and rabbinic method of the argument and exegesis in the context, raise problems as to the applicability of this verse to the question at hand; an appeal to it might in the end prove too much. Then, too, it rather seems that the term "broken" which Jesus uses here refers not to the objective accuracy of Scripture but to the way in which it is regarded by men; he is saying, "Scripture cannot be lightly set aside, cannot be flaunted or disregarded." The verb Jesus uses has this meaning elsewhere in this Gospel. At any rate, too many questions surround this verse for us to ask it to disclose Jesus' own theory of the inspiration of the Scriptures (even assuming that he could properly be said to have had one).

The subject of the total historical reliability of the Old Testament as such is a topic on which Jesus does not speak. However, he acknowledged the Old Testament as God's Word. In the sense of being a true witness to revelation—"testifying of him"—and hence having the utmost spiritual, ethical, doctrinal authority, ". . . scripture cannot be broken . . ." Jesus set his seal upon it. In the sense of its being factually accurate in all particulars, Jesus had nothing to say.

The Credentials: The Bible as Its Own Authentication

And, strangely, most of the learned arguments for the verbal inspiration of the Scriptures rest finally on what the Bible says about its own inspiration. One highly regarded study, echoing the argument of B. B. Warfield, puts the matter this way:

> The basis of faith in the Bible is the witness the Bible itself bears to the fact that it is God's Word, and our faith that it is infallible must rest upon no other basis than the witness the Bible bears to this fact. If the Bible does not witness to its own infallibility, then we have no right to believe that it is infallible. If it does bear witness to its infallibility then our faith in it must rest upon that witness, however much difficulty may be entertained with this belief. . . . The doctrine of Scripture must be elicited from the Scripture just as any other doctrine should be. . . . The real question then becomes: What is the witness of Scripture with reference to its own character?[11]

As an initial reply, of course the infallibility of the Bible cannot be accepted on its own authority. If it claims inerrancy, it can only be taken seriously as its own witness if it is already regarded as infallible on other grounds. Its own claims might be one of the points on which it is in error. If the *Book of Mormon* claims infallibility for itself (and I am not sure that it does), it is not for that reason infallible. This argues in a circle.

But this argument is not as childish nor as easily answered as these few sentences would seem to indicate. It has become in some conservative circles a highly sophisticated and very involved line of thought. It is perhaps unfair to deal with it briefly, but let me see if I can condense its principal thrust.

Cornelius Van Til is probably the figure most associated with the amplification of this argument. He admits that understanding the Bible through the Bible is argument in a circle. But he replies that this is not as scandalous as it may appear, for all argument is circular. That is, Van Til says, all positive statements imply a system resting on certain presuppositions and including a whole view of life. This system is not always worked out by each thinker, but it is always there in principle. Now, for Van Til, the great division among such opposed systems is that between the Christian and the non-Christian. Between these there is complete antagonism. "According to one theory God is the final court of appeal; according to the other theory man is the final court of appeal."[12] These two cannot be reconciled. A person either makes himself determinative of everything, even of God, or lets God be determinative, even of himself. Thus, either we learn about God from ourselves, and this is idolatry, or we learn about God from God. So God in his self-revelation is the presupposition of all thought. And for Van Til, God's revelation means the verbally inspired Scriptures. "Thus the Bible, as the infallibly inspired revelation of God to sinful man, stands before us as that light in terms of which all the facts of the created universe must be interpreted."[13] There is a deep impropriety, then, in critical study of the Bible. "We cannot subject the authoritative pronouncements of Scripture about reality to the scrutiny of reason because it is reason itself that learns of its proper function from Scripture."[14] And again, "For the believers, Scripture is the principle of theology. As such it cannot be the conclusion of other premises, but it is *the* premise from which all other conclusions are drawn."[15]

What about this argument? Van Til does make a valuable point when he puts the authority and the cruciality of revelation so clearly in the fore. He certainly says well that only God knows God, and only God can reveal God, and if we are to know God it must be through God. He is also on defensible ground in subordinating reason so sharply to revelation. These points, however, are pretty much what Karl Barth, Van Til's *bête noire*, has also been saying; they are the common coin of contemporary understanding of revelation. The disagreement comes when Van Til makes God his principle, and revelation his principle, and then makes Reformed theology and an infallibly inspired Bible a part of the same circle, the finality of God inhering throughout.

It is this equation of God, revelation, his own system, and the statements of the Bible literally construed that is highly doubtful. Does the Christian revelation of God (which must be final) demand a verbally infallible Bible as its necessary implicate? Is it the purpose of the Scriptures, as part of the revelatory movement, to give perfect propositions disclosing the mind of God? Van Til would say, "Yes, the infallible Bible is a part of the circle in which God in his self-disclosure is both beginning and end. For that is what the Bible teaches about itself."

So it seems that if we are to question this equation we must give some attention to the so-called "claims" of the Bible for itself. B. B. Warfield and the symposium *The Infallible Word*, usually cited as the most weighty authorities on this subject among modern conservatives, draw their case largely from this source. Indeed they are frank to recognize the futility of any outside attestation of biblical authority and inerrancy. So we may well ask: What can the Bible be said to claim for itself?

For one thing, just as an introductory consideration, it would be impossible for the Bible to make any "claims" for itself as an entity. "The Bible" itself (Old Testament or New) did not exist as a single literary unit capable of being talked about until some generations after the writing was done. So the notion "the 66 books of the canonically received Scriptures are verbally inspired and inerrant in the original writings" simply could not have occurred to anyone in the biblical period.

But, to proceed to the more specific texts that are cited as constituting "claims":

(a) All of the New Testament passages that speak of "the Scriptures" as inspired refer, of course, only to the Old Testament—and only to it insofar as its canon was settled, a matter not made final until after the New Testament period.

No New Testament passage "claims the rank of inspired Scripture for the writing in which it occurs, or defines the works to which it attributes inspiration."[16]

The one passage which is often cited by Fundamentalists to involve the New Testament in such "claims" as are made, viz., 2 Peter 3:15-16, says only that the writings of Paul (and only they, and possibly only the apocalyptic or eschatological passages in them) are: Scripture, difficult, and often misinterpreted. These "claims" are not in dispute.

(b) It is customary among Fundamentalists to lean heavily

on the conscious "claims" of the Old Testament prophetic writers. "More than 3,800 times the writers of the Old Testament introduce their messages with such statements as these: 'The Lord spake,' 'the Lord said,' 'the word of the Lord came.' "[17]

This characteristic formula of the prophetic consciousness when it said, "Thus saith the Lord," is equally present in the claims of charlatans, false prophets, and ancient oracular utterances. By its use a speaker clearly claims to be a prophet. But the use of this formula does not in itself demonstrate that the speaker was properly entitled to use the phrase—one of the few who was right in the claim the formula implies. Its presence, in itself, proves little. It is a prophet's authoritative way of indicating his identification with and insight into the divine purposes—his message was not his own; something not himself possessed him when he prophesied. It is, of course, true that through the Old Testament prophetic utterances, "the Word of the Lord," did come; they were inspired. But saying this does not relieve the mystery of what the formula means. H. Wheeler Robinson once said:

> In that spiritual temple of Israel of which the prophets are the essential builders, there is also a dark chamber as the Most Holy Place, over which are the words, "Thus saith Yahweh." If we could penetrate its mystery, we should know the last secret of personal religion.[18]

So when those who are making "claims" for the Bible assume that they know exactly what this formula intends—that the divine inspiration was such as to overrule the fallibility of the human speaker, that Almighty God was literally speaking Hebrew—they exceed the denotation of the words themselves. It will not solve the matter merely to say (even to say repeatedly and emphatically) that the words mean just what they say, for that is the point in question. Nor will it prove very much to say, "You don't mean enough by these words. I don't know exactly what I mean, but I mean more than you do." When all the arguing is over, "the last secret of personal religion" remains a secret still. The prophetic consciousness is a mystery at least as unilluminated by anything contributed by conservative scholarship as by anything contributed by others. The true prophets were men of God; they were possessed by the word of God for their time; and they spoke with the authority of men laid hold of by the Lord. But the "claim" that the words were so given by God as to exclude the free, responsible, and fallible work of the human instrument is not a necessary implication from the use of this formula, which in itself is a convention of the ecstatic prophetic manner.

(c) Two New Testament texts are examined in elaborate detail by the Fundamentalist apologists, and it may be questioned whether the conclusions they reach do not exceed the data.

The first of these is 2 Timothy 3:16: "All scripture is inspired by God and profitable for teaching, for reproof, for correction, and for training in righteousness."[19] This sentence states clearly enough that all Scripture (leaving unstated the scope of the writings so designated but doubtless referring to the Old Testament) is inspired by God and profitable for Christians. These "claims" are not seriously denied. The manner of the inspiration or the exemption of the resultant writings from error is not discussed.

To weight one Greek word (theopneustos—"breathed by God") too heavily here and to make it teach an elaborate theory of plenary inspiration and freedom from error makes it bear more freight than it will safely carry. Aside from this one instance, this is not a biblical word. That is, it has no history of development as a biblical term in the theology of the Old Testament and the New. It does not appear in the Septuagint or in the teachings of Jesus or anywhere else in the epistles. So there is no biblical use to establish its exact theological meaning. Concepts of "inspiration" from the classical world are of no help. A clue may be had from the poetic image in this word. It suggests the picture of man made from dust of the earth and breathed into life by God. But the fuller theology of inspiration must be understood in the perspective of revelation as the Bible shows it to be. How does God show himself to men? How does God speak? How is he heard? The biblical point (or points) of view in these matters must provide the guidelines within which the exegesis of 2 Timothy 3:16 will hold proper bounds. At the moment, of course, I cannot develop these great questions. But I may at least suggest that this one verse (the main verse used among Fundamentalists as a proof text for verbal inspiration), by itself, says nothing about inerrancy, offers no theory of inspira-

tion, and can at most be one of the verses that will take its
explicit meaning only from a more ample investigation of the
total biblical concept of revelation.

(d) The second of these texts is 2 Peter 1:21: ". . . no
prophecy ever came by the impulse of man, but men moved by
the Holy Spirit spoke from God." This verse refers at least explicitly to the prophetic portions of the Old Testament, and any
extension of this thought to the entire Old Testament or the
entire Christian Bible must be by inference, not by clear statement. Concerning the prophetic Scriptures, this verse says that
their ultimate origin was in the Holy Spirit, not in the will of
man. This is certainly a good way of putting the distinctive feature of the prophetic consciousness. St. Paul felt the same way
in his own preaching of the Cross (e.g., 1 Cor. 2:13). But it is
only by inference that the verse from 2 Peter can be taken to
support the theory of inerrancy; that particular subject simply
is not under discussion.

(e) Sometimes Revelation 22:18-19 is brought into the series
of "claims": "I warn every one who hears the words of the
prophecy of this book: if any one adds to them, God will add to
him the plagues described in this book, and if any one takes
away from the words of the book of this prophecy, God will
take away his share in the tree of life and in the holy city, which
are described in this book." These verses are a closing warning
against tampering with the text of the Apocalypse by addition
or subtraction. This stern warning is a literary device modeled
after Deuteronomy 4:2 and 12:32, and based on the assumed
divine givenness of the vision. It says, in effect, "When I was 'in
the Spirit,' the Lord granted me this vision—a thing which was
beyond my control. I have reported it to you fully and accurately
just as it was given to me. Let no one presume to alter it." Most
writers of visionary literature must have felt a noble jealousy
rather like this about their work. Such a final cursing is not, in
fact, at all unique. Many commentaries give extensive parallels
from the literature, Jewish and Christian, of the period surrounding the New Testament.[20] The presence of such claims and such
cursings does not, of course, mean that any or all of the writings
in which they appear are the infallible Word of God. As a further consideration, it appears to me that factual "inerrancy" as
such is hardly a relevant category in the case of apocalyptic

literature. In what sense does one establish the inerrancy of a statement about a beast with seven heads and ten horns? Nonetheless, of all the New Testament texts produced by Fundamentalist apologists in defense of verbal inspiration, this one seems to be the one that most nearly constitutes a "claim." But of them all it is the one which in substance claims the least.

This may not be the entire list of the "claims" which the Bible is alleged to make in its own behalf. But it certainly includes the ones that bear the greatest weight in the case, and the whole cannot endure if these are withdrawn. No one of them nor any combination among them teaches that "the Scriptures of the Old and New Testaments are verbally inspired of God and inerrant in the original writings." This is a late formulation imposed on "proof texts" which, rigorously construed, "claim" nothing of the kind for the Bible.

However, these texts and scores of others, as well as the consistent faith and usage of the church, do attest the *fact* of the specialness of the Scriptures. That is, these writings have been so guided by the Spirit of God that their witness to the significance of the saving events is without substantial distortion. These writings are our unique report of the events *as seen by faith*. They report the fact plus the believing response to the fact; thus, they "contain all things necessary to salvation." They were written from within, and for, the covenant community; and the church has received her faith from, and corrected her faith by, them. They are, as no other writings are, "the Word of God." The testimony of Scripture and church is also clear that the message of the Bible is a unity: Christ came not to destroy but to fulfill. The New Testament scheme of redemption draws its interpretation as it creatively reenters the patterns given in the Old Testament "Scripture." This much is "claimed" and agreed. But a statement of the precise extent to which the quality we call "inspiration" obtains, a theory of how it operated, or a categorical claim to inerrancy is simply not to be had from the Bible itself. The only biblical basis on which such claims as the Fundamentalists advance can be made is to say that the fact necessarily implies a certain theory—that, by definition, inspiration must be propositional and errorless. This is exactly the implication that I question. At this point I am only saying that it goes far beyond the biblical data themselves.

A short time ago I came unexpectedly upon a remark—from so unimpeachable a source as Wilbur Smith—in the *Moody Monthly* which conceded this very point. Smith was reviewing the recent conservative symposium *Revelation and the Bible*; in the course of his discussion of a disagreement among the contributors as to the basis for the belief in biblical inerrancy, he gave his judgment: "One must grant that the Bible itself, in advancing its own claim of inspiration, says nothing precise about its inerrancy. This remains a conclusion to which devout minds have come because of the divine character of Scripture."[21] His second sentence could be questioned by other minds no less devout who conclude in favor of the fallibility of Scripture because of its divine-human character. But the first sentence quoted strikes me as a beam of clarity that was not "getting through" ten years ago. I am subject to correction on this, but I do not think that among Fundamentalists it has been generally and widely admitted that the claim of inerrancy rested *not on Scripture itself but on an interpretation of Scripture.* If this was being said privately, at least it was not being said in the pages of the *Moody Monthly.* This means, of course, that the movement which has claimed to be supremely and consistently biblical, and which has accused everyone else of abandoning biblical authority in favor of mere human reason, now (at least through one spokesman) grants that the chief cornerstone of its distinctive position is itself not "scriptural" but "a conclusion" of "devout minds." This striking concession seems to me to cut the ground from under the Fundamentalists' exclusive claim to base inerrancy strictly on the Bible's own claims. A doctrine of verbal inspiration and factual inerrancy claims in the name of the Bible more than the Bible claims or could claim for itself.

II. THE LEGITIMACY OF CRITICISM

A further reason for rejecting the Fundamentalist notion of the Bible is that it seems to most scholarly observers to be a false account of the data. Our construction of the biblical story and our understanding of the nature of Scripture must depend not on some a priori judgments of what they ought to be but on a free survey of the facts as they tell their own meaning. Having looked at the case that Fundamentalists have developed for their views, and found it shaky indeed, let us look at the work of the century of critical thought which has tried to approach the Bible without the Fundamentalist prejudgments.

I cannot pose as an expert on biblical criticism, but it is evident to me that the critical reconstruction of traditional notions of the classification, origin, date, structure, sources, authorship, and unity of the biblical documents rests on solid foundations. It is, as all scientific truth is, a provisional body of conclusions—subject to continual review and correction. But in this expected process of change, whether the direction be radical or conservative, we can anticipate no surrender of the scientific attitude and no return to the conclusions offered by prescientific authority. There will be advance—just as Einstein built on Newton—but there will be no return to Ptolemy.

Now if, in good scientific procedure, the conservative opinions have been tried as hypotheses and found to be in many cases untenable, what has been lost? Most of what has been cleared away is the accumulation of long uncriticized traditions about the literary organization of the Bible. Why do Fundamentalists reject the authority of tradition in general and yet make a great issue over certain positions about the Bible for which no authority can be claimed except ancient editorial convention? There is much the same kind of evidence for Jeremiah's authorship of Lamentations, or for the unity of Isaiah, or for the Mosaic authorship of Genesis, or for the Matthean authorship of the First Gospel, or for the Johannine authorship of the Fourth, as there is for the immaculate conception: viz., something someone thought would be fitting—if it were true—was said to be true and was then repeated as a fact until in time it came to be a profanation to call it into question.

Is Genesis 1-12 historical or mythological? Was the Song of Solomon written with any other relationship in mind than that to some fair Juliet? Is the Fourth Gospel reconcilable with the first three, or the first three with one another? The answers are in the realm of literary judgments. They can supply an informed opinion as to what genre of literature we are reading. There is no author's preface to Genesis saying, "I, Moses, having heard from God of things which long antedated my own day, take pen in hand to write exactly fifty chapters of sober, literal prose, giving a precise account of the world from the primal chaos to the death of Joseph." Lacking such a preface, we are obliged to inquire of the literature itself as to its character. We must do so taking into account the methods of writing and transmission, the literary conventions of the time, and the beliefs and influences which must come to bear on any writer.

As we extend this inquiry, we must be prepared, as good critics, to take into account such things as meet us on the first page of the Old Testament, where we find two narratives of the creation (Gen. 1 and 2), with their different sequences, different names for God, different accounts of the creation of woman, different literary styles, different pictures of God. We must be prepared to take into account such things as will meet us on the first pages of the New Testament in the artificial genealogy of Jesus in Matthew or the attribution of words of Malachi to Isaiah in the second verse of the Gospel of Mark. For every page, honest investigation must be free to give the most reasonable account of whatever it finds.

Such an investigation, if it is really willing to let the documents tell their own story, will often find just such observations as the dual account of creation in Genesis and the formal arrangement of the Matthean genealogy to be its most revealing clues as to the origin, intention, and meaning of the books being studied. The nature of the writings must be concluded from the writings themselves; we cannot approach them assuming that we already know, from some unassailable tradition, exactly what they are and what they are intended to convey.

Furthermore, such an investigation must always be aware that it is dealing with religious literature. In the case of the Gospels, for example, critics discovered that they were dealing not with biographies but with something new—Gospels. And these writings had to be judged as such, not by standards derived from outside their real intention. Sensitive criticism can discover how inextricably faith is mixed with history and can thus lead beyond externals.

But primarily criticism is concerned with literary and historical judgments, and its work in these matters is of inestimable help. For the Bible is the literature of two communities, ancient Israel and the apostolic church. In this literature there are the variety of life and the organic growth of a living community's self-expression. Try to imagine, for a parallel, a book we may call *An American Grab Bag*. It has in it the life of Washington—

part from Parson Weems and part from Douglas Southall Freeman. It has American history woven from Charles Beard and from Stephen Vincent Benét's *Western Star*. It contains our Constitution; some of our laws; the pledge of allegiance to the flag (both with and without the "under God" phrase); some Paul Bunyan "tall" stories; some Civil War songs and stories and speeches (a few from each side); some essays by Emerson; some of Lincoln's speeches; sections from *Moby Dick* and *The Scarlet Letter*; some poems on democracy by Whitman; some selected wise sayings by Franklin and others; Wilder's *Our Town*; some selected great letters; some love-song lyrics; and a couple of good short stories—one patriotic, one romantic. Now, imagine that this rather sizable book comes out not as a complete jumble but printed in a somewhat illogical order, all as prose, in double columns, with every sentence or so starting at the margin and numbered, and with no explanation of what you are reading or any assurance that within any section of the book you will be reading the same sort of thing for long. This book is to be preserved and given to people living two and three thousand years hence, to give them an idea of what it meant to be an American. Imagine what theories might find support in this data. I do not mean to say that the selection in the Bible is as arbitrary as that in the *Grab Bag* or that the editorial process has led to an unintelligible result. But I do mean that the Bible presents us with something that, at least for the modern and critical mind, needs explanation. Some kind of a guide needs to tell us what we are reading. If criticism seeks to do this, it should be encouraged. The biblical documents are not self-explanatory, and the traditional judgments are often unreliable.

But again I should emphasize that the critical process cannot pass on whether or not what we are reading is the Word of God and should evoke our final trust in its message. Is the Pentateuch the product of a single author or of a composite tradition? The answer must be given by a documentary analysis, and the reality of neither the creation nor the fall nor the moral law is touched by the decision. Was Isaiah 40-66 by the son of Amoz written before the Exile or by some person (or several people) writing after it? The answer rests on the analysis of the nuances in the internal evidence and on the probabilities in the critical balances. But the great Servant Songs of renewal through suffering remain as profound one way as the other. Is the Letter to the Ephesians the work of St. Paul or of someone else? The answer again depends on a critical weighing of the facts. But its great summary of a cosmic redemption in Christ through the church is unaffected by the outcome. If St. Paul wrote it, we have the high point in his theological insight. If someone else did, we have two witnesses, rather than one, to the Pauline Christian doctrine.[22] God is still Creator, Judge, and Redeemer, whether it is said by one man writing history or by generations of men chanting myth, whether it is said by an apostle or by someone whose name we do not know. No matter of actual consequence to the biblical message or the Christian creed stands or falls with the critical decisions.

This is not to say that with questions of demythologizing and the relation of fact to faith in the fore as they are in our time a critic does not move very quickly from his critical or literary judgments into matters of theology. However, though the line between them is not sharp, the two kinds of issues—the critical and the theological—are distinguishable. Here I have only sought to defend the legitimacy and value of the critical enterprise. If our faith is true, its truth will be witnessed to in every real discovery. Critical questions need cause no fear. In fact those who believe most implicitly that the Bible is the Word of the Creator and Redeemer should be the most free and confident in asking it to disclose its nature and development as a literature. Panic over such questions would seem to betray a lurking distrust.

If you happen to show this new letter to your Fundamentalist friend, he will at least know that we minions of the Tempter these days, if not very bright, are at least very busy.

Perhaps some constructive ideas about the Bible, revelation, and authority can be the subject of another letter. For the present, this must suffice.

Cordially,
Spermologos

THE KNOT
IN THE THREAD

O Theophilus,

Since I last wrote, I have been trying to put in order some positive ideas about the Bible, to complete the business left unfinished then. Now your most recent letter seems to move right on into those questions—the big questions of revelation and authority—that were untouched in our discussion of criticism.

Having dismissed the idea of verbal inspiration, I do not want to appear to say that only stupid people would believe it. You and I know very well that devout, brilliant, and well-informed people do hold the theory of verbal inspiration. I only mean to say that intelligent people would not hold it unless they misunderstood the issue and unnecessarily feared the alternatives.

I think it is true, and occasional expressions of theirs seem to concur, that the crucial reason why most Fundamentalists believe in verbal inspiration is their fear that lacking an objective, infallible authority one has no alternative but what they call "subjectivism." That is to say, they think that once criticism is allowed to judge the Bible in any respect the order of things is upset—the Titans have challenged the gods; man's vaunting pride has put itself above the Word of God. The expected logic of this reversal is that eventually human reason, having put itself first, will try to be self-sufficient and do without the Word of God altogether. In a passage I referred to previously, Hordern spoke of the fear of "creeping humanism." Are we not leaving a firm rock for a foundation of sand when we suggest the competence of human reason to stand in judgment in any way over Holy Scripture?

This is the way the issue shapes itself for many thoughtful Fundamentalists. As such, it is a serious matter. You were pretty dramatic when you wrote, "If Elisha's axe head did not float, is the alternative atheism?" Perhaps, however, the choice does appear to a concerned Fundamentalist in terms rather like that.

With this as the problem, let me try to describe what I take to be a consensus of recent thinking about revelation as it bears on this issue of "subjectivism."

I. HEBRAISM VS. HELLENISM: THE BIBLICAL POINT OF VIEW

We begin with a contrast between the Greek mind and the Hebrew mind. Of course, the Bible is Hebraic in its outlook— both Old Testament and New. However, the scholasticism of which I have spoken as the method of Fundamentalist theology, with its formulation of an ultimate system of truth—purportedly that of the Bible—is an intrusion into Christianity of an essentially alien genius from the classical world. The Greeks were intellectualists. They sought truth, believing that the man who *knew* would be the good man. They discovered the mind. Aristotle's defining philosophy in some respects completed the Greek quest; Dante called him "the master of those who know." The conservatives' insistence that in the Bible we have a single system of permanent, general truths which are the thoughts of God would seem to be a Hellenized conception of the nature of the Bible.

On the other hand, for the Hebrew the ultimate good was not understanding; it was knowing God in his self-revelation. The biblical writers thought of revelation not in terms of propositions but in terms of dynamic acts of God in history. (To be sure, in the postexilic world of scribal traditions, the insights of the prophets were institutionalized into an elaborate system against which both Jesus and Paul battled. But the really creative eras of the biblical faith—the prophetic movement and the apostolic generation—were quite different.) According to the Hebrew mind, God does not impart to man in discourse certain permanently true ideas; rather, he reveals himself to men through dramatic actions of deliverance and judgment. The place of revelation is within the stream of history. This in itself is revolutionary. History is not illusory or meaningless. It is not a cyclic trap, as it was for the classical world. It is not a finite realm from which to escape into union with the Absolute, as it tends to be for the religions of the East. History is rather the medium through which the Creator's purposes and redemptive movements are carried out. The faith of a Hebrew went back not to speculation about the nature of being but to certain things that happened. In and through particular divine events of history, God had worked out his will and shown himself mighty. His actions are disturbing; they show our distance from him— yet they summon us to obey. The Bible is fundamentally an account of a continuous history. It does not contain a system of universal truths good for all times and all places; it tells the dramatic story of the acts of God. It is a literature growing out of the concrete experience of the two covenant communities, the Hebrew nation and the apostolic church.

When a Hebrew was asked about his faith, he did not reply with a catechetical definition of God, using adjectives beginning in "omni-" and "un-." He recited certain stirring events:

> We were Pharaoh's slaves in Egypt; and the LORD brought us out of Egypt with a mighty hand; and the LORD showed signs and wonders, great and grievous, against Egypt and against Pharaoh and all his household, before our eyes; and he brought us out from there, that he might bring us in and give us the land which he swore to give to our fathers.[1]

And when Christians of the apostolic generation declared their received faith, it was not a discussion on the two natures of Christ. It, too, was a recital of divinely charged happenings:

> For I delivered to you as of first importance what I also received, that Christ died for our sins in accordance with the scriptures, that he was buried, that he was raised on the third day in accordance with the scriptures, and that he appeared . . .[2]

Such a summary should be compared with the sermons in Acts; they are similarly narratives of the saving events.[3]

The Christian creeds, too, tell a story; stress is on the verbs "conceived," "born," "suffered," "crucified," "buried," "descended," "ascended," "sitteth," "will come." Further, in addition to their use as tests of orthodoxy, the creeds were forms for a Christian's confession of his newfound faith at baptism. In their origin, intention, and original use, creedal statements were not merely for definition and theological controversy but for the active commitment of the soul in the most sacred of moments.

The Bible is not an "ism" or a world view; it is the story of men acting in confrontation with God. The great men of the Bible are not men of contemplation, but men of action—men who left all and followed: Abraham, Moses, Elijah, David, Jeremiah, Peter, and Paul. Contrast this with the Greek schools and porches where men sat and talked about the ultimate nature of things. Jesus himself, the center of the divine drama, was not a contemplative type. You may have seen pictures of Buddha, serene, seated, his hands together, in union with the ultimate. There are even statues showing him lying down in contemplation. I venture that you never saw a picture of Jesus lying down! He is traveling, engaging men in talk, healing, expelling the moneychangers, weeping in Gethsemane, on trial, crucified, risen —he is God's servant, and God's will is never static. The song at the birth of John the Baptist puts it this way:

> Blessed be the Lord God of Israel,
> for he has visited and redeemed his people . . .

This "visitation," this "day of the Lord," this divine action, is, for biblical thought, the revelatory thing.

II. ACT AND INTERPRETATION

However, the revelation is not action alone. It is action interpreted by words. Sometimes the interpreting word is intimately associated with the act to which it refers; sometimes it follows it—even by several generations; sometimes it precedes. But always revelation is the divine action plus the faith-interpretation.[4]

Thus, in characteristically biblical or Hebrew prophetic experience, God's actions are not revelation apart from a human response. God's self-disclosure begins with himself, but the purpose of the process is its completion in the human commitment of faith and obedience.

The Bible, one should observe, reports this response. Its literature recounts sacred history and prophetic proclamation— these are the declaration of the Word, the divine challenge. But its literature also contains praise, prayer, and ethical instruction (sometimes of a surprisingly prudential sort)—these are the human response. If the redemptive events declare who God is and what he has done, the Psalms, the Wisdom literature, the Letter of James, the ethical portions of St. Paul, and the like, tell what man is—or they tell what man ought to be because he has been addressed by God. The distinctively biblical note is God's initiative in historical events; but significant portions of the Bible are also concerned with the human reply and the form it takes.

Much of modern theology has found it helpful to think of this divine-human intercourse on the analogy of human encounter. The two are comparable, for in revelation God does not give information about himself; he gives himself—Person to person. Similarly, all personal relations go beyond mere information. Any information gotten in a scientific way—sociological, physical, anthropological data—is beside the point when one person meets another. All I can know about another person by careful observation will not enable me to know the person unless he acts. He is still a "thing," an object of scrutiny, until he makes a self-revelation. My wish to know him will be forever frustrated unless he discloses himself by actions and words— actions made intelligible by words; words made real by actions. Only then does he step out of "thinghood" into "personhood."

When the living word is spoken, it calls for a response. I am addressed compellingly, and I must answer. I am a different person because a new person has addressed me. I must relate myself to that other self on the terms set by his address.

Now, to return to the biblical revelation, this is the way God speaks. The acts of God reported in the Bible narratives —the acts in the great Gospel drama—were seen as revelatory by prophetic witnesses. The happenings were not reported objectively by men who stood unrelated to them in their saving significance. Rather, they were reported by witnesses within the covenant, by men who felt the infinite demand upon them of the living God who disclosed himself.

When the prophetic interpreter has become so possessed by the revealing act that he has seen it in its divine or divinity-bearing meaning, his interpreting words, too, become a part of the "Word of God." The prophetic word becomes itself an occasion for the furtherance of the revealing purpose. Being "from faith," it can call out "to faith." It is "inspired." It is a God-given interpretation of his own mighty acts.

Thus, through the biblical record, the redemptive action

touches us. Because in the act of witness-bearing the prophet stood before God and believed, his words form a classic body of witness whereby the living Word can be uttered today. These words have their authority and significance *as witness.* As historical reporting, they may be inaccurate. As science, they may be dated and naïve. But, as witness to the redeeming activity of God, they are final, self-authenticating, and carry the authority of the God whose Word they are. Through the Bible we are confronted, not with "beautiful thoughts," not with long-ago and faraway stories, but with a living God who calls us to faith and obedience.

Since he respects our freedom, his Word can be rejected. It then becomes not salvation but judgment, not grace but wrath. And it leaves us not better but worse; not more but less truly human.

So the Bible is two things inextricably mixed. It is history, the sacred history of divinely charged events. And it is faith—the meaning of the events as they were apprehended in their divine significance by believing men. It is God confronting man in the particularity of history. And it is man believing where he cannot see.

III. THE BIBLE AND THE GOSPEL

This view of the Bible puts the Scriptures, their use and significance, into a perspective different from that of Fundamentalism.

It is not the case that the Bible is from end-to-end "the documented revelation of God" (Warfield's phrase). The neo-Evangelicals have been most urgent in denying a "dictation" theory of inspiration. They would like to deny that any intelligent conservative ever held it. But they nowhere explain how the more cautiously stated view they do advance differs in effect from the crudest notion of "dictation." They may well reject the term; but they still cherish the thing. Carl Henry, for example, writes (italics mine) :

> The Bible is no mere record of revelation, but *is itself revelation.* Revelation is inscripturated. . . . The inscripturation of special revelation is the *objective culmination,* therefore, of God's redemptive disclosure in special historical events and in propositions communicated to chosen prophets and apostles. *This identifica-*

tion of written sentences and propositions with special divine revelation—the recognition, that is, of the Word in the form of the words—evangelical Christianity holds to be not merely the historic Christian view, but an indispensable element in a proper Biblical theology.[5]

Is not this, even without the word "dictation," the identification of God's Word with the sentences of the Bible? To be sure, Henry's view of inspiration would allow for the responsible use of the faculties and personality and experience of the penman. But when he defines the Bible and its significance as he does, he might just as well not have made this allowance. If this consideration is put in or left out, it comes in the end to pretty nearly the same thing.

Rather than taking the Bible as the "objective culmination" of the revelatory process and sitting down to collate its propositions, I suggest that we look into and through the Bible. We are to let it witness to us of something beyond itself. It is not a picture to be admired. Rather, it is a window onto a landscape in which God is seen in redeeming action. Or, more truly yet, it is a door whereby we step out into the redeeming purpose of God. There is a central story in the Bible to which the Bible testifies and from which the Bible derives its authority. We are confronted by this central story, and it is a lifelong and devastating task to learn this story on its own terms. Much more than grammar and history is needed. The "culmination" of revelation is not a book but a believing person, not sentences but the new society in Christ.

Behind the Book is the process of the divine revealing-redeeming activity in events (sometimes more, and sometimes less, central) interpreted by faith (sometimes more, and sometimes less, perceptive). The God Jehovah enters human life as Creator, Lawgiver, Judge, and Redeemer—the long process of his self-disclosure drawing cumulatively to the point where he no longer sends his emissaries; he comes himself. The incarnation is the climax of the redemptive acts. As such it has an absolute quality. In this act, the action and the Actor and the interpreting Word are one. In this act, the divine initiative of redeeming power and love and the human response of loving, trusting obedience were both made perfectly. All other actions of God, then, are completed and explained by this one. Now this great divine drama, as it involves men in itself, is witnessed to in the biblical record. The Bible is not a source book of proof texts disclosing the thought-life of the Almighty. It is a body of witness, given by those who could do no other—". . . the word of the LORD came to me: 'Son of man, speak . . .' " As such it calls out to our faith.

As the biblical witness confronts us, we become contemporary with the redemptive events. We stand before the incarnation, the Cross, the resurrection, Pentecost—yes, and the second coming. "The Kingdom of God is at hand." "Now is the accepted time." The redemptive history becomes creative in our day. Our aim is not to bring the Bible to terms with the thought of our day; rather, our aim is to bring ourselves and our calling for our day to terms with the redeeming purpose as it is disclosed in the Bible.

Modern theology seeks roots within *the Bible, understood biblically.* It tries to reject, insofar as possible, interpretations of the Bible by principles and methods outside its own genius. It is biblical, not by making a prison house of the letter of the Bible, but by discovering "the strange new world within the Bible."[6] This is a difficult task, for we, no less than the prophets, are uncomfortable in the presence of God revealed. We find "the strange new world" uncongenial to our instincts and opinions. The biblical revelation uncovers the deep distortion within us. We will often say, "Depart from me, for I am a sinful man, O Lord." "Woe is me, for I am undone." Revelation demands nothing less than the redirection of life; "repent, and believe the Gospel." But it offers, too, deliverance, confidence, and promise.

Finality, then, belongs to the Bible's central message. The drama of redemption—the emerging Gospel—gives a criterion of value within the Bible itself. Thus, if the barbarous ethics of Judges or the imprecatory "hate songs" in the Psalter or a vindictive vision in Revelation seems remote from, or even opposed to, the emerging Gospel, we need not defend any of them. There are degrees of value and divergent points of view within the Bible— nothing is gained by saying that there are not, for even the most convinced Fundamentalist reads his Bible as though he realized there were. But there is also within the Bible the criterion of judgment. There is that in the Bible by which the Bible is judged.

This point will bother many Fundamentalists. For one of

the charges against "modernism" has been: "How can you use
Jesus to judge the Bible when you only know about Jesus through
the Bible? And if the Bible is unreliable, you can't even have
Jesus undistorted." This is a poser after which many a Fundamentalist apologist has sat down in triumph (in his own class-
room). But it does have an answer. The experience of judging a
work by an inner principle of the work itself is not unfamiliar.
Let me cite a story you may have read in David Ewen's *Dictators
of the Baton.*[7] Arturo Toscanini was conducting a performance
of a work by Verdi. During rehearsals he had made a slight ritard
in a passage where none was indicated in the score. Toscanini
did not usually take liberties with interpretation, but he in-
sisted on this one. After the performance, the composer, who
had been present, came backstage and asked first of all how
Toscanini had known that he had wanted a ritard at just that
point. He had felt it needed but had not indicated it in the
score for fear conductors would overdo it. Now Toscanini was a
critic of the printed score (and an accurate one in the sense that
he rightly caught the composer's intent), but he was so on the
basis of musical data he knew only through the printed score. He
was sufficiently in sympathy with the inner meaning of the music
he had learned through the score to be able to question the
score itself. I should say that the task is easier in the case of the
Bible, and not incomparable. A central message can make itself
so clear that by it the form in which it comes can be questioned.

Now, when Packer says that for the critical view "the supreme
authority is undoubtedly Christian reason, which must hunt for
the word of God in the Bible by the light of rationalistic critical
principles,"[8] I wonder if he can be serious. He may very well be
describing what some rationalistic critics have done. But their
results were obtained because they were rationalists, not because
they were critics. It is the aim of kerygmatic, biblical theology,
as Packer apparently does not see, to read the Bible in the light
of its own Gospel. Any theological reading of the Bible must
have some perspective, some first principle. It is possible to try to
take these from within the Bible rather than to bring them to it
from the outside. So the devout critic seeks to read the Bible,
not by the "supreme authority" of his reason or by what some
norm of science or logic says must or must not be, but under the
authority of the biblical Gospel. Forsyth was wont to distinguish

between the higher criticism informed by literary scholarship and the "highest criticism" informed by grace. This "highest criticism" I take to be the task which the newer theological study of the Bible has set for itself.

IV. THE GOSPEL AND SUBJECTIVISM

The view of the Bible which, in Henry's phrase, identifies its "written sentences and propositions with special divine revelation" thus neither allows for the fallibility of the Bible nor states the Bible's distinctive authority and greatness. The Bible, I have contended, is a body of witness, confronting us with the saving Gospel. And in that Gospel we are personally confronted by the living God.

How do we respond? We believe; we obey; we acknowledge the absolute claim of the God who has spoken and who speaks. In the biblical witness much of the idiom may be embedded in a cultural conditioning which raises problems. In our believing there will be limitations of our environment and of our spiritual obtuseness. Yet as much of us as possible submits as much as we can to as much of the biblical revelation as a reverent listening makes clear.

Acknowledging God's absolute claim is the deepest and most determinative thing we ever do. I suggest distinguishing in it three levels.

First of all is *faith* itself, a trust, a sense of infinite debt to Christ. Such faith is a step, a leap, a venture, an action. Man's response to God, no less than God's address to man, is by action before it is by word. (This is not to say that some real personal actions which commit one's innermost self cannot be carried out by words—for example, a declaration of love, marriage vows, or an oath of office.) What the Gospel seeks from us is not assent to a body of propositions but a radical redirection of life. I am sure you can weigh the difference between an "act of faith" and a "statement of faith." The Gospel gives us not a new set of opinions but a new Lord.

Next are *religious actions and utterances*: worship, prayer, witness, sacrament, confession of trust, and devotion. These are still pretheological. They are not theology; they are the material out of which theology is made. They are the recital of decisive historical events, the images, symbols, and myths which carry ultimate authority and meaning for Christian faith and life. Propositions made at this level come from a need to adore, to pray, to confess, and to obey rather than from a need to define. Perhaps this is why prayers, liturgies, and hymns of other eras and cultures are or can be living vehicles of Christian devotion, while speculative formulations from these same eras tend to be dated or irrelevant. The biblical writings belong for the most part on this level of what have been called "the immediate utterances of faith." They are, of course, not systematic; they are occasional writings, written from positions close to the dynamic happenings to answer particular needs. That is why the words of Scripture are susceptible to many interpretations in many different systems; and yet they keep their renewing, correcting vitality.

Only thirdly, in this analysis, comes *theology*, the necessary articulation, through conflict within and without the church, in systematic form according to some key concepts, of the meaning inherent in the biblical and religious facts and faith. Since Christian thought can go awry, we may consider the growing tradition of orthodoxy (the creeds, councils, confessions, and the like) as the believing community's attempt to define its own faith in such a way as to preserve its redemptive significance.

By distinguishing these three levels in the Christian response to God I do not mean to propose some kind of irrationalism. I only mean to suggest that the heart of the revelation of God is his personal apprehension of a man. It is given supremely, as William Temple pointed out, in a Person who wrote nothing but left us dependent on the witness of followers. Those who have been apprehended have been introduced to a dimension of mystery—"blasted with excess of light." They cannot respond in impersonal, academic, exhaustive definitions. The only appropriate response to one who knows and cares and gives and loves infinitely is by personal trust and commitment. The only appropriate utterance is not doctrinal, creedal, catechetical statements but the confession "Abba, Father." This need not be irrationalism; it is only putting first things first. All later theologizing is an attempt to reckon with something given by God which will always be greater than its formulations. Whatever uncomplimentary names conservatives might have for such an attempt to affirm mystery, I venture that some could also be found for any theology which denied or ignored it. It seems an inevitable part of the very idea of revelation.

Neither am I saying that there is an antagonism between faith and knowledge or that these three levels can be tidily parceled out in experience. Human nature is too unified to permit such antagonism or division to persist. Just as faith becomes strong and creative, it must theologize. I only contend here for a recognition of an order. In doing so I do not think that I am tilting at windmills, for many of the terms which are crucial and divisive in the Fundamentalists' disputes with others and among themselves—for example, dispensation, verbal inspiration, substitution, atonement, satisfaction, deity of Jesus, second coming, premillennialism, bodily resurrection—are not biblical terms; they belong to the third of the levels I have distinguished; they are part of the speculative understanding of faith. They are not an indispensable or integral part of the activity of faith itself in devotion, fellowship, witness, or obedience. For the moment I am not suggesting that any of these terms is untrue, useless, or unimportant. I simply mean to say that the issues surrounding these terms and others like them will not be seen in perspective except by the recognition of their secondary place through some such order as I have suggested. The religious dimension is prior to and cannot finally be dictated to, or exhaustively explained by, the theological; it strains against, refashions, or often breaks any forms into which it is confined.

Now the question must be raised in its sharpest form as to whether or not in distinguishing this religious dimension of belief and commitment from an ordered body of propositions, and in according it primacy, we end in "subjectivism." Most Fundamentalists would reply, "Clearly, you do." But the very posing of the issue in these terms indicates a slip into a Greek way of thinking. (There is ground for interpreting the history of Christian thought as an attempt to keep the Christian revelation from the control of Greek philosophy, while at the same time being under the paradoxical necessity of employing Greek thought in theologizing.) The very subject-object antithesis is a characteristically Greek problem. The Greeks were observers of life, subjects; they sought to understand the world and men, objects. By contrast, in the biblical view we are not detached spectators of life; we are responsible participants—called to decide and to obey. This real life of commitment to a self-disclosed God takes place (as do all of the deepest experiences of life) at the disappearing point of subjectivity and objectivity. We live most intensely at the point where the exterior world is becoming interior and where the inner world is gaining outward expression. The subjective-objective bifurcation belongs to reflection about life rather than to living, to speculation rather than to active commitment.

The Bible describes a divine-human encounter which belongs on what we have learned to call "the existential level." It is certainly not purely objective, for I am decisively involved in it, and so are you, and what we are creatively involved in is not objective to us. But neither is it subjective, for it comes to us from without, and that which meets us from beyond ourselves is not the product of subjective processes. In this central factor in biblical faith, the subjective-objective tensions are transcended.

The objective character of Christian faith is given in that it roots in revelation. Revelation rests on God's initiative. Into the world of the human and the relative has come a Word of God. And any theology which believes that God has spoken and which is informed by his utterances has taken the first and most decisive step away from subjectivism. Its Gospel is God's Word to man, not man's words about God.

So far Fundamentalists would agree. The difference with them comes at the discussion of the locus of revelation. Fundamentalists seem to say that the really significant, "culminating" locus of revelation is a book. "The Word of God" equals the Bible. Most modern theologians, on the other hand, would maintain that the locus of revelation is sacred history—a historic process culminating in a historic person. This redemptive act is the revelatory thing. "The Word of God" equals the saving event.

The "objectivity" of the revelation is given in its historic character, for history is, if anything is, objective. For a crude parallel, take Cornwallis' surrender to Washington at Yorktown. It was a decisive event for this nation's political liberation. It happened, and we can know it happened, share in the consequences of its decisive character, and, as unapologetic Americans, share some of the same thrill of it as the contemporary patriots did, even though no single record remains of it that is "verbally inerrant." In other words, lacking an infallible account of the event does not leave us completely in doubt as to whether or not it happened or what it means. Facts of history are never sub-jectively determined.

But neither is history completely objective. Though events happened without my making them, and though I cannot alter them, I am part of the conditioned historic process myself. His-tory relates to me; it is never strictly past; for me, history is present, too. History must be history as known; it elicits a re-sponse and becomes *my* history. Human history is always a record with a meaning.

The necessity of response to history is supremely true of the biblical narrative. Revelation must reveal; redemption must redeem; the good news is not good news until it is heard—until it communicates. There must be a human response to the divine initiative. The whole activity of God implies a free response on the part of man which allows the divine activity to become creative of a new life and a new society, the church. But this response, too, is given. The deepest mystery of Christian experi-ence is that what is most freely our work is most really God's work in us. The exterior biblical witness and the internal testi-mony of the Holy Spirit coalesce. No man confesses that " 'Jesus is Lord' except by the Holy Spirit."

So, at the point of the divine-human encounter there is an ultimate authority which is neither objective nor subjective. It is the deepest thing in human experience, and hence it is akin to the subjective realm. It is, however, at the same time a thing *ab extra,* whose origin is in a grace I receive and in a faith which is a gift; hence it is akin to the objective realm. It is at the same time the work of God and my work. Here is an authority which is not the dehumanizing idolatry of an "objective" au-thority, and yet not the vanity of a "subjective" authority. This encounter brings together two things: (1) a work of God which is not complete until it is consummated in a human response, and (2) a human experience which is not self-explanatory, but which points beyond itself to an act of God in Christ for its only finally satisfactory *raison d'être.* This insight reorients theology around the fundamental biblical paradox: "I live, yet not I, but Christ lives in me." The vital center of faith is in this encounter, and all theology, if it is to be valid, must arise from and answer to its latent implications.

V. FUNDAMENTALISM AND OBJECTIVISM

We have examined the Fundamentalist charge that to discard verbal inspiration leaves no logical alternative but "subjectivism." I have suggested that the charge is unjust to the spirit of modern theology and that this way of putting the issue is superficial.

Now I would like to ask about Fundamentalism's view of authority. Apparently, Fundamentalist theorists do not shrink from a goal of "objectivism"—an external norm providing an absolute, perfect authority. But we should inquire, "In practice do Fundamentalists have such an 'objectivism,' or are they, without admitting it, in the same world of mixed subjectivity and objectivity in which the rest of us live and think?" The absolutism of Fundamentalist claims would seem to need qualification. Even the most convinced Fundamentalist uses the Bible with a great deal of selectivity—he has some principle of valuation by which he judges the contents of the Bible; he is a critic. Moreover, when asked why he believes the Bible so implicitly, he can only give an answer based on personal judgment. And in the responsible choice of one authority rather than another, the absolute externality of the authority disappears. An authority for anyone depends on an act of faith, an individual judgment—this is not perfect objectivity.

Furthermore, the appeal to an objective, infallible authority is not as pat a solution to religious problems as its apologists would have us believe. It is claimed that without an absolute external norm we are left with relativism; we have no final arbiter for our opinions. But does the Bible, even under the "highest" view of its external authority, provide such an arbiter? Among those who appeal to this same infallible authority in the interest of avoiding subjectivism, there are disagreements amounting to downright contradictions—all claiming the same biblical sanction. Put in a room all of the groups which agree on verbal inspiration (and one would have to include the Roman Catholics and many of the sectarian groups, all of whom agree neither with one another nor with the Fundamentalists), and, even among the evangelicals present, brother would be divided against brother. The dispensationalists and their subspecies all excommunicate one another; they only close ranks when opposed by the antidispensationalists—all based on a verbally inspired Bible. Calvinists and Arminians appeal to the same infallible guide and

get different answers. Even a common adherence to an inerrant
Bible plus a massive Reformed theology does not keep an issue
such as common grace from opening deep conflict. Infallibilism
has not delivered religious groups from relativism.

These observations suggest that Fundamentalists are better
Christians than they are theorists. They claim to seek and to
have an "objectivism." This would be, were they to obtain it,
as serious a distortion as the "subjectivism" they fear. The fact
that they do claim and seek it does a certain amount of damage,
to be sure. But the fact that they do not attain it is something
of a counterbalance. I, for one, cannot but be happy over their
failure to secure the thing they seek. But I wish that in view of
the actual impossibility of serious Christian theology being
totally subjectivist or objectivist they would stop calling others
by abusive names and revise their theory to correspond with the
very real and necessary subjective ingredients in their (and everyone's) practice. We are all partly subjectivist or we would not be
Christian theologians at all. R. C. Moberly once observed, "What
we really love is never wholly without us." I can be quite objective and scientific for a while; I can observe and weigh probabilities. But in the end, as Pascal reminds us, I must wager. And
having done so, when I turn to reflective thought, *the fact of
my having wagered* is thereafter a primary, determining datum
for my theologizing.

In our ambiguous world, objectivity and subjectivity are
never exclusive possibilities. One way of looking at the ministry
of the Holy Spirit is to say that he is the bridge of this gap.
He is at once the inner life of God and the inner life of a Christian. He is within us and beyond us. The cleavage between objective and subjective is not an illuminating or a Christian distinction when the Spirit's work is taken into account.[9]

VI. CHRISTENDOM BY THE LIGHT OF THE CROSS

Now, a revelatory encounter is the final thing in Christian
faith. It carries the absolute stamp of God himself. It is an
ultimate authority which lets faith be faith (not demonstration)
and God be God (not a tyrant). It carries the self-authenticating
power that is as near as we get to religious certainty. Faith shows
itself to be faith, to be transcendent in its ultimate reference, by
the very freedom and authority with which it questions every
form which it creates and by which it is communicated.

Putting the central thing at the center brings to a single burning focus the Christian point of authority, of revelation, of redemption, of obedience, of community, of devotion, and of mission.

This central, final thing is the critic of all else that may claim our trust. It sits in judgment over the "objective idols" of Fundamentalism and over the "subjective ideals" of Liberalism.

Let me explain this judgment by using a term which I think will carry a more specific meaning for you than "divine-human encounter." Let me put it in terms of the centrality of the Cross —especially as it bears on three other final authorities which are claimed by Christian groups: the Bible, the objective finality of the Fundamentalist; the church, the objective finality of the Romanist; and Christian experience, the subjective finality of the Liberal. No, let me add a fourth: theology, the objective finality of the confessional orthodox.

First of all, what do I mean by "the Cross"?

As used in the New Testament, "the Cross" came to have a far wider meaning than a particular wooden instrument of Roman execution. It came to denote the death of Christ in its saving significance. It carried with it not simply a historical reference to Jesus but also an evangelical reference. "The word of the Cross" was the Christian Gospel. So, the terminology of the New Testament, and of later writers who caught its spirit, passes freely from "the Cross" as a historic event in the procuratorship of Pontius Pilate to "the Cross" as that event is interpreted triumphantly in the Gospel and the experience of the Holy Spirit in baptism and life. Vocabulary stretches around the historical, transcendent, and personal foci, for all are mutually interdependent.

Underlying all of our view of the centrality of the Cross to other things is *the centrality of the Cross in history*. History enshrines the Cross. The Cross belongs to the sequence of the historic movement. "Every 'word' of God is a fragment of human history," wrote H. Wheeler Robinson.[10] The Cross is woven into our common human motives and conditions. When God became man, he did not violate the conditions of the historic process. Rather, he worked through them. He was incarnate as a particular Jewish man of a particular time. The Cross is tied into the fabric of human life throughout.

But the Cross is above history. History enshrines its own

judgment. History is not known or redeemed from within itself.
No point or selection of points in the linear sequence can give
the pattern of the whole. The linear is met by the perpendicular.
And the point of their meeting does not so much take its meaning from the sum of the other points as gather into itself and
give meaning to the totality of the historical movement. There
is a decisive event in which the meanings emergent within history
are revealed by action of that which intrudes from without. "He
came unto his own." The eternal and divine enters the temporal
and human in Jesus Christ to say clearly what God had tried
to say all along in human history. When this happens, the moral
heart of history stands revealed. The linear key to history (the
Kingdom of God) grows out of the perpendicular key (the
Cross). Because of the Cross, history is a judged process. The
sense of things derives from the Cross, where the Creator became
Redeemer.

This centrality of the Cross in history is fundamental. The
topics which follow are but special cases of this basic view
of history.

The centrality of the Cross in the Bible: The Bible enshrines the Cross. The Cross has gripped men and driven them
to bear witness to itself. The Bible is their witness. There is no
knowing the Cross without the biblical record in which it is embodied. The story, in the end, is one: the preparation for, the
events of, and the consequences following Christ's death and
resurrection.

But the Cross is above the Bible. The Bible enshrines its
own judgment. The Bible has its decisive, authoritative value
only as mediator of the Gospel. But in the Bible that which
falls below the Gospel is condemned. Whatever in the Bible is
ethically other than the holy love of God as disclosed in the
Cross is manifestly unworthy of defense (though it is often worthwhile to understand and even to recognize ourselves in that of
which we do not and cannot approve). The Cross is the stringent
measure of value within the Bible itself. Legalism, moralism,
unworthy conceptions of God and providence, the barbarous
"revenge code" of Queen Esther, spitefulness, self-righteousness
—these (all of which are found, without disapproval, in the
Bible) fall before the Gospel of self-sacrificing love. The Cross
is the touchstone for "disentangling the divine revelation from

the popular religion."[11] It helps us see in the Bible that which is sub-biblical.

The centrality of the Cross in the church: The church enshrines the Cross. The church is constituted in the Cross and draws its validity from its union with God's redemptive movement. The Cross expresses itself continuously and corporately in the history of mankind.

But the Cross is above the church. The church enshrines its own judgment. The Gospel is that without which the church cannot be the church. But the privilege of this identification with the Cross presents constant moral demands. Over the whole life of the Body and between each of its members is the Cross. Ecclesiasticism, partisanship, divisiveness, pharisaism, high-pressure evangelistic bullying, superficiality, false pious poses, cheapness, vulgarity, triviality, activism, self-satisfaction, complacency, sentimentality—these betray the Cross. They are not merely ungentlemanly or in poor taste; they are false to the human condition as the Cross is not. Lord, have mercy upon us.

The centrality of the Cross in Christian experience: The Christian heart enshrines the Cross. The deepest confession of the Christian is "I am crucified with Christ." The identification, through faith, with Christ and his Cross gives Christian experience its authenticity and certainty. A Christian "glories" in the Cross. The Cross lays hold of a man and makes him its own. St. Ignatius calls Christians "branches of the Cross."

But the Cross is above the Christian heart. Experience enshrines its own judgment. Anything self-seeking is the contradiction of the self-offering of Christ, and it stands condemned. The great penitents have been the great saints. As we grow closer to the Cross, we grow in a divine discontent with ourselves. Expressions such as "keep smiling" or "I am saved and satisfied" raise a question as to whether the Cross in its purity could leave anyone so self-content. Has *agape* transcended *eros*? Is God serving man, or is man serving God? "Repent ye," as Luther put it in the first of his theses, means for "the whole life of the faithful to be an act of repentance." Consecration is our response in kind to Christ's sacrifice for us. God in grace "made the first sacrifice, to which all man's sacrifices are but response. Our best is but the faint echo of His. And we can never come to a depth of sacrifice where God has not been before us and outdone us. If we make our bed in Hell, He is there."[12]

The centrality of the Cross in theology: Theology enshrines the Cross. The Cross comes to us not as a puzzle but as an answer. It is an answer, however, which requires elucidation. It has vast implications. Theology is the necessary rationale of the Christian faith. God has revealed himself by the Word —the principle of intelligibility in the Godhead—and his revelation has meaning and gives meaning. An untheological or anti-intellectual faith is timid and superficial—usually resting uncritically in the worst heresies of its intellectual environment. It is a faith false to its own potentialities. The meaning of the Cross provokes us to inquire further. Such inquiry will not rest without some solutions, and these are theology.

But the Cross is above theology. Theology enshrines its own judgment. The Cross is not only God's answer to human questions; it is God's question to man, requiring man's answer. So, that in theology which is not derivative from the point of origin, the Cross, stands condemned. The Cross, not logic, is determinative. The intellect must answer to the evangelical reality, not vice versa. Anything in theology which is academically true but evangelically false stands judged. Logical consistency and systematic tidiness are not the supreme criteria of truth in theology; the Cross is. Philosophical forms must be broken in order to fit the shape of the message of the Cross. Theological method is not to build upward from certain philosophical a priori expectations of what must be but to build outward from the existential crisis where God is met in Christ and his Cross. When theology works in this way it may leave some philosophical "loose ends," but justice will have been done to the moral problem at the point at which God himself gives the nearest thing we have to an answer to it—the Cross. Better to be morally adequate even though intellectually incomplete than to have it the other way around.

Thus the "final authorities" of Christendom, subjective or objective, fail. Rome trusts in an infallible Pope who does not define precisely when he is speaking ex cathedra and when he is not. Protestant Fundamentalism trusts in an infallible Bible— but in the nonexistent autograph manuscripts. So when the Romanists say "Pope" and the Fundamentalists say "Bible," these qualifications assure us that we are not talking about reality—the Pope who actually speaks or the Bible we actually have. The established systems of confessional orthodoxy are too intellectualistic, polemic, and dated. The Liberal's ultimate authority, experience, without a given Word of God, is quicksand. But each of these authorities points beyond itself—it is a witness—to something more ultimate, permanent, and final in which it participates and through which God has spoken. And in the effectiveness of its witness is its value. Church, Bible, theology, and experience all in their way point to the Gospel of redemption; and they must point in such a way as not to obstruct the line of vision. Not until we rest in the Gospel-rooted faith does our final certainty derive from God and from nothing less.

There is an old story of a tailor who divulged a piece of great wisdom. He observed that before a person begins to sew he should be sure he has a knot in the thread. I have tried to say where I have learned to secure my thread.

Cordially,
Spermologos

IV

THE
CHURCH

The Church is Catholicke, universall, so are all her Actions;
All that she does belongs to all. When she baptizes a child, that
action concernes mee; for that child is thereby connected to that
Head which is my Head too, and engraffed into that body,
whereof I am a member. And when she buries a Man, that action
concernes me: All mankinde is of one Author, and is one volume;
when one man dies, one Chapter is not torne out of the booke,
but translated into a better language; and every Chapter must
be so translated; God emploies several translators; some peeces
are translated by age, some by sicknesse, some by warre, some by
justice; but Gods hand is in every translation; and his hand shall
binde up all our scattered leaves againe, for that Librarie where
every booke shall lie open to one another.

JOHN DONNE, Devotions XVII

THE MEANING
OF THE CHURCH

O Theophilus,

You cannot but be correct. A Fundamentalist who abandoned
the objective, external, absolute authority of the Bible might be
in a pretty chaotic state. You asked, "If the security of the simple
answers is gone, isn't something essential to satisfactory religious
experience taken away and nothing put in its place?" I appreciate
your reminders about "the man in the pew." To be sure, the
discussion cannot stop where my last letter left it.

The way in which you put the question suggests that we are
dealing not with an academic but with a personal question. The
central crisis over verbal inspiration is by no means isolated. A
change at that point requires much readjustment elsewhere. So
we must look at your bewildered Fundamentalist's (or ex-Funda-
mentalist's) personal problem of dislocation and loss of identity,
for this is what is involved. His belief in the existence of an
infallible, objective authority had focused much of his way of
life and thinking. His attitudes and emotions were deeply involved. The view that authority rests in an infallible Book had
given to all religious matters an appearance of simplicity. A ready
answer seemed to be available for every question; it was merely
a matter of knowing the apt texts. This seeming simplicity had
put into his hand—and into the hand of each "Bible-believing
Christian"—the sure oracles of God. He could carry his final authority in his pocket. He could dispel all doubt, derive all certainty and comfort, and vanquish all opponents by the Book.

The seeming simplicity is deceptive; the Fundamentalist view
of the Bible (as we have seen) is simple neither to define nor to

defend, and it does not answer all questions (indeed, no view does). But it seems to do so, and for most people that is as good as though it did. So intimately are basic attitudes bound up with his theory of the Bible that, for a Fundamentalist, serious doubt of the factual accuracy of the Bible sends shock waves through the whole religious experience.

I recall a vivid passage quoted in Dickie's *Revelation and Response,* describing "the way in which many people have felt that their faith was shaken when the idea of plenary inspiration of the Bible was withdrawn from them."

> I am comparing . . . in my own mind religion made thus familiar to us to a fire-lit cottage at night, enclosing a sailor's child. The blinds are down, the darkness is shut out, the flickerings of the hearth give a friendliness even to the shadows in the farthest corner. The child sees everything intelligibly adjusted to its needs. If it is hungry, there is food for it in the great mysterious cupboards; and when it is tired, it knows that there is a room above, where a pillow of rest awaits it, to be reached by a narrow stair. We are like such a child, who, having taken its cottage for the world, suddenly opens the door, and finds itself in a night like this confronted by all the stars, and by all the thunderings of the sea. Will these realities of the Universe provide us with a new home which, compared with the cottage of Christian miracles, will be a palace? Or will they leave us roofless, with no home at all? That's our question in general terms, isn't it?[1]

The fear of loss need be only temporary. But for it to be so, a searching readjustment must take place. For in Fundamentalism the Bible does not stand alone. The final authorities are *the Bible and the individual.* And these are so linked (in theory and in experience) that a modified conception of the Bible must involve a modified conception of the individual and of the relationship between the two. Otherwise, a still-Fundamentalist individual with an other-than-Fundamentalist Bible will feel himself shaky indeed.

The trouble with such a theory is that it expects the Bible and the individual to do something that neither can properly do—to live apart from the faith community. One gathers that for many persons who have moved away from Fundamentalism such movement has involved a rediscovery of the church. In a sense, a theology of the church is the largest gap in Fundamentalism—ecclesiology ranks as the forgotten doctrine of the movement. You are right that a basic need of the soul is at stake, but perhaps the need may be met by Christian community rather than by a magical view of the significance of the Bible. At least we might test such a thesis by examining the corporate note in Christian faith.

I. FUNDAMENTALIST INDIVIDUALISM

To begin in a negative way, we may observe that Bible-piety tends to be individualistic. Not only are the individual and the Bible the highest theoretical court of appeal, but Bible reading means private Bible reading; prayer means private prayer; salvation means individual conscious conversion; being "in Christ" is thought of as an individually realized religious experience, the "Spirit" as an individual empowering.

Look at the songs of Fundamentalism (always a good index of popular religious life): "That will be glory for me," "I shall see Him face to face," "My sins are gone," "I'm so happy . . . ," "I'm saved, saved, saved," "Love lifted me," "He holds my hand," "Now I belong to Jesus," "Safe am I . . . ," "My Lord is real, yes, real to me . . ." Shall I extend the list, or is the point clear enough? These distinctive products of the Fundamentalist movement show its undeniable individualism. Do children still sing that shameless chorus: "For me, for me, for me, for me. There's a mansion there for me"? Is not this original sin set to music and taught to the young?

According to this view the Christian pilgrimage is made alone. God's salvation is individually directed. His help is in an individual companionship. The way is the lonely route of personal sanctification, personally attained. And the goal is a mansion built for one.

The Fundamentalist theory of the church is most often that of "a voluntary association of baptized believers." (The phrase in quotation marks was a seventeenth-century Separatist watchword defining a "gathered church.")[2] This makes the "saved" individual—self-sufficient, self-contained, Bible in hand—primary. The church is a fellowship created by the act of several of these individuals, agreeing to terms of association. This doctrine is the ecclesiastical counterpart of the contract theory of the state.

An individualistic theory of community seems always to lead

to social atomism and to divisiveness. For what has been created by "voluntary association" is free to be destroyed by "voluntary disassociation." Each person is equally sovereign, and nothing in the nature of the community annuls his fundamental self-interest. The fissiparous tendencies of Fundamentalism have often been noted and lamented.[3] With this view of the church, however, such division is almost inevitable and almost praiseworthy.

A leading symptom of a diseased state of spiritual community is the "Bible church" phenomenon. A few malcontents from the traditional denominations organize a "pure" church with no heritage, no internal cohesion except common contempt for the churches they left, no external ties, and no theology. A congregational polity is adopted which lets the members call a preacher and dismiss him in a moment if he says something distasteful. The sacraments are all but disregarded. The denominational churches are contemned. Everyone fancies himself a Bible expert, so when any defect of doctrine or of spirit appears he is qualified to go to the edge of town and start a competing Bible church purer than the first. I know of no feature of the Fundamentalist world which brings its individualism to a clearer focus than does this proliferation of "independent" churches.

II. COMMUNITY AND HUMAN NATURE

A critique of this feature must be thorough and evangelical. For these "independent" institutions are the result of a partial Gospel, and a curative must come, not from expediency, but from a more ample Gospel.

Just as the social contract theory of the state rests society on the fiction of a primal covenant between dissociated individuals (such isolated individuals never existed; such a contract was never made), the individualist theory of the church rests it on an unreal abstraction. It says that first there were unrelated individual believers; then these produced the church. This premise of an unrelated individual believer is like the premise of a three-legged biped. It is self-contradictory. To be a Christian is to be in relationship. There is no encounter with God in Christ that is not at the same time encounter with the church.

We can begin with human life in general, for here, no less than in religious life, there is no such thing as an individual-in-isolation. "No man is an island, entire of itself." Any theory of civic, social, economic, educational, or spiritual life which begins with an examination of "the individual" begins with an abstraction. There are only individuals-in-relation. This is the rule of nature and of grace. A person in isolation is not human. A faith in isolation is not Christian.

There is, to be sure, a certain realm of life's privacies where the individual transcends the group. The dignity and the freedom of the human self are never exhausted by a description of conditioning external relations. A man is more than his social environment. But the individual and his groups interact.

The individual is born into an already existing family. His membership in it (perhaps the most important relation he ever has) is one of the given factors in life—he is not consulted. Immediately he begins the lifelong task of coming to terms with his family. He is a citizen of an already existing community and an heir of a mind-shaping culture. Through baptism he may be made a member of the church of the centuries. He begins life within social relations. It took two people to bring him into life. It takes many more to sustain him.

For some time, perhaps for a third of his lifetime, a person is a passive or dependent member of his society. If he eats, it is because someone provides for his feeding. If he is clothed, it will be by others. If he learns, it is by being taught. If he prays, someone gives him his words.

Gradually the period of passivity merges into a period when a more active contribution can be made. A person's individuality and creative leadership emerge. He can extend help and acceptance to others. He can shape the forces that others will inherit.

Later years may bring a return to dependence on his society.

No claim of society can or should regiment or crush the ultimate freedom of personhood—it is a mysterious and sacred thing. But the development of this personality to its greatest potential of individuality and self-dependence is an achievement made through the discipline of responsible membership. A person's greatest contribution is only made by a free but discriminating acceptance of his heritage. In and through the interrelatedness of life, personality becomes humanized and fulfilled.

There is, then, a polarity in human life between the claims of individuality and the claims of society—between man as a unit and man as a member. If either pole is given exclusive priority, the result is harmful. Any collectivism which submerges the individual in the group or any individualism which regards the corporate side of life as optional is a doctrinaire perversion of the actualities of experience.

III. COMMUNITY AND THE BIBLE

If social involvement is a real part of the natural realm, it is no less a part of the life of grace.

Individualist Christianity has taken over the Bible as its divine sanction. Hooker said of the followers of Bible-piety in his day, "When they and their Bibles were alone together, what strange fantastical opinion soever at any time entered into their heads, their use was to think the Spirit taught it them."[4] But the Bible, no less than the individual, cannot stand alone. The Bible is the Book of the church. It is written in the plural pronoun. If Fundamentalists use and read the Bible individualistically, they can only do so because they misunderstand it.

Bible and church—the Book of a people and the people of the Book—are inseparable. How are they related?

The Old Testament was the literature of a people. It was Israel's mythology, chronicle, hymnbook, law code, devotional guide, rule of conduct; her inspiration and her rebuke. The New Testament was the literature of a people. Its writings assume the believing community and are written "from faith to faith." They appeal to an already received tradition. The church existed for a generation before St. Mark's Gospel and for twenty years before St. Paul's first letter. The New Testament documents came from real crises in the faith and life of the apostolic church. The Bible, Old Testament and New, was conceived within the womb of an active community. The Book did not drop full-grown from heaven. It did not emerge in a vacuum.

Criticism has done much to increase our realization of the interdependence of Book and community. The Old Testament in its present form is seen to represent not only the creative work of individual writers but also the editorial work of representative schools of Hebrew thought, prophetic and priestly. It is the slow deposit of the stream of Israel's corporate life. Not for nothing was one of the first great books in English on Old Testament criticism called *The Old Testament in the Jewish Church* (by

W. Robertson Smith, written in 1881). The New Testament
has been shown (largely through form criticism) to owe much
of its pattern and content to the preaching and teaching practices of the first-century Christian community. Stories, sayings,
and formulas were remembered, repeated, treasured, and passed
on in part because of their usefulness in the life of the early
Christian fellowship. The kerygma itself and other confessional,
sacramental, narrative, instructional, and ethical elements had
a place in the living work and witness of the church before they
found their place in written form in the New Testament. Criticism has thus brought the writings and the fellowship into an
increasingly meaningful relationship. The Bible, in its origin,
selection, preservation, and interpretation, is bound up with the
life of the covenant people.

The persistent unwillingness of Fundamentalist students to
give serious thought to the preliterary age of the Gospel, or to
face the problem of the canon, indicates that at the points where
the relationship of Bible and church leans most heavily on the
church as a living society, rather than on the Bible as a finished
authoritative document, the Fundamentalists are not at home
with the serious questions at issue.

What is "Scripture"? What is properly included in "Scripture"? Who said so? On what grounds? The Fundamentalists
profess a position based solely on the authority of the Bible.
But they must look outside the Bible for a definition of the contents of the Bible.

The church of the early centuries, in the face of heresy, drew
three safeguards to define its tradition, or *paradosis*. They were
the canon of the New Testament, the creed, and the episcopal
succession. By what reasoning do Fundamentalists virtually
disregard the second and third of these and stake everything on
the first, when much the same source and authority is responsible
for all three? (Similarly, they have accepted the decision of a
post-Christian Jewish council as to what is properly in the Old
Testament.) Once an element out of ecclesiastical tradition is
used as authoritative, such authority is in principle admitted.
The question then is, Why be so arbitrarily selective in using it?

It is not difficult to point up weaknesses in much thinking
(Roman Catholic and Reformed, conservative and liberal) about
the relation of Bible and church. But where and when their

positive interrelatedness has been appreciated, it has provided a
sense of proportion which has moderated extreme ideas. If, by
the Spirit, the continuing fellowship is the interpreter of the
Bible—entering and validating the biblical faith in each generation—it will be clear that some things are obviously central in
the Scriptures while other things are decidedly peripheral. The
Bible is only seen rightly when seen in its native communal context.

And the "man in the pew" whose needs you insist we keep
in mind need not necessarily study the critical views, radical
and conservative; he need not enter the intricacies of the discussion of what inspiration does or does not mean. It is fundamental to the view I have been presenting that knowing God is
both more important and less complicated than knowing how we
come to know him. So matters of biblical and theological method
can be presupposed rather than preached. If the man in question is really "in the pew," he is in the locus where the Bible is
heard and used believingly. In the worship, thought, life, and
work of the church, the Christian attitude toward the Bible is
maintained—a matter far more fundamental than theories about
it. The Bible is the living Word of God in the innermost heart
of the believing fellowship. Book and people are as interrelated
today as they were in the apostolic generation or in the time
the canon was determined or in any time between then and now.

IV. COMMUNITY AND THE GOSPEL

However, neither the Bible nor the church is ultimate. Each
is a witness pointing beyond itself to God and his act in Christ.
Both are products of the Gospel. And the Gospel—the saving
movement of God in history—always involves community.

It is unfortunate that the term "social gospel" has been identified by Fundamentalists with a humanistic conception of redemption as this-worldly meliorism. This is unjust to the theological
realism of many of the greatest apostles of the social gospel.
Furthermore, it spoils a good phrase. We need some terms that
will indicate that the Gospel is by its very nature a societal message. It is corporate before it is individual. "The flight of the
alone to the Alone" is neo-Platonic, not biblical.

From the startling old stories of early Genesis, to the white-
robed multitudes of the Apocalypse, the Gospel is corporate. "It

is not good that the man should be alone" is the divine sanction for marriage and family. The question was asked: "Am I my brother's keeper?" And the questioner was self-incriminated. "Cain went away. . . . and he built a city," and his city has persisted. But alongside it has grown the pilgrim fellowship of Abel and those who, like him, have witnessed "by faith." And the struggle between these communities—the one of selfish exploitation, the other of self-giving love—is the moral core of history.

Abraham was the father of a family and a nation. The great men of the Old Testament—lawgivers, judges, kings—were related to a people. The prophets were God's spokesmen to the nation. Their message might have been received in relative solitude, but it always sent them back into the heartbreak of responsible relation to their people. (Revelation is always to the individual for the group. And, finally, the elect group is a witness for all mankind. In this way, whatever solitary element may be in prophetic experience is delivered from the snobbishness of non-biblical mysticism.) The hope of Israel was shared by the humblest Hebrew, as he belonged to the elect community.

In recent decades, biblical scholars have realized the significance of the Old Testament conception of "corporate personality." The clear distinction between the individual and the social unit has been a late development in human thought. In the Old Testament, personal terms are often used for corporate entities. The "I" of the Psalter, for example, is thought by responsible scholars to be at times the elect nation more truly than a devout individual. The ambiguity as to whether the "Suffering Servant" of Second Isaiah is a person or a community probably comes from the fact that the two were not clearly separated in the mind of the prophet himself. The reference of a term like "Christ" or "anointed" passes readily from the community to the representative person of the community ("Thou wentest forth for the salvation of thy people, for the salvation of thy anointed," Hab. 3:13). The prophetic outlook assumed the solidarity of the people in sin and in covenant.

In the New Testament Jesus chose twelve companions. He spoke of twelve thrones—anticipating a "new Israel." He announced his message in terms which were sometimes like a kingdom and sometimes like a family; but always they were corporate. The ethic he proclaimed was love—implying society and relationships for its exercise. The picture in the Gospels is always of "Jesus and his people."[5]

However, none of the sons of Adam was a worthy Messiah of the Kingdom about which Jesus taught. He himself was that. He alone was Son of Man and Suffering Servant—in all the richness of the personal and corporate significance of these Old Testament terms. He identified himself with the expectations and the sins of "many." On the Cross, and beyond, he was alone, yet he was representative of the whole of the people of God. He was the Kingdom, the church, the Israel of God.

The incarnation was the establishment of a beachhead of the Kingdom in mankind. Pentecost was its initial breakthrough, its outward burst of power. After Pentecost, the apostles taught and carried with developing insight a new, redeemed fellowship constituted in Christ with him as Head. Sometimes Christ is spoken of as over against the church and distinct from it. But sometimes the term "Christ" includes the church, Head and Body.[6] The unity of the fellowship in Christ was not something to be created; it was something which existed in the very nature of the dependence of the church on her Lord—Christ is not divided. There is one Spirit; therefore Christ's Body, the Spirit-created *koinonia,* is one. But the unity could be lost; man did not create it; but he had a part in preserving it. This unity—basic though it was—was not a uniformity. Within it a great diversity of functions was apparent, for the Spirit who filled the community gave gifts to the fellowship, providing richness and variety in its life.

Fallen man is by nature a stranger to true community. Sin, as self-centeredness, is a separating thing. Man's quest for community is undone by his self-destructive, exploitative tendencies. But against this tragic brokenness of the human family, the Christian Gospel brought the uniting force of God's love in action—a community summoned by his own humility. Corporateness based on grace—on the form of a servant—had immediate ethical implications. The gifts of the Spirit were for the well-being of the body, not for individual exercise. Forgiveness, love, sharing, mutual deference, and gentleness were the Christian answers to the ruin caused by pride and self-directed interest.[7] The witness to the reality of the new age was that the oneness of the Church included both Jew and Gentile; this fellowship was potentially universal.[8] In Christ man could learn what it meant to say "we."

This society of redeemed mankind is the goal of God's purpose for all men. The faithful of all ages are necessary to one another—" . . . apart from us they should not be made perfect."[9] And ultimately (St. Paul ventured) the redemption of the sons of God holds the key to the renewal of the cosmos.[10] The Christ who was raised to the right hand of the Father held promise of the restoration of all things—what was promised to Abraham and to Adam would be consummated in Christ. And in this cosmic redemption all those would share who drew their life from union with him. Heaven, in Scripture, is never solitary. It is always "many mansions," "a great city," "a multitude no man can number." Its songs are in chorus. Nature, grace, and glory (to employ an old theological distinction) are all realms where the divine purpose is corporate.

This hasty sketch of the biblical idea of community may indicate the way in which the fellowship is bound up with the whole scheme of redemption. Bishop F. R. Barry once said of the church, "It is part of the Gospel which it preaches and an essential element in its own creed."[11] I hope that his remark now makes some sense to you, for it summarizes what I have been trying to say. The church is not an optional extra. It is an integral part of the good news.

V. THE GIVEN ELEMENTS OF THE COMMUNITY

The church, then, is a gift. It is a divine creation in Christ and the Holy Spirit before it is a fellowship of men. "Its first members did not construct it, but joined it," wrote William Temple.[12] The divine initiative in the Gospel is reflected in the church, the elect community.

I like to think of this givenness of the church as God's meeting man in the legacy of Christ. Let me explain what I mean by citing four inseparable aspects of the divine-human life of communion. What did Christ leave? Not primarily a body of teaching. Little of his teaching was original, and while it is forever true and of the utmost authority, all of it is pre-Easter and pre-Pentecost. The intuition of the church (following St. Paul) has regarded the fact of Christ himself and what he did as more important than his words. Thus his legacy may be thought of as consisting in (1) himself, (2) a fellowship, (3) the sacraments, and (4) a mission; or, more exactly, himself in the fellowship which is sacramental and missionary.

First, then: *himself.* The New Testament develops rather fully the theme of the communion of the church with the ascended and living Christ. There is no solitary Christ in the New Testament. Christ is source of vitality (John 6:48-57), pattern and goal of the church's maturity (Eph. 4:13-16). "Abiding" in Christ is life and productivity (John 15:4-5). Christ, perfected through suffering, communicates strength and growth to those still imperfect members in union with himself (Heb. 2:10-18; 4:14-16; Col. 2:19; Eph. 4:15-16). The church is thus in utter need of Christ. But Christ is represented by St. Paul in a daring passage as incomplete without the church (Eph. 1:23 and J. Armitage Robinson's commentary). There is a completeness of Christ's work and suffering which it is the privilege of the struggling church to make up (Col. 1:24). A deep exchange of sympathy takes place between Christ and his church. Christ is touched by human infirmity (Heb. 4:14-15). He suffers with the suffering church—imprisoned, athirst, naked, persecuted—Christ is there (Matt. 25:31-46; Acts 9:4-5). When at worship (Matt. 18:20) or witnessing (Matt. 28:20), Christ is with his people. The sonship conferred through Christ dignifies suffering and assures a shared triumph over sin and death (Rom. 8:16-17).

The church, for its part, reciprocates the divine self-giving by basing its sacrifices of personal and public devotion on the historic events of the life and passion and triumph of Christ by which redemption was won. The yearly cycle of Advent, Christmas, Lent, Easter, and Whitsunday is a living recollection of the saving events. The Mishnah says, "In every generation a man must so regard himself as if he came forth himself out of Egypt."[13] And in a like manner, the Christian fellowship identifies its unworthy devotion with the perfect human self-offering made by Jesus Christ.

H. B. Swete has summarized this profound union well:

> The fellowship which springs from this unity [with Christ] is an interchange not simply of words or acts or sympathies, but of life: the life of the Incarnate is passed into His Saints, and their life is, in a mystery, merged in His, and identified with it.[14]

Second: *a fellowship.* Jesus left a community constituted by his choosing and representing the investment of his deepest work—the embryo of the worldwide church. This nascent church had a strong sense of a shared life—"all things in common" is the striking phrase of Acts.

Faith is never solitary; love is never solitary. Both imply relationships. No one can be a Christian in isolation. He needs the fellowship to nurture him, and he needs it to provide a sphere for service. Faith is an introduction to the fellowship of those who, knowing themselves accepted in spite of themselves, can learn the humility to make them accepting of others. Security, support, discipline, order, service, charity, patience, understanding, freedom—these are all learned in a shared life of community. A compelling logic lies in this statement from 1 John: ". . . he who does not love his brother whom he has seen, cannot love God whom he has not seen."[15]

There is a mysterious interplay of forces in compassion, understanding, and intercession among the members of this worldwide fellowship. Each is needed by all; ". . . we are members one of another."[16] Entering this family, one dies in order to live; he renounces his self-centeredness in order to find his true selfhood within the divine order ruled by grace. This self-forgetting spirit of the fellowship can help people who differ to learn from and appreciate one another, for each realizes that "No man is able to understand more than a tiny fraction of the unsearchable riches of Christ; he needs the supplementing contribution of his neighbor's apprehension."[17] Teachability is a mark of the Spirit. The mutuality of the life of the Christian community was described well by P. T. Forsyth:

> Each has wealth to give and room to receive the rest. We grow by such mutual interpenetration. Hearts swell into each other. We assimilate each other. We know as we are known. We live ourselves into each other. We rise to each other, or we stoop to raise. None without the rest can be made perfect.[18]

But this fellowship is more than a worldwide body of the now-living. It is a potential "partnership between those who are living, those who are dead, and those who are to be born."[19] In Christ there are no dead. The faithful are united in worship, prayer, and interest on a level which physical death cannot interrupt. As a consequence, we must be interested in the unity of the church not only in the spatial dimension but also in the temporal. Any union now which disregarded continuity with the past would betray the full dimensions of the common life.

This world-embracing, age-embracing fellowship bears through history to each generation the mighty redeeming acts of God. It is the "realm of redemption."[20] And "outside the Church there is neither salvation nor remission of sins."[21]

Third: *the sacraments*. Our Lord left no systematic account of doctrine. He left no detailed plan for church organization. He left no casuistic specifications about conduct. But "on the night in which he was betrayed," under the most solemn circumstances, he gave an observance with instructions for its perpetuation—evidently intending it to be the focal point of the corporate life of his followers and their way of communion with himself. This sacrament has in some unique sense remained enshrined over the centuries as the central, distinctive, and most hallowed act of Christian worship.

In this sacrament, the church finds herself in the presence of the whole redeeming history. Her Lord is not a dead martyr in whose memory she holds a memorial. In the recalling of him, he is present. The church stands before the incarnation, the Cross, the resurrection, Pentecost, and the *parousia*. She sups with her risen Lord at the lakeside. He is ever "known to them in the breaking of the bread." The church is in touch with the life beyond death; she eats the bread of heaven.

In the important passage in which the church has found Christ's legacy in his "commission" there is the command "go, baptize." The first Christian sermon came to its climax with "Repent and be baptized." Baptism was, thus, from the beginning, the normal means of Christian initiation. Here again, in sharing in the legacy of Christ, one shared Christ himself. For he, too, was baptized. And he took that baptism to be an acceptance of his mission; his "baptism" symbolized for him his obedience, his work, and ultimately his saving death. Hence, when a Christian was baptized, he was linked with a rite which already signified the death and resurrection of his Lord; he died and rose again in Christ.

Thus, in the early church, a part of the givenness of the church's life was the sacraments. They were rich in the most profoundly evangelical significance. In James Denney's famous dictum:

The truth seems . . . to be that both of the Sacraments are forms into which we may put as much of the gospel as they will carry; and St. Paul, for his part, practically puts the whole of his gospel into each.[22]

Possibly in no area of its life has the church so conspicuously declined from the New Testament as in its loss of sacramental realism. This is true of both the Roman Catholic tradition and the Reformed tradition—though in different ways, of course. And the devaluation of the sacraments would seem to be conspicuously true of Fundamentalism. The ministry of the Word has become all-inclusive. The Word provides the means both for entrance into and for sustenance within the believing community. The sacramental ministries, while they may at times be taken seriously and observed frequently, have no meaningful role to play in the economy of salvation. They are reduced to vivid illustrations of aspects of the Word, and their integrity is lost. Whether the Word is thus illustrated or not is regarded as of no special consequence; the Word remains self-sufficient.

This is only a special aspect of the general loss of a significant doctrine of the church. If the life of the community is important, the sacraments will be important. Every fellowship of men, secular or religious, develops a cultus—a focus of common action. When it meets, it engages in common acts which will be creative for the life of the fellowship in proportion to the closeness they bear to the point of the deepest cohesion of the community. In the Christian church, if the common actions when the community meets are not sacramental worship, as its Lord intended, they will be something else. However, any such change risks a narrowing and a disproportion in the common life. Out of the searching discussion and experience of the Church of South India, Bishop Newbigin observes "the whittling away of the sacraments":

When this happens the Church becomes something very different from what is given in the New Testament. When we allow ourselves to be more rational or more spiritual than Christ who gave us these two sacraments, we violate the nature which God has given us, and we take upon ourselves more than we were meant to bear. When we claim to possess a religion so spiritual that we can see past these visible signs to their meaning, and therefore can dispense with them, the inevitable result is that we lose a certain simplicity and a certain awareness of ultimate mystery which belong to the very heart of man's true response to God. Seeking to rise above the ordinary limitations of humanity, we become something less than human. What God has done for us in Christ, what we have to rely on, is much more than we can formulate in detailed statements or appropriate in conscious religious experience. The heart of our life in Christ must therefore be a sort of casting of ourselves upon those visible and tangible assurances which He has given us. He *has* sent forth His Church, given to it His Spirit, and furnished it with these visible and tangible means of His presence. Even the wisest must in the end become as a little child and accept what He has given, ever seeking to enter more fully into its meaning, yet ever knowing that the reality infinitely exceeds that part of it which he has grasped.[23]

Fourth: *a mission.* Our Lord left behind him a task. The church was to be no self-content society living for itself and resting "safe in the arms of Jesus." In the Gospels, a "commission" is given in connection with Jesus' departure from his followers. And only in discharge of this mission, only in its sentness, its apostolate, is the church truly the church. Some of us have almost added to Holy Writ the statement of Emil Brunner that "The Church exists by mission as fire exists by burning." As, in the name of Christ, the church bears the reconciling Word to men estranged from God, it is truly "the extension of the incarnation." Someone has put it well by saying that the church lives for the sake of those outside it.

The Word of the Cross must be brought to the world. The business of proclamation is paramount. But the proclamation of the redemptive Word is not just the preparation of a sermon. It is a style of life which is itself the "Word made flesh." The church is the present, decisive act of God's redemptive movement. In proclaiming the saving events—the life, death, and resurrection of Jesus Christ, the coming of the Holy Ghost, and the *parousia*—we make them redemptively relevant to the life of our time; we become contemporary with them. The eternal purpose of God reaches out for men in the realm of time "through our Gospel." "So we are ambassadors for Christ, God making his appeal through us."

We have traced some of the features of the divine-human life in the church. Christ gives himself. The fellowship, in ministering this Christ by word and sacrament, is delivered from becoming a club. The sacraments belong to the ordered life of the Christian fellowship, and that saves them from being magic. The word, too, derives from the Cross, and that saves it from being mere ideology. These are the given elements of the legacy of Jesus Christ to his church.

You may have remarked that I have made no mention of the Holy Spirit, who is certainly conspiciously mentioned as part of the legacy of Christ in the discourse in John 13-16. But in reality I have been talking about nothing else. For it is by the Holy Spirit that the ascended Christ lives in the fellowship. It is by the Spirit that the sacramental communion is maintained and effective witness and service are rendered. The communion of the church with God and of Christian with Christian is deep, loving, and creative because of Christ and the Spirit's witness to him. The Holy Spirit is not properly one item among several that Christ left for his followers. Rather, the whole legacy of Christ is administered by the Spirit—it *is* the Spirit. He is given in his gifts.

This discussion may have indicated to you what is available to "the man in the pew"—if the patient fellow is still there! We meet him with an invitation to the family of God. He is asked to enter the redeemed relation to God through Christ in the fellowship of the church—with all the dull, struggling, failing lot of us. In this setting he finds forgiveness, support, and a mission for his life. This does not offer the comfortable rigidity of a fixed "position," but it gives the strength of life in a growing, living organism. Such an invitation cannot provide infallibility— in fact, things can be pretty trying at times—but it does offer reality.

This strikes me as the better bargain.

Cordially,
Spermologos

THE
IMPLICATIONS
OF CHURCHMANSHIP

O Theophilus,

Yes, of course. I am being too abstract and theological about the church. As you remind me, the church is not only a divine fellowship, "the household of God"; it is also a human institution, determined in many ways by its time and place, and made up of the perverse, disagreeable lot of us.

In fact, it is just because the church is involved in history that we can come to terms with it. The institutional side of the church's life is not a regrettable compromise; it is part of its humanity.

Our task, as I see it, is to accept institutional forms—worship rites, organizations, witness and service programs, budgets, educational standards, and the like—as part of our humanness. But, as far as possible we must keep all these institutional features of our common life sacramental. That is to say, about all of the aspects of the church's life, however much they may look like the work done by some other institutions, there must be a certain "strangeness." All the things the church does should point beyond themselves. They serve the purposes of and are under the judgment of a Kingdom which is "not of this world."

This task of making our institutional life sacramental, I should say at once, is one in which no one is ever completely or permanently successful. It is the never-ending demand upon us. We must be related to our time but not dominated by it.

Now let me take up the little list you made of the "externals" of church life and examine them as they appear in Fundamentalism. I am persuaded that an inadequate theology of the church (as described in my last letter) has led to inadequate practice. The institutional structures and programs of Fundamentalism have not taken seriously the significance, givenness, and corporateness of the church's essential life. Were they to begin to do so, the results might have to be revolutionary.

To take the topics on your list one at a time:

Evangelism. A passion for evangelism has, of course, been one of the strengths of Fundamentalism. I do not want to belittle in any way this dedicated effort. I only want to suggest that a fine thing is often cheapened unnecessarily by an apparent separation made between evangelism and the church.

Fundamentalist evangelistic procedures characteristically assume a wedge driven between Christ and the church. The evangelists appeal to men to find Christ in a tent at the edge of town—a tent which has only been put there because the churches are said to have failed. The professional evangelist has come to run in competition with them. As "saved" once and for all, a convert may or may not unite with a congregation, but in either case he is reported in the statistics of the meeting. I tried to indicate in my previous letter that such a wedge is driven mistakenly. Christ is not one thing and the church another. The church, to be sure, is made up of sinful men and women, and Christ stands over against it as Judge. Nevertheless, Christ is to be found *in the fellowship,* not outside it. He judges it so severely because it is his own. The New Testament envisions a divine-human community deeply united with a divine-human Lord: "For it is from the head that the whole body, as a harmonious structure knit together by the joints with which it is provided, grows by the proper functioning of individual parts to its full maturity in love" (Phillips' translation of Eph. 4:15-16). Christ lives in the church, and the church lives in Christ. Any evangelistic effort which in practice separates the two is doomed to ephemeral results and ineffectiveness. "The Spirit *and* the Bride say, 'Come.'"

The evangelistic effort of Fundamentalism seems to have accepted such a separation between an experience of Christ and an experience of the church. This basic error in strategy shows up in three ways which come to mind at once: inefficiency, inhumanity, and manipulation of people.

Let me illustrate evangelistic inefficiency by citing the youth movements of Fundamentalism. Youth for Christ, Young Life, Word of Life, I.V.C.F.—in fact all of them that I know—normally do their work apart from the organized life of congregations or denominations. The groups may meet in a church building, but their effectiveness seems not to suffer if they do without even this loose tie. This tactic is defended on pragmatic grounds—"The churches are stuffy and slow moving," "The churches do not understand young people." So the youth movements proceed without reference to the churches, the clergy, the sacraments, the wider fellowship and mission. Now one should acknowledge that in our secular society we need evangelistic experiment, and we should be prepared to take the Christian Gospel, life, and fellowship into the community and its subcultures rather than expect modern pagans to be attracted by the characteristic activities of conventional church life. However, the more venturesomely we experiment, the more urgent is the necessity of keeping close ties with the sustaining life of the stodgy, but apparently indispensable, churches. Youth groups, lacking such clear ties, can teach only an attenuated Christianity. How can young people study the whole faith or the whole Bible and omit the most immediate of spiritual realities—the natural environment of Christian life—the church? Further, such groups are doomed, by their self-imposed isolation, to short-term results. Their appeal is intended solely for young people. However, young people can at best make up only an artificial community; they are but a part of the Christian family and should not be encouraged to think of themselves as the whole. If their religious activities have been conducted independently of the church, when the youth-oriented appeal loses its charm, the newly super-annuated young people are cut adrift. There is no clear transition for "alumni." Surely part of good evangelism is the conservation of results. This can best be assured by keeping it in or at least close to the churches. Anything less involves bad theology, introduces a divisive factor into Christian life, and wastes a great deal of effort, enthusiasm, and dedication.

What I mean by the "inhumanity" of much Fundamentalist evangelism may be seen in the implications of a phrase everywhere used and nowhere criticized, "saving souls." You may have heard a comment which Herodian often makes—that this expression suggests that the object of salvation is some "disembodied ectoplasm." What, of course, is invited to Christ in any evangelism worthy of the name is not a soul, but a man, a person —a person in all his humanity. Christ claims him not just for a momentary religious crisis but for the whole range of his personhood. His social, vocational, family, political, and intellectual life must be converted. Salvation means to have the whole of one's historic, concrete, unitary humanity related to Christ so that he can work patiently over the years. He does his teaching, sanctifying work in and through the church living in the world. In her fellowship we learn to love others as he has loved us; through her work we are directed in channels of responsible obedience. An evangelism which contents itself with "souls" alone and with religious categories exclusively can easily be an escape from the full claim of the very Christ it seeks to present.

Further, I have suggested that Fundamentalist evangelism is guilty of manipulating people. Its mass techniques have been developed so as to control large groups of people, play on their most vulnerable fears and insecurities, and lead them to suspend their critical faculties. Any evangelism which deprives a person of his full right to think and respond freely and with integrity is sub-Christian. One cannot but observe from the sincere but cliché-ridden "testimonies" rendered by new converts that somewhere along the line someone has been putting words in someone else's mouth. Even that Fundamentalist evangelism which protests that it is not "high pressure" seems to me to be guilty of a kind of "ideological imperialism." It is solely a one-way process—the evangelist has a little body of final answers (drawn, of course, from what "the Bible teaches") which the convert must repeat on his own as evidence of his being saved. Such a one-way process lacks humility in its witness for Jesus Christ; it tends to turn Christ into the evangelist's private property. A properly Christian evangelism must preserve the dignity of the person addressed, must love him, not use him. The true spirit of evangelism is a willingness to listen sensitively as well as to speak; it enters the human hurt sympathetically before it brings healing. A great modern evangelist has commented thoughtfully in this connection:

An evangelist who in the process of evangelism does not himself learn more about Jesus Christ from the man to whom he is talking —a man who in the process of evangelism does not himself learn more about Jesus Christ from the situation to which he has been sent, is not engaged in evangelism. He is engaged in propagating Christianity, which is a very different occupation.[1]

Christian Education. In Fundamentalism, despite extensive interest and experience in work among children, the conception of Christian education remains generally what one might call "rabbinic." That is, it seems to regard the imparting of information—Bible content and orthodox doctrinal propositions—as its principal goal. It disregards the importance of the life of the community for the sustained nurture of persons.

This defect could be corrected by rethinking the relation of Christian education to the living fellowship. Is there not a deep theological significance in our common, human, social context? Do not the love and care and redemptive action of God reach the child through his natural or "primary" communities? The church and the family, as Reuel Howe has put it, need to speak love and acceptance and discipline through the "language of personal relationships."[2] Such a quality of fellowship introduces the trusting, but young, child of God to his Lord within the redeemed community where Christ lives. Such a community ministers justification by faith—the "acceptance of the unacceptable"—in the very character of its life together. The propositions to articulate all of this may follow in due course. But knowing and loving God no more needs to wait for the idea of God than knowing and loving one's parents waits for the idea of parents.

If primacy is thus accorded to the personal, there are implications for curriculum:

The task of Christian education is not to teach theology, but to use theology as the basic tool for bringing learners into the right relationship with God in the fellowship of the Church.[3]

Such an emphasis involves the educator in far more than a knowledge of Bible and theology. Not only must he know content; he must know persons and know them in their interpersonal ways of relating. It would seem that there should be some radical methodological difference between the Christian education of a child and that of a parrot. If life precedes the understanding of life, curriculum will be based not on the academic ordering of content but on the relevance of Christian theology and Bible to the living questions of growing persons. The great words of the Gospel—sin, judgment, forgiveness, reconciliation, holiness, righteousness, love, joy, humility, sacrifice, hope, obedience—are not academic terms; they are existential words to be learned in the doing, deciding life within redeemed Christian relationships. They must be lived—and lived in community.

The dreadful attempts to force St. Augustine's conversion pattern on six-year-old children still seem to go on among the child-oriented groups of Fundamentalism. Spiritual counselors can only wonder who is going to repair the damage done by someone's good intentions.

Worship. Fundamentalists are churchgoers. Yet, despite their tradition of disciplined, faithful church attendance, they have an impoverished sense of worship. The worship of God is the characteristic thing the Christian church does when it gathers. It is the turning of our restless hearts to the God who made us for himself. It delivers us from a mere superficial activism. It is the one activity we share now with the realms of glory. But the theologians and pastors of the Fundamentalist movement have not taken this primary Christian action seriously—in fact they seldom speak of it.

I sometimes have thought I detected a groping for a sense of the primacy of worship in the reference commonly made by pastors of Fundamentalist churches to the midweekly prayer meeting as "the most important service of the week." This reflects a sound intuition. What the church has to say to God is prior to anything she has to say to men—in fact the church has nothing at all to say until she has first listened. But if this communion with God is the most important action of the common life, why not have it at the most important hour of the week? The same intuition that recognizes the primacy of a meeting for prayer on Wednesday condemns by implication an exclusively preaching-centered service for Sunday morning.

In practice, the Fundamentalist worship I know falls into two categories. In some quarters, it is marked by an essentially secular, vaudeville atmosphere. In others, a heavy-handed, severe, unlovely, lecture-hall atmosphere prevails—strongly suggesting that truth and beauty are enemies. When I set the two categories side by side in this way, a remark of Roger Hazelton's comes to mind: "A fever or a chill may alike be symptoms of a diseased condition."[4] (One observes that a good many Fundamentalist churches, evidently wanting to have something for everyone, practice both styles of worship—lecture hall with black gown and immense dignity on Sunday morning, vaudeville with xylophone and frenzied indignity on Sunday evening.)

Fundamentalist worship in the lecture-hall tradition places all the emphasis of the service on the prophetic person and his message. Such a stress—despite the dignity and the learning with which the preaching office, at its best, is invested—is one-sided. It errs in the direction of wordiness and intellectualism. It is too cerebral. Words in orderly, academic discourse seem to exhaust a topic; they define; they categorize; they isolate and distinguish. In this word-centered form of worship, there is seldom a proper sense of mystery and there is little realization of the awesome aboveness yet tender nearness of God—we only know that God is great and man is small because we say so. But, in speaking to his children, we should not confine God to only what the leader of our worship is capable of verbalizing. Where the ministry of words is intimately linked to the ministry of the nonpropositional —adornment, color, bodily posture, symbol, action, music, silence —the individual both gives and receives more than would be possible through conscious verbalizing alone. There is a kind of considered shape—a movement, a rise and a fall, a progression toward a goal—in the worship of the great liturgical traditions that meets the individual participant at unexpected places of need. Form is not evil; form is humanity; it is civilization; it is the precondition of freedom. Through a worship which mingles the verbal and the nonverbal, the Word of God can reach us in our wholeness. It is characteristic of symbol that it suggests more than it states; thus the frank acceptance of symbolic ingredients in our worship is a reminder—more eloquent than words—that "our knowledge is imperfect and our prophecy is imperfect."

But the "warming" of the chilled form of Fundamentalist worship does not mean an imitation of the more feverish form. The vaudeville style of Fundamentalist worship has provided us with the spectacle of enthusiastic choristers, trombones, barber-shop quartets, marimbas, and the like pressed into unaccustomed roles in divine worship. (I once heard the pastor of a respected

Fundamentalist church whistle, to organ accompaniment, a verse of a hymn at a Sunday morning service! This was met with numerous ejaculations of "Amen, brother.") This tradition has set stale rhymes on "me," "free," and "tree" to marches, waltzes, two-steps, and ballads. Such a use of the "nonpropositional" is most successful in appealing to the feet—an organ not hitherto regarded as a center of spiritual receptivity!

In this connection may an observer who has long since lost personal contact with such things and is dependent on what he hears on the radio be permitted a remark on the appalling lapse of taste in Fundamentalist music? The tradition as I knew it a number of years ago was, it seems in retrospect, "corny," but tolerably sincere. The music tended to be of about the quality of "Clementine," and it had about it some of the flavor of the tent meeting and the country hoedown. But it had a certain measure of integrity—after all, there are moments in which even "Clementine" can be persuasive. Now, if I am to believe what I hear, the musical world of "evangelicalism" has taken a most incredible turn. Slick, syrupy strings with chimes try to do something for old Gospel song tunes without inherent musical distinction—"Clementine" arranged by Mantovani, as it were. And the newer "Gospel hits" are in the tradition not of the tent meeting but of the musicals of the Friml and Romberg era and occasionally of the cabaret. The words are often ludicrously erotic, the music indescribably cheap, and the rendition frankly "torchy." If the neo-evangelicals want to convince the world that they have taken on new depth and relevance, let them stop beating the ecumenical movement and start doing something about their music. It presently seems to be a sign of inner decay.

A recovery of a sense of worship among Fundamentalists would also, I think, have an effect on ecclesiastical architecture. With some exceptions the buildings most characteristic of the Fundamentalist movement are of the "tabernacle" type. They are derived from the structures designed for the Billy Sunday campaigns. They feature a "platform" and a place in the front for a large and conspicuous choir. They often are fitted with theater seats (perhaps their one bit of meaningful symbol!), and they nearly always have a cheap and temporary look. Such buildings are essentially auditoriums designed for oratory. They are not "carved prayers" built with integrity to be in themselves sacrifices of praise to God. They are not buildings derived from the demands of an action of corporate worship within them.

If the unspoken accompaniments of worship are not claimed for God, if they are not "the Word made flesh," the implication seems to be that God reaches us only through the conscious processes. This baseless notion leaves the deepest portions of life to be shaped by quite unchristian influences. For if churches give no nourishment to the life of the imagination, the imagination does not die. Rather, it flourishes on a diet of prevalent secular images and myths.

But along with this concern for the dignity of the nonpropositional, I am concerned about what the downgrading of worship does to the identity of the worshiping congregation. In any kind of "preliminaries and sermon" pattern, attention is centered on a man—the staging of his entry and the ability of his personality, dogmatism, passion, and wit to hold the congregation and carry his point. The worshiper, from his side, comes to be entertained or edified. He is essentially an individual coming to "get a blessing." This is subjective, particularistic, and preoccupied with self; it is not corporate worship. The worshiper comes for what he can get. This misses the primary note of adoration. By contrast, a sense of worship as the principal business of the Christian fellowship means that the worshiper comes to take an active part in what is by nature a corporate action. The active part he takes may be different from that taken by another minister of the service, but neither is more or less necessary than the other. No one is a passive listener. Each expresses by his participation the fact that he is a member—not an isolated, self-dependent believer, but a sharer in the life of the community within which he can become what he most truly is.

Having said so much that is critical, perhaps I should not drop the subject of worship without a positive suggestion. I think that any Christian worship can have a self-correcting factor within it if, as a normal thing, the whole of worship regularly culminates in the sacraments. The Word and the sacraments ought to be regarded as interdependent. "The Word of God" is depicted in the Bible as a powerful, effectual, creative, lifegiving agency. As such, the Word is not adequately represented in the faith community by words alone. There must be "the Word made visible" in actions, and actions made significant by words. If the proclamation of the Word within the fellowship were normally followed by the breaking of bread, there would be a deliverance from individualism, subjectivism, and intellectualism. Here would be a place where the church holds communion with her Lord under tokens of bread and wine—the element of inexpressible mystery is present; the concrete, non-propositional has been introduced by Christ's own institution. In the sacramental recalling of the death and resurrection of Christ for the sins of the world there is a touchstone for detecting that in our worship which is—by cheapness, sentimentality, sensationalism, and the like—unworthy of this association. I think that the restoration of the sacraments to their due place in theology and practice would introduce a criterion into worship which over the course of time would be conducive to greatness and would tend to make the inferior wither away.

Fellowship. In the quality of fellowship, too, I think that a recovered sense of the church would have a marked effect. And again the effect would be to complement an area in which Fundamentalism has to its credit some real achievement. There is presently throughout Fundamentalism a sense of cohesion—a thing made all the more remarkable for its not being organized in any movement-wide way. In some of the fellowships, crusades, and corporate efforts among Fundamentalists, a common life is shared creatively and deeply in and under the Spirit of God. However, in the atmosphere of Fundamentalism, the sense of fellowship tends to become narrow and stereotyped. It gains its power and discipline by the same exclusiveness by which it loses its comprehensiveness, its richness, and its source in love.

Although there is no over-all organization in Fundamentalism, there is a phrase (or an idea corresponding to the phrase) that seems to mark the life of the movement so characteristically that it may be a key to the weakness I have in mind. Throughout Fundamentalism there seems to be an insistence that everyone, as a condition of his acceptance, be able to say, "I know the Lord Jesus Christ as my own personal Savior." This formula provides a kind of unofficial admissions policy for the movement.

This insistence should be open to question on Fundamentalism's own ground, for it is not strictly biblical. The customary phrase cannot be traced in any concordance. Perhaps, the closest that St. Paul comes to the Fundamentalist idea "Christ died for me" is in Galatians 2:20 (". . . the Son of God, who loved me and gave himself for me"). The Bible suffers from its being read exclusively in the light of this "personal" emphasis. Books and passages that are radically corporate are made over and read with a particularistic, individual thrust. (For example, the Letter to the Ephesians is sometimes considered by Fundamentalists as "The Wealth, Walk, and Warfare of the Christian." But the letter is not interested in anything so abstract as "the believer" and his individual union with Christ. Its subject is the church, not the individual Christian; it is plural, not singular.) There are some deeply personal passages in the New Testament, to be sure, but the overwhelming emphasis is corporate rather than individual—God loved the world, Christ gave himself for the church. Union with Christ is union within his Body. The legitimately biblical individual emphasis has simply run away with things in Fundamentalism and distorted the nature and place of the historic community.

This practical admissions policy is open to another sort of criticism. The kind of experience required to qualify a person to say, "I know the Lord Jesus Christ as my own personal Savior" —a conscious, datable conversion—means that those who have had such an experience, articulated in those terms, have a deep religious crisis in common. And if they make this the criterion of entry into the fellowship, the resultant community life can be intimate. Having a common experience, the members understand and accept one another. But they tend to exclude those who do not claim this same experience or do not express an equivalent experience in the approved terms. This leads to a fellowship that I call *intensive*. But such an emphasis misses what I could call an *extensive* unity. An extensive unity avoids the spirit of "We few, we happy few, we band of brothers," for its point of unity belongs to the givenness of the fellowship. Any religious fellowship based on human choices or human experience is bound to become "clubby," for it is determined by preferences. It can too easily become an extension of egoism in that it is a group formed of "me" plus "my kind." The Christian community must rest finally not on "I choose" but on "I am chosen." It is constituted by the mysterious regeneration of the Holy Spirit, not by any specifiable human experience. As one of the profoundest Christians of our day has said, "Christian brotherhood is not an ideal which we must realize; it is rather a reality created by God in Christ in which we may participate."[5] Since the basis is given in grace and not acquired by merit, the fellowship is potentially universal—as no community based on choices or experience could ever be. Our acceptance and sympathy must be no less wide than the brotherhood.

Now there is nothing wrong or pathological about the intensive or cell-type fellowship. It is probably necessary as a way to bring like-minded Christians into effective groupings that are not organized from the outside. Real life-changing and society-changing work has been done, or at least initiated, through just such informal groups. But neither is there anything inherently Christian about such groups. The sense of intimacy and dedication to a cause can be sacred, but at root it is a neutral human characteristic reproduced in some degree by such other cell-type communities as lodges, radical political groups, and the comradeship of a local tavern. The fact that the Spirit uses this type of fellowship at times does not mean that whenever this type of fellowship is present the Spirit is controlling it. Further, when the intensive is the only style of fellowship that is recognized, it becomes restrictive, narrowed, and self-conscious. It tends to congratulate itself: "What we have here in our little intimate group—and only it—is the 'real' Christianity."

The spontaneous, irregular, intensive style of fellowship needs badly to be set within the extensive type, which can provide it with a larger, more objective context. Only a fellowship which refuses to define itself narrowly and exclusively can bear witness to a Christology and an ecclesiology such as this of Forsyth's:

> It was a race that Christ redeemed, and not a mere *bouquet* of believers. It was a Church He saved, and not a certain pale of souls. Each soul is saved in a universal and corporate salvation. To be a Christian is not to attach one's salvation to a grand individual, but it is to enter Christ; and to enter Christ is in the same act to enter the Church which is in Christ. Faith in Christ is faith in One Whose indwelling makes a Church, and Who carries a Church within His corporate Person.[6]

A further quality I observe in the Fundamentalist sense of fellowship (and again the requirement of a "password" may be a mischief-maker) is a tendency to restrict the variety of the community. Only certain experience patterns are common in Fundamentalism, with only a few idioms for expressing them. Only a few vocations are open for those who wish to take their Christian commitment seriously. We should expect as a mark of vitality an endless diversity in Christian life, sanctity, and vocation; God seems to avoid uniformity. A preference for uniformity of experience and expression loses the color we might expect to find in the whole range of the human community restored to the ground of its being in God. Such a narrowing reinforces the middle-class orientation of Fundamentalism; it tends to mediocrity and imitativeness. Surely more than one temperament, more than one class, more than one culture, was included in Jesus' invitation. More than one should be in ours. There is a depth, range, and fullness of community which can never be discovered until all arbitrary stereotypes are abandoned. Halford Luccock once remarked on the impossibility of whistling a symphony!

In this connection, Carl Henry's claim comes to mind—that the Baptist reassertion of the principle of "a regenerate church membership" is one of the lasting contributions of evangelicalism.[7] The issue he raises has been a live one since the sixteenth century, and the lines along which it is argued have hardly changed. I think that Henry reflects the general preference of conservatives, Baptists or not. I question, however, whether the thing that Henry has in mind is attainable. The Baptist policy seeks to achieve this "regenerate church membership" by admitting to baptism only those whose regenerate state is certain. But who is to establish the certainty? There is, of course, the possibility of attaining a "converted church membership" if a certain definition of "converted" is used. This, as a matter of fact, is what a strict Baptist scheme achieves. Regeneration is a divine mystery. Conversion is a human experience—accessible to the religious psychologists. The two are surely not unrelated. But neither are they identical. So, in effect, the practice Henry prefers secures an "intensive fellowship" of those who are satisfied with the account of one another's religious experience. Their adult dedication is assured, and their corporate effectiveness is great. But, after twenty years, is even the most scrupulous Baptist congregation prepared to examine its register of baptisms and declare that its criteria of "regeneration" were accurate? It, no less than any other church body, must reckon with the problem of "unconverted church members." It has its pastoral heartbreaks as all others do. The perfect church is beyond our clumsy powers of discrimination to create here.

Church Order. It is hard to say anything completely applicable about the preference for church order among Fundamentalists. For questions of church order are, within limits, matters of dispute among them, and Fundamentalists come from several traditions of polity. Nevertheless, there seems to be some correlation between Fundamentalism and the more loose and congregational types of order. Most of the churches and denominations which have been created by Fundamentalism, and hence represent its own genius, are of the independent sort. But it must be questioned here as to whether or not this preference for an atomistic church order does not reflect a deficient sense of community. In view of the essential corporateness of the church, can particularistic organization be defended as expressing the Gospel? Groups which establish independency in the interest of freedom are actually more vulnerable than others to the peril of tyranny. Bureaucracy or dictatorship can come in the actual back doors of groups which have thrown ordered cohesion out their theoretical front doors. A brilliant leader can acquire a following and more absolute power to dominate his group than would be possible in a structure which had accepted a considered and balanced order as part of its real life.

You have often commented about the welter of "faith projects" in Fundamentalism, begun by startling personalities (and often bearing their names), and each taking its own way. These can be hastily organized, easily exploited financially, and irresponsible in their abuse of devoted followers. Each makes converts who have no way of sensing any relatedness in Christ to all other Christians. There is no reciprocity between the body of converts and the parent body of mission supporters. I am persuaded that the egoistic statesmanship behind these independent mission projects is devoid of a sense of the church. The leaders are not so much shepherds as cowboys. After all, is not the frequently advertised claim to be a "faith" venture in itself invidious? To distinguish one's group on this basis implies that other Christian projects not so distinguished are working, praying, and giving in the service of God without faith. The difference is not between faith and the absence of faith; it is between, on the one hand, faith that works with unity, planning, discipline, and sometimes a mote of wisdom or daring (albeit often with the most provoking slowness) and, on the other hand, faith that works without checks against competitiveness, rashness, and irresponsibility.

If the corporateness of the spiritual fellowship is important, church order is not less so. For while organizational structure may be a means to an end, and hence theoretically subordinate to the end of "the perfecting of the saints," it is a means which holds within itself the power to safeguard or to destroy the conditions whereby the end can be achieved.

If the theological discussion in my previous letter is at all correct, atomistic church order needs rethinking. However, I do not plead here for any special form of polity. Although I am not prepared to say that all forms of church order are equally desirable, it does seem clear to me that God uses all of them. Any form can embody more than it does of the meaning of the great church, and changes can be made from within when a given form seems unequal to the strain of this essential mission. Thus for the present it may be enough to submit that a person in a tradition where independence and freedom are cherished must be careful to maintain his heritage in responsible freedom. On the other hand, a person in a tradition that stresses organic cohesion must watch against the domination by rules. Both types of structure are open to the perils of bureaucracy and conformity. Both can become either conservative or adaptable. Both can encourage or kill (by laws or pressure) the delight God seems to take in divine madness, in the irregular, in the charming nonconformist, in the odd and perplexing occasional "troubadour of God," in the disturbing prophet. Both emphases can be means of grace for those who are wise enough to use their characteristic strengths and overcome their characteristic weaknesses.

Denominational Relations. The spirit of antidenominationalism is all too characteristic of Fundamentalism. In some places there now seems to be a more statesmanlike rapprochement with major church bodies, but in other parts of Fundamentalism the matter worsens. Of course, the completely Fundamentalist denominations are regarded with general favor. But the few "evangelicals" who by some mischance are in one of the major

Protestant bodies are made to feel that their best line of godly duty is to oppose its whole program vigorously and to be either apologetic for it or disruptive of it. The real loyalty is to the nondenominational crusades, missions, and movements that unite Fundamentalists and make all denominational and parochial loyalties secondary.

Although the picture of American Christianity is not altogether inspiring, the spirit of bewailing the "apostate denominations" does not make it more so. It almost seems that every move in denominational or ecumenical affairs will be met with ill-tempered comments from Fundamentalists—no matter how "neo" and reconstructed they may claim to be. Certain portions of the evangelical press have made a profession of attacking the actions and the motives of the most respected leaders and councils of the Christian world. One marvels at the sustained attitude of bitterness, smallness, and misrepresentation. Are such spokesmen sincerely persuaded that denominational and ecumenical statesmanship is always wrong, or are they caught in a posture from which they must oppose such leadership no matter what it does? One sympathizes with Forsyth's distrust of "a Church of those who object to Churches."[8]

No denomination is about to repeal the Apostles' Creed. The denominations and ecumenical councils of Christendom have repeatedly evidenced their essential orthodoxy. They do not need defense. But even if it were apparent that a wholesale defection from the received faith were under way, what would it prove? The vitality of a church is attested, not by the confessional conformity of its clergy, but in the ability of the body to reform from within. The amazing thing about the church is not her purity—from the Apostles to the present it has never been pure, and there is probably no sin of greed, pride, ambition, or cowardice of which it has not been guilty. The amazing thing is the way the Spirit calls the church back time after time from its bypaths. The ecclesiastical Cassandras crying doom and "apostasy" give up on the churches much more easily than God does.

But on another level, there is again the charge of egotism to bring against those who disparage, from some personal pinnacle of spiritual insight, the work and witness of the churches. They assume themselves led by the Spirit, but they cheerfully deny his

leadership in the case of others. They dogmatically enlist followers, but they themselves have never learned to follow. This is
not only a strange kind of conceit; it is also a quite mistaken
assessment of our real position as Christians in the middle of
the 20th century. If the Spirit of God is speaking now to Christians, when did he not so speak? Try though we may, we cannot
begin Christianity as though we had no antecedents. We stand
on the shoulders of others to reach even as high as we do. We
are heirs of a Christian tradition. We can acknowledge it and
work gratefully from it—not uncritically, but toward the conservation of its best and the correction of its defects. Or we can
repudiate it and imply by so doing that the Spirit who speaks now
to us has never truly spoken to others. This latter has been the
choice of too many Fundamentalists. They choose to be "planters"
and not "waterers." Denominations, to be sure, are not ideal; our
divisions are foolish and disgraceful. But we do not need still
more confusion. Each tradition enshrines a facet of the Gospel,
and without the fragmented witnesses the Body would be the
poorer. Each tradition represents something older, larger, and
wiser than ourselves. A genuine recognition of the corporate
side of Christian life will tend to lead us into our existing heritage, not away from it—not into it, of course, as to an ultimately
satisfactory resting place, but into it as to a tradition which represents, better than no tradition, "the pulse of the timeless in
time."[9]

This series of discussions may have suggested to you the bearing of the corporate emphasis on some of the weaknesses of
Fundamentalism. I should repeat that in these practical, pastoral,
frontier aspects of the church's life there are no final, guaranteed
answers. We all are groping, experimenting, succeeding, and failing. The trouble in talking with Fundamentalists has been that
they have assumed their way of meeting these problems to be the
only right one—thereby allowing them to despise others. I have
contended here that they are in the same struggle as all of the
rest of the church; that they are in some ways not showing up
very well; and that these flaws tend to be related to the absence
of a sense of the real meaning of the church.

When Christians know themselves as parts of a divine-human
fellowship—as parts related to one another, not as pills in a
single bottle, but as organs of a living body—they have a per-

spective for constructive endeavor. Only as *church which knows itself to be church* can enduring work be done.

Shrunken views of the Kingdom are crippling. The church is part of the great procession of the faithful—from Abraham to the *parousia*. She is alive and changing—adapting to emergent needs. She contains the weak, the humble, the mistaken, and the sinful. She is seldom true to the gift of God within her. She betrays her Lord fully as often as she reveals him. Yet Christ loves her. He gave himself for her. He has made her his household, his bride, his people, his temple. And some day he will present her, cleansed and perfect. Meanwhile, she is his "body"— his instrument for his work in the world. Under him she is prophet and priest to mankind. He has hazarded the Gospel on the church.

Cordially,
Spermologos

V

THE
TRUTH

All active mass movements strive . . . to impose a fact-proof screen between the faithful and the realities of the world. They do this by claiming that the ultimate and absolute truth is already embodied in their doctrine and that there is no truth or certitude outside it. The facts on which the true believer bases his conclusions must not be derived from his experience or observation but from holy writ. . . . To rely on the evidence of the senses and of reason is heresy and treason. It is startling to realize how much unbelief is necessary to make belief possible. What we know as blind faith is sustained by innumerable unbeliefs.

ERIC HOFFER

SOMETHING
ABOUT OBSCURANTISM

O Theophilus,

You are right, I am sure, that the meaning of the old accusation of "obscurantism" is confused these days. Not only so, but
this charge—when used against Fundamentalists—seems to strike
an exposed nerve; conservative spokesmen leap to the defense
whenever it is made. Obviously the topic needs more thought.
In fact, if there is a good discussion of the term anywhere in
print, I do not know of it.

I have a few ideas which will not settle the confusion, but
they may carry the discussion a bit further along.

I. THE MEANING OF THE CHARGE: PAST AND PRESENT

One can readily understand Fundamentalists' offense at the
charge, for it is a serious one. Let me venture a thesis: In effect,
the charge of "obscurantism" means that those against whom
it is made are accused of deliberately (though not necessarily
always wittingly), as a matter of religious principle, and in the
name of Christ, calling darkness light and light darkness. Obscurantism is the interposition of some consideration or other between an observer and reality so that neither truth nor error is
recognizable. It is any dogmatic preconception which would
render unimportant the question of truth. It is the rejection, on
religious grounds, of the world as it is. The issue is searching.
It is a spiritual, not merely an academic, matter. The charge
should not be made lightly.

The dictionary defines obscurantism as opposition to progress,
enlightenment, reform, or inquiry. So discussion of obscurantism

involves, inevitably, certain implications as to where "truth" and "progress" are to be found and what the competence of the human mind really is. For it is against these that obscurantism takes its definition. This consideration accounts for the shift in the meaning of the charge. In recent decades in theological thought there has been a decided change in the kind of truth sought and in the way of seeking it. As a consequence, there has been a change in the meaning given to "obscurantism."

You may well be right about the original form of the charge. Behind the term as used a half century ago was the conflict between Liberal optimism concerning human nature and perfectibility and the Fundamentalists' counterassertion of original sin. In that period the Liberal believed in the goodness and the rationality of man. He seemed to feel that if only the true and the right could be made clear enough they would commend themselves to men universally and provide the deepest of all motives for harmonious action. Encouraged by this faith, the Liberals set about to revise the social order, the church, the Christian faith, and the human soul. To those involved in this forward-looking program, the Fundamentalist insistence on human perversity seemed like an obscuring of all that made life and duty intelligible and hopeful. To those who took Liberal idealism as their light, Fundamentalism could only seem to be a "bedarkening."

For their part, Fundamentalists played the villain's role with unfailing enthusiasm. Their distrust of human nature, human accomplishment, and human reason soon became outright anti-intellectualism. Learning was regarded as a cunning wile of the devil, a thing to be warned against, not used. The seminaries—which still, in my memory, were, in a common play for laughter, being dubbed "cemeteries"—were condemned wholesale. If only a spokesman stood for "the old-time religion," he was listened to, regardless of his methods or his competence. Self-appointed experts—sometimes little more than charlatans—were acclaimed as the latest oracles on science and the Bible. Hysteria and personal vilification were the preferred apologetic forms. Superficial and shoddy scholarship was granted uncritical acceptance. There is probably no charge related to obscurantism which cannot be substantiated over and over again out of the voluminous polemical writings of Riley, Norris, Shuler, Bryan, Rimmer, Price,

Brown, and a score of others. But I need not document this. The "repentant Fundamentalists" are doing that, and it comes more graciously from them than from me.

In those formative days of Fundamentalism the issue was quite clearly drawn on these lines. The Liberals were the champions of reason, of science, of criticism, of "the newer thinking." The Fundamentalists, on the other hand, seemed to cling to the old formulations, the old critical opinions, the old science. They were so persuaded of the wrongness of unaided reason that they were willing to defend their orthodoxy in defiance of evidence. They affirmed the miraculous, the irrational, without apology in an era that worshiped natural law. For Fundamentalists, the Lord of the supernatural realm was willing to stop the sun, send a universal flood, create the universe in 168 hours, or kill some people in judgment and raise others from the dead in mercy. And Fundamentalists geared their apologetic to demonstrating that he had, in fact, done so. They sought to establish "the reasonableness of supernaturalism."[1] To the Liberal, however, it seemed evident that the God thus described by Fundamentalists was at times capricious and immoral. It was further obvious that the Bible had had a long literary history and had assimilated elements from the religions of its surroundings—the "supernatural" of the Fundamentalists was often filled with superstition and with primitive features for which parallels could be found in Frazer's *The Golden Bough*. It had become evident, too, that the universe and man were of vastly greater antiquity than a literal reading of Genesis would suggest, and that there has been a traceable development in the history of organic forms. These doctrines were all so apparent to the Liberal that the intellectual life of the Fundamentalist seemed to be forever in the shadows—it rejected the proper claims of reason and enlightenment.

But in the present day the roles are to some extent reversed. Now Fundamentalists may find themselves the champions of reason, while their critics defend the irrational.

The reason for this is that the center of theological discussion has changed. A generation ago theological inquiry sought, by means of scientific criticism, to recover the "historical Jesus." Too often the quest was for a Jesus shorn of the miraculous and the divine mission with which faith and dogma had invested him. This inquiry expected that such a Jesus when found would be a man very like our own enlightened selves. The strangeness had been imposed upon him by others. But critics themselves long ago showed that the closer we get to Jesus seen in his own context, the greater is the distance between him and ourselves. "He passes by our time and returns to his own," said Schweitzer. He must be heard and understood on his own terms. There never was a Jesus without theological significance. The eschatological setting for his life and mission is present in our earliest sources. With these observations, scientific criticism worked itself out of the crucial job in biblical and theological studies. It had shown that the message *about* Jesus was not superimposed on the message *of* Jesus. Hence, the center of the theological task shifted from historical criticism to biblical theology.

In other words, we have come in half a century from a period which was primarily scientific or historical in the questions it raised and the answers it gave, into a period which is primarily theological in aim. Two quite different methods of thought dominate these periods. Each kind of thinking has its own definition of obscurantism. And in each period Fundamentalism has seemed to be in the wrong. In the scientific period, obscurantism lay in twisting facts to fit predetermined conclusions, in opposing new light, in making interpretations and critical opinions into dogmas divinely revealed. In the theological period, obscurantism lies in treating theological formulations as complete and final, in absolutizing a rational structure.

In the earlier period, Fundamentalists were accused of being arbitrary and irrational in the scientific realm, where the human reason is competent to judge. In the later period, they are accused of the *hubris* of overconfident rationalism in a realm where the limitations of human reason should be recognized. If they are bewildered at being berated first for insufficient trust in reason and then for excessive trust in it, their bewilderment is certainly understandable. At one moment they are derided for defending all sorts of irrational conclusions. The next moment their opponents are using terms such as "ecstasy," "paradox," "existential," "teleological suspension of the ethical," and "nonpropositional." They are now the apparent irrationalists, and the Fundamentalists are accused of having too much faith in reason.

The sharpness of this change has been accentuated by the course of thought within Fundamentalism. In the first generation, as I have suggested, the scholarly strain of Fundamentalism was quickly outshouted by the definitely, avowedly anti-intellectualist strain, which for several decades held the floor. But, as the second generation problems have come to the fore, the anti-intellectualists are being discredited in their own circles—they had led the movement into disrepute. The scholarly strain is reasserting itself in the leadership of the movement. This strain maintains a rationalistic approach, so, just when rational theism is faltering in theology at large, it is being reaffirmed in conservative circles. The interaction of these two recent trends is certain to make the charge of obscurantism denote its new meaning in its acutest possible form.

II. THE REFUSAL TO RECOGNIZE ERROR

I maintain, however, that the terms of the quarrel are no longer determined by a difference on the reality of sin. That sin is real is agreed by both sides. It is no longer the case, if it ever was, that everyone except the Fundamentalists believes in the perfectibility, the indefinite educability, of man and that the Fundamentalists' solitary rejection of these tenets marks them as obscurantist. Quite the contrary, a spokesman like D. R. Davies can say, in his pungent way:

> Trust in human nature, which results in the most appalling sentimentalism and in the most incredible shallowness about life and history, may be true or false; may be a beautiful creed or not; but whatever it is, *it is not Christian*. On the contrary, it is the most utterly anti-Christian view of life and man which has ever appeared during the two thousand years of history since Christ. It severs the very lifeline of the Christian religion.
>
> Whether Christianity be true or false, whether or not it has any further relevance to our world, it does not regard evil in man as an unfortunate accident, as a mere incident in history, which future progress will overcome. Evil in man is fundamental. That famous rock-bottom ego is devil, not angel.[2]

Davies rejects the idea that evil is the result of unfortunate factors outside the essential personality of man. He insists that evil is fundamental in man as we know him.

A statement more forceful than this would be hard to find in Fundamentalist hamartiology's most breast-beating pages. In fact, there is room for the fear that vital realism may pass over into a sterile pessimism so that one of the needs of the moment is to reaffirm Christian sanctions for the dignity of personhood and the truth of reason, lest some of the gains of Liberalism be lost. At any rate, original sin is not the issue. It is agreed upon in at least similar forms by both sides.

The quarrel is over the selectivity with which the doctrine is applied by Fundamentalists. Several quite gratuitous exemptions are made in the application of original sin. These exemptions support illusions fully as unreal and as sub-Christian as any of the dreams of the most idealistic Liberal. These exemptions make a sort of Protestant parallel to the immaculate conception —a gap, an exception, somewhere in the solidary pattern of human sin and error. I would like to suggest three of these.

First of all, the Fundamentalists exempt the biblical writings. This exemption is a priori. It seems to be assumed, before the fact, that if God is to speak to his creatures, the divinity of his Word must somehow imply the infallibility of the vehicle. A recent writer has put this explicitly:

> If . . . the Biblical records were produced by men directed and controlled by the Holy Spirit, then we have every reason to believe that the facts and doctrines recorded in the Bible are free of those imperfections and blemishes that characterize all purely human productions.[3]

This does not follow. Take for a parallel the manner of personal conversion. The very Spirit of God may graciously and mysteriously be communicated to another person through me. But that does not imply my infallibility. It only implies the actuality of a tolerably transparent witness to the Word of God—possibly through a theology less than orthodox or a spirit less than saintly. Grace puts its treasure in "earthen vessels." Can it not do so in the case of the Bible? Its writers bore effective witness to the saving events of God's redemption, and we are utterly in their debt. But must that imply their exemption from the common human shortcomings in piety, logic, historical information, theological acuity, and neighborly charity? The refusal of Fundamentalism to reckon the biblical documents among the failing, erring run of human works, subject to the same judgment we are, is one facet of the obscurantism charged against the movement.

The biblical writers bore witness to their Gospel—but they themselves were under the judgment of the Gospel they brought. They claimed no more for themselves—"But *even if we*, or an angel from heaven, should preach to you a gospel contrary to that which we preached to you, let him be accursed" (Gal. 1:8; italics mine).

But Fundamentalists will not have it this way.

Have they weighed the import of their claim? They are, fittingly, rather reticent about the psychology of the inspiration they claim for the Bible. But this reticence comes after some affirmations of the meaning of inspiration which cannot but have general implications as to method. James M. Gray's statement in *The Fundamentals* is still, I think, representative:

> Moses, David, Paul, John were not always and everywhere inspired, for then always and everywhere they would have been infallible and inerrant, which was not the case. They sometimes made mistakes in thought and erred in conduct. But however fallible and errant they may have been as men compassed with infirmity like ourselves, such fallibility or errancy was never under any circumstances communicated to their sacred writings.[4]

These terms are not some critic's parody of what Fundamentalists say. This is sober, refined Fundamentalist dogma. This adventure of speculation (wise above what is written in a dozen ways) we are to believe is the teaching of Scripture about itself. This doctrine asks us to suppose that for a period of time and for a specific purpose God set aside the conditions of the humanity of certain of his children; he abridged their freedom to err. He qualified the authentic relation between a writer and his work. Even without the offensive word "dictation," does this not present us with the spectacle of God's treating his children as tools, instruments, things? Packer admits as much when he defines inspiration as "a divine activity . . . which involved human writers as a means to an end, but which actually terminated, not on them, but on what they wrote."[5] Has he looked critically at his expression about God's *using* "human writers *as a means*"? Man was not made for the Bible, but the Bible for man! This logic decrees that God, instead of submitting to the law of the human, temporarily overrode it. In order to produce an errorless book, he carried these writers outside the human condition. He destroyed "the form of a servant," and then, the writing done, he remade it. Strange, capricious God! Strange, improbable doctrine! Heresy! Begetter of heresies!

This presumed exemption of the Bible from error I have discussed at length in earlier letters. I only cite it here as a form of obscurantism. It is a form, however, which leads to others. The explicit exemption from error of one's ultimate religious authority cannot but lead to further, closely related forms of obscurantism.

One corollary of the Fundamentalist view of the Bible has been this: Since the Bible is not subject to error of fact and must not be criticized, whenever a conflict appears between supposed Bible-truth and supposed science-truth, this conflict must be decided in favor of the Bible. The traditional form of this conflict has seemed to assume on the part of the Fundamentalists: (1) that the universe cannot be the creation of God unless its making was instantaneous, and (2) that the Bible cannot be divine unless it is all "prose"—factual, literal, and journalistic. These two bits of superstition have mutually reinforced the case for the obscurantism charge.

Fundamentalists have repeatedly yielded their most rigid opinions over the years to allow for the findings of science. But, at best, "they have made only minor concessions and adjustments, and then with the utmost reluctance and at the latest possible date."[6] It does seem to have come about within the last few years that a Fundamentalist leader can hold some form of a theory of evolution without risking excommunication. Surely it is about time. The possibility of a kind of evolutionary view compatible with a Christian doctrine of creation was established shortly after the publication of Darwin's *Origin of Species*. Huxley's conclusions from Darwin's observations were never the only legitimate ones. However, among Fundamentalists no possibilities were open other than sustained hostility between Genesis and science. Any modification of this is still a recent and hesitant development.

This process of reconciliation with geology and biology—a process which had moved hardly at all for most of the life of the Fundamentalist movement—made a major stride a few years ago. In 1954, Bernard Ramm published a significant study, which made a more thorough revision than anyone had made before, of the strange assortment of dodges that Fundamentalists (Ramm calls them the "hyperorthodox") had collected to "harmonize" science and Scripture.[7] He observes that most of the conflict has been based on what had wrongly been taken to be the meaning of the Bible. The arguments of the hyperorthodox have been drawn not from Scripture but from faulty, arbitrary interpretations of it. He is willing to allow that the language of the Bible on cosmological matters is naïve, nonscientific, "nonpostulational," and conditioned by such limiting factors as the writer's time, place, and cultural outlook. Thus he is able to loosen the hermeneutical procedures that had led literalism into serious conflicts in the past. In short, his book is an able critique of some long-cherished nonsense; it brings the discussion in Fundamentalist circles into the twentieth century—a major stride. Fundamentalists, we may hope, will hear fewer crank flood geologies or "gap" theories from now on.

Far as he has gone, Ramm remains a conservative. Nevertheless, his removal of the worst of the crudities of Fundamentalist apologetic opens fresh and unexpected possibilities. In his own circles his book met with great hostility from some readers, but it received a grateful welcome from others.

Once Ramm has said that the statements of Scripture on cosmology are not revealed, veridical, scientific statements to be literally construed, one of the major barriers to intelligent conversation has come down. Obscurity has begun to yield to light. Scientific issues are now (if Ramm's lead is followed) to be decided on scientific rather than on exegetical grounds. One could disagree with any or all of Ramm's conclusions on the antiquity of man, the flood, and the like, or on his interpretation of certain biblical passages, and still recognize gratefully the significance of his achievement.[8]

The trend continues. In a more recent book review, Ramm states approvingly that a book maintaining that "the general sequence of rock formations and appearances of living forms as described in the average book on paleontology is correct" has been published by a Dutch writer of unimpeachable orthodoxy. But, even in the year of our Lord 1959, a century after Darwin's *Origin of Species,* Ramm has to introduce this book to his constituency as "a real shocker."

A second major exemption from the effects of sin is made by Fundamentalists in the case of their own theologians and biblical interpreters. You comment in your letter, in defense of Fundamentalism, that "leaders of Fundamentalism, far from being intellectually obscurantist, devote a great deal of energy to the rational systematization and defense of the faith." So they do. I would not question the energy or the rationality of their formulations in themselves (any more than I question the ability of a devout Mormon acquaintance of mine—a Ph.D.—to use his mind on religious matters). Obscurantism does not lie only in failure to think; it lies in reluctance to open the primary questions that anchor thought in the real world and keep it from becoming artificial. It lies in the untroubled contentment with one's present opinions and the refusal to review them freely in the light of what offers itself as new truth. On reading the publications of the "conservative" press, one has the feeling that its writers assume a fixed body of absolute truth, final, divine, unquestionable, and firmly in their possession. This oppressive presence of the final truth, finally formulated, is everywhere in Fundamentalism. With it goes a stifling lack of ideas.

There is a vast presumption in this claim to possess a divine truth or a revealed system. It assumes: (1) that the divine oracles are completely discontinuous with and distinguishable from all other truth; (2) that there is a single, consistent theological system in the Bible; (3) that Fundamentalist exegesis has discovered it; and (4) that Fundamentalist systematics reproduces it. These are all highly questionable assumptions.

The claim that "my system" equals "the true system" equals "God's system" implies certain things about the nature of God, about the nature of man, and about human knowing. These are made explicit in Van Til's *Defense of the Faith*:

> We may safely conclude then that if God is what we say he is, namely a being who exists necessarily as a self-complete system of coherence, and we exist at all as self-conscious beings, we must have true knowledge of him. . . .
>
> As God created us in accordance with his absolute rationality, so there must be a rational relationship from us to God. Christianity is, in the last analysis, not an absolute irrationalism but an absolute "rationalism." In fact we may contrast every non-Christian epistemology with Christian epistemology by saying that Christian epistemology believes in an ultimate rationalism while all other systems of epistemology believe in an ultimate irrationalism.[9]

This I would call obscurantism of the kind that overrates rather than underrates the capacities and the situation of the reason. It is an overdeveloped intellectualism rather than an anti-intellectualism. It may be a noble faith, and it has had learned supporters over the centuries, but it goes far beyond anything said or clearly implied in the Bible or unambiguously suggested in experience. It is speculative. This absolutism is an interpretation of Scripture, not scriptural data itself. These formulations are one thing, the Scriptures another. The God of these formulations (i.e., "a self-complete system of coherence") is one God; the God of Abraham, Isaac, and Jacob is another. To equate the Scriptures with any metaphysic or epistemology is a perilous venture. It implies that no one can understand the Gospel except through skill in using the thought-forms of Western culture. This, in turn, means that the more philosophical skill a person shows, the better Christian he is—a kind of modern Gnosticism. When this "absolute rationalism" is made the criterion for discriminating between what is and what is not "Christian epistemology," Van Til and his colleagues say, in effect, that Christianity is a philosophy.

Now I do not want to equate Christianity with relativism or irrationalism, just to counter Van Til's argument. But I would like to suggest that there are some methodological factors relating to the Bible and to theology which seem to be overlooked in any claim to a final system. These factors, if properly regarded, can translate the virtue of humility into theological principle. These factors, when overlooked, leave a system open to the charge of methodological pride—the claim to know as God knows.

A claim to absolute truth overlooks the vast hermeneutical problem inherent in any attempt to turn the Bible's dramatic, concrete, historical, prophetic religious utterances (nonsystematic and nonspeculative in character) into propositional, general, systematic form. This attempt must always be made by the church, but it can never meet with complete success. The attempt is a never-ending task, for there is always a tension between the biblical message and any nonbiblical form into which it may be put.

The mention of the crucial place of hermeneutics suggests some of the most significant modern questions. They are the

questions raised by Rudolf Bultmann and his school. Whatever
reservations we may have about his solutions, we can be grateful
to him for posing his questions so energetically. He has made us
aware of the great difference there is between the world view of
the biblical periods and places and the world view of the most
reluctant post-Copernican. (For that matter, I think a case could
be made that there are somewhat divergent world views within
the Bible itself.) He has made us ask how separable the biblical
message is from its setting in a now dated cosmology. In general,
Fundamentalism has been so convinced that the Bible is self-
explanatory that it disregards hermeneutics. As one recent writer
puts it, "It [Fundamentalism] tends to quote rather than explain,
in other words it burkes the real problem of exegesis."[10] But the
problem will not vanish because it is ignored. It is not the purpose of the Holy Spirit in inspiration to supply scientific information; he does not impart a distinctive, finally true
cosmology. Each age's cosmology is so integral a part of its own
thinking or common sense that it cannot be overridden without
violating the Spirit's customary accommodation of the human.
Our modern cosmology is (or cosmologies are) not final. None
in the past has been final. Yet in terms and symbols appropriate
to each, the redemptive word has been uttered. So doctrines such
as creation, miracle, heaven and hell, incarnation, ascension, and
coming again must be restated in full awareness of the difference
between our assumptions and the assumptions of the period in
which these mythological conceptions were born.

I have used the term "mythological." This expression is, for
most Fundamentalists, a block. They are unaware of how much
"demythologizing" the most literalistic of them have done as
over against the Christians of a few hundred years ago. (Everyone is a "modernist" if the right standard is applied.) The intention of the category "myth" need not be frightening. The
Bible sets its narrative and, for that matter, all of human life in
a framework beyond history. That is, it says that human life and
history are not self-explanatory; they take their meaning from the
God and the eternal in which they are set and which touch
them at every moment. However, the only way the human mind
has of talking about that which is beyond history and experience
is by language taken from within our common experience. However, such language is used in a nonliteral way. It is used as

symbol, metaphor, myth. It is the stuff of imagination. When we use ordinary language to refer to extraordinary reality, we usually alter the literal meaning of the terms we use—we heighten some things and de-emphasize others. Thus, the language may be true and not true—untrue on a literal level in the interest of fidelity to truth on a nonliteral level.

Surely the most effective illustration of this in modern theological writing is Donald Baillie's parable of maps.[11] He compares the attempt to put our experience of God into theological propositions with the attempt to draw a map of our spherical world on a flat surface. The attempt must be made, and more than one way of doing it has been accepted. But each such two-dimensional map (while helpful and convenient and not completely misleading) is wrong; and any two such maps solving the problem on different principles of projection will disagree at every point. If we know that they are intended to represent the surface of a sphere in handy form, and if we let the various kinds of projections correct one another, we shall not be seriously misled by them. In a somewhat similar way, the Bible describes our human life and history as confronted at every moment by eternity. But the language used for the realm of eternity is ordinary language used in such a way as to be literally incorrect and even at times paradoxical or self-contradictory. On the one hand, we have in the Bible places, dates, and historical people acting in quite common ways. On the other hand, we have God working for six days and then resting; we have the sons of God holding counsel in heaven; we have the Lamb that has been slain appearing in the midst of heaven; we have heaven above the earth and hell below it and a great deal of "coming down" and "going up" taking place. These two kinds of biblical language interpenetrate—and never more so than when the divine redemptive purpose gathers to a concentration, as in the birth, life, death, resurrection, and ascension of Jesus Christ. Thus the Bible is full of human experience and the language appropriate to it, but it is also full of symbol and metaphor, which are the ways we use to refer to that which is beyond descriptive experience.

Now, in a day in which the setting assumed by the ancient symbols is no longer part of our cosmology, our astronomy, our maps, our histories—no longer a living part of our imaginations—

we are forced to interpret. We must interpret in such a way as not to "explain away" the radical confrontation which the language was meant to suggest. We dare not reduce the biblical symbols to some nonsymbolic "explanation" which renders the image no longer necessary. But we must interpret. We cannot use biblical words and suppose uncritically that we mean by them exactly what the Bible means. We cannot say them very loudly and suppose that because they are from the Bible they carry conviction and power. The biblical symbols must be translated for us, just as we translate the images of our Western Christian thinking when we take the Gospel to a completely different culture. Thus the questions of symbol and of communication, the fundamental questions, must be raised. Without them we are inexcusably glib when we say, "The Bible teaches thus and so."

Furthermore, the claim to a final system overlooks the conditionedness of any system of doctrine. There is no single, disembodied system of Christian truth; there is only the thinking of Christian people—Reformed, Thomist, personalist, existentialist; clear, confused; now with one emphasis, now with another. There is no final theology because there is no final theologian. We could not, even with an infallible book in our hands, construct a system good for all times and all places. Since we cannot live in any world except our own, any system we produce is conditioned by our time and place; by personal ability, inclinations, and training; by theological and cultural fashions and traditions; and by political, social, and ecclesiastical currents. The great and learned man can in part transcend these limitations, but not even his system is final. All are partial, fragmentary (though often helpful) formulations—mixtures of truth and falsehood, the enduring and the transient, the eternal Word through the broken words. One can only marvel that the *noetic* effect of the fall of which Van Til makes so much seems, in his own theology, to have exempted not only St. Paul but also John Calvin, the Westminster Assembly, and Van Til!

But this conditionedness which has been cited here as a limitation is also an opportunity. We are not called upon to formulate a final system of truth. We are called upon to minister the Word in the midst of our very particularities, occasions, and limitations. We are asked not to address the ages but to face the real questions of the real people of our own time. The more sensitively and perceptively we do this, the more likely we are to say something that will outlast our brief moment.

I think a case could be made that the most significant milestones in the history of Christian thought—apostolic, patristic, Reformation, modern—have been in writings of an occasional sort—tracts for the times—rather than in system-making efforts. The church is called to witness, and theological thought when it is most truly itself is the servant of that calling.

Now, it may be that a given Christian, sensing a call from God in his own specific circumstances, will be led to create a systematic treatment of theological themes. Such a system when complete may be a great achievement, but it will be his system, not *the* system.

Oh, so you read that article by Warfield to which I referred in a letter a while ago. You are right in saying that I only cited the first part of his argument. Toward the end, in a short paragraph, Warfield does include a disclaimer to being in full possession of final truth:

> It is not imagined, of course, that this reflection [of the truth] can be perfect in any individual consciousness. It is the people of God at large who are really the subject of that knowledge of God which systematic theology seeks to set forth.[12]

He adds that sin distorts the perception of truth so that theology progresses and is only perfected when the saints see God as he is. Thus, the partial apprehension of truth by any individual thinker and the conditionedness of any formulation of truth within history have not been unrecognized by the conservative theologians. Theoretically, every Christian in his right mind acknowledges his fallibility. But this insight has often—as in Warfield's article—been put in an appendix at the end of the statement of method. This approach seems to be: There is an absolute truth which discloses God's thinking finally—oh, yes, by the way, we are incapable of knowing this final truth perfectly. Objectively, the final truth is thought to be "there." But, subjectively, our appropriation of it is imperfect.

Now, I have been trying to say that these two sides cannot be so neatly separated. The imperfection of our knowing cannot be left as a mere afterthought to a discussion of the perfection of a certain objective something to be known. This imperfection must be taken into account from the beginning. It will be present necessarily at every point. The only truth we have is *truth as known*—truth apprehended by a finite mind. This recognition of the limits within which human thinking must work cannot be tucked into a corner of one's epistemology or applied more rigorously to others than to oneself. We always need such a guard against our tendencies to theological presumption. It is a gift of grace to know our own intellectual limitations.

The Fundamentalist set of mind seems unwilling to rest in anything short of geometric, demonstrable certainty. Van Til places much hope in Christian conversion and the sure impartation of a "new nature." But who is prepared to say that he does not still "know in part"? Every theologian is still a man, not God; still in history, not in the *parousia*. As long as this is the human situation, any claim to a final system is presumptuous. Any attempt to exceed or to be delivered from the necessarily fragmentary, tentative nature of human knowledge is a kind of obscurantism.

The Fundamentalists' third serious exemption from original sin is the area of *social institutions*. Here the exemption is proclaimed, not as in the case of the Bible by a doctrine stating it, not as in the case of a final theology by a claim implied, but in this case simply by a failure to bring an area under Christian criticism. When it is not seen that the Christian message brings a withering criticism against a particular social structure, the presumption is created that the social structure is somehow Christian and happily wedded to the Gospel.

Fundamentalists, as is evident to nearly all observers who have some measure of detachment, are overwhelmingly rightist politically and conservative socially and economically. The movement is a socio-economic phenomenon as well as a religious one. The Midwest and the South, two strongholds of political and social reaction, are also the "Bible belt." The symptoms are often crude, flag-waving, Billy Sunday "Americanism" or vigilante attacks on purportedly "pink" ecumenical leaders. But the same attitude can just as well be shown in learned discussions demonstrating the essential identity of Christianity, the ideals of certain selected founding fathers, and some supposed laws of the market. The Bible is wrapped in the flag and the package sealed with a dollar sign. With only a few prophetic protests, this is the inclination of the "conservative" group. *Christianity Today* has expressed itself often on political, economic, and social questions; and, after reading the quite predictable opinions of such writers as Howard Pew, Irving E. Howard, V. R. Edman, Representative Judd, or Senator Knowland, one can see that the trend is unmistakable. Surely L. Harold DeWolf is neither incorrect nor intemperate in observing: "There is little in that journal which would disturb even the most conservative defenders of wealth and special privilege."[13]

Whether the case is made with or without footnotes, Christianity is identified with the bourgeois outlook. Most of Protestantism has belatedly repented this identification and is trying to undo its mischief. Fundamentalism has yet to recognize the problem at all. The sins which are assailed in Fundamentalism are the personal sins—intemperance and the indulgences of the flesh. But there seems to be little awareness of the larger evils of the institutions which can sanction a pattern of greed and exploitation. What alarms are sounded are very one-sidedly for the rights of free enterprise and individualism against government control—surely a not unworthy cause. But there seems to be a failure to realize that competing individuals and businesses can be just as predatory as can governments and trade unions— and without the political check which government has of answerability to all the people. Fundamentalists have regularly shown interest and compassion for the victims of society—skid-row "rescue" work—but much less awareness of the deeper problem of the forces by which our society creates and maintains its victims. I have heard, as you have, the "profit motive" and competition canonized in terms that seem oblivious to the relation of these economic patterns to the fundamental Christian diagnosis of the disease of mankind in terms of selfishness. Surely a kind of blindness is present when "self-interest" is made a Christian virtue and "welfare" becomes a vice.

It will not do to say: "The apostles did not analyze their social structure with a view to correcting its abuses. They were saving individual souls. Any dabbling with social betterment deals only with symptoms. We must proclaim the forgiving love of God." This line of argument usually defends a line of action that is even more restricted to symptoms than the one it opposes.

For, if Christian social criticism is not the ultimate solution to
the human dilemma, it is at least less superficial than merely
personal piety. Modern man defines himself in his social, economic, and political contexts. If the Gospel is to be relevant to
him, it must be relevant to him in context. The present race
impasse in the North and the South, for example, has a way of
demonstrating the moral bankruptcy of a piety and an ethic
which speak to individuals but fail to declare the Lordship of
Christ over individuals-in-context. We cannot argue from the
model of the apostles; they were doing missionary work in the
first century. We can only guess what they would do in the midst
of twentieth-century Christendom. But once we attempt to meet
our problems in the same spirit and under the same Christ as
the apostles served, failure to carry our criticism and responsibility into social areas tacitly proclaims acquiescence in them as
they are.

Besides, I think the whole contention so commonly made
among Fundamentalists that the only way to make a society
better is to convert the individual members to the Christian
faith needs to be challenged. It is certainly true that a society is
made what it is—good or bad—by the actions and character of
its members. But it is also true that persons are shaped as individuals by the social structure in which they live. The most
elementary decencies are often impossible and the most debased
behavior all too possible for certain people, not because of their
excessive depravity, but because of the dehumanizing effect of
their social environment. Thus it seems to me to be quite legitimate to begin from either end. The Christian conversion and
nurturing of individuals and the liberalizing of society interpenetrate. To reach a person in his wholeness, we cannot abstract
him from his communities. Evangelism which seeks to do so is to
a great extent self-defeating. So, responsible concern for the
liberties, rights, opportunities, graces, and compassion of a social
order is a legitimate part of Christian outreach. It is fully as
legitimate as a ministry to individuals, for it is a part of the
same thing. The Christianizing of persons and the Christianizing
of institutions are inseparable.

Of course, no political or social program is explicit in the
Christian Gospel. Christianity is not an economics any more than
it is a philosophy. There are general, overarching aims of Chris-

tian social ethics, but no party has a monopoly on these. However, this much can be said categorically: One who believes with all his heart that this world and its fabric of institutions is sin-ridden can, if he wants to be a responsible Christian, be many things; but the one thing he cannot be is a complacent conservative. He may wish to keep the values of the old in all that is new. He may wish for gradual rather than for revolutionary change. He may cherish our traditional institutions of democracy as a check on the sinful abuse of excessive power. He may (along with the greatest conservatives) respect, as things divinely given, the nature and the ordering of the cosmos, of man, and of society. He may sense a providential moral governing of history. But he cannot accept the *status quo* with a quiet conscience. He cannot presume to baptize and place above criticism such things as economic individualism, unbridled competition, and doctrinaire capitalism. The failure of Evangelicals to realize that the Christian faith stands in judgment over capitalism (the system, not merely its abuses) is, in a way, just as much "mixing religion and politics" as is the work of the Christian Socialists. It accepts with silence a mixture already present, but this is as eloquent a way of teaching a social or a political doctrine as any could be. If a Christian prefers, as he may, democracy and capitalism to any of their alternatives, his passion for them must include a thorough, godly criticism.

Let me add that the political Liberal who exempts his doctrinaire theorists and social planners from self-interest, corruptibility, and fallibility is as arbitrary as the Fundamentalist who exempts his bourgeois society. A Liberal who idealizes the future is as unchristian as a conservative who idealizes the past. Christians who uncritically equate their religion with socialism are as utopian as those who equate it with capitalism. The faith which should help us criticize our illusions can be twisted to support them instead. And it can be twisted to the left as well as to the right.

These three areas—an inerrant Bible, a final theology, and a divinely sanctioned politics—may suggest what I mean by the selectivity with which the Fundamentalists apply the doctrine of original sin. In view of these exemptions, I question whether or not Fundamentalists really believe in sin with the rigor they profess. They obviously do believe it as an article of assent, but they have not courageously followed out its implications. They leave convenient absolutes in thought and life, hoping for a measure of security thereby. They fail, as St. Paul did not, to "conclude all under sin." They have not brought all of life under the criticism of the Christian analysis of human nature. One aspect of Fundamentalist obscuration is just these blind spots— this failure to accept the fact that all of human life is under judgment; this insistence on seeing perfection where there is no perfection. It would be a first step away from obscurantism for Fundamentalists to recognize the limited, conditioned nature of every human goal and achievement and to be willing to live maturely within the terms set by that recognition. John Donne once adjured the seeker for truth to "doubt wisely." Where there is pretension to perfection in Christendom, wise doubt has a sacred ministry to perform.

With that comment let me send this letter on to you. I have in mind some other things to be said about obscurantism. But this letter is enough for now. So, while you are reading this I shall regroup my forces for the next engagement.

Cordially,
Spermologos

SOMETHING MORE
ABOUT THE SAME

O Theophilus,

Now that I have your letter in hand, let me resume the subject. But before I turn to your comments about the moral aspects of obscurantism, I would like to conclude a line of argument implicit in my previous letter.

I. THE REFUSAL TO RECOGNIZE TRUTH

There is another side to obscurantism. It surprised you that I questioned whether or not Fundamentalists really believe in sin. I want to question now whether or not they really believe in grace. This may be still more surprising.

This reverse side of the issue comes from the paradoxical nature of man. We must be prepared to see, as Pascal has it, the "greatness" and the "wretchedness" of man.[1] There is no place in human life wholly without God. There is no place where that of God which is present is not twisted and perverted by sin. Ironically, Fundamentalism fails to see the pervasive good just as it fails to see the pervasive evil.

In practice, Fundamentalism largely limits God to religion. It gives little attention to dignifying or criticizing the hours outside of church work. In church, though one hears much of the evangelical message and the evangelical experience, the form of Fundamentalist piety drastically narrows and trivializes these. The God of the Bible is not only Redeemer; he is also the one who makes and conserves all things and who leads his universe to its destiny. The redemption of sinners rests finally on the identity of the Redeemer with the Creator. If, in the interest of

exalting the evangelical message, the work of Christ as Redeemer
is so emphasized that it is not closely connected with and based
on the wider, cosmic activities of the Godhead, eventually the
evangelical message itself is impoverished. The preoccupation
with religion on the part of Fundamentalists is, in the long run,
self-defeating. As William Temple remarked: "It is a great mistake to suppose that God is only, or even chiefly, concerned with
religion."[2]

If God is truly Creator and Conserver of all, any men who
are engaged in creative and conserving work are doing the work
of God. Wherever men reverence and preserve life and order,
they are God's servants. Where by conscientious labor new truth
is sought and found in any field, it is God's truth, and it is of
his mercy that it is found. Is there not a kind of Cross—a self-
offering—in humility before the truth? In teachableness? And
is there not a kind of resurrection—a new and higher life
through surrender—in finding the truth? In learning?

The tendency in Fundamentalism to restrict the sphere of
God's activity leads to obscurantism through the rejection of
many fields where he is manifestly at work.

For example, Fundamentalists have largely rejected biblical
criticism. Very grudgingly and quite belatedly, they have made
some minor critical concessions. But they remain largely shut off
from the new light that has been shed on the history of revelation now that we can see biblical origins in their religious and
cultural contexts as previous generations could not.

It is strange that Fundamentalists, with their great biblical
interests, have simply dropped out of the debate on critical
matters. They could have contributed much. Most of the very
radical critical views once advanced by rationalistic scholarship,
sometimes in the interests of discrediting the biblical faith, have
had their day. Modern criticism is carried on within the believing
fellowship to elucidate, not undermine, that very faith. Many
judgments in the New Testament field have moved in the direction of earlier dates and greater respect for the historicity of the
records than was once the case. In the Old Testament field, the
stress on primitive origins and the insistence that all the creative
age of the distinctively Jewish emphases came late, in the period
of the prophets, have been modified. However, these developments, which are in directions that conservatives would generally

approve, have all been made without their contributions entering into the change of direction.

Furthermore, in the rediscovery of the apocalyptic element in the biblical perspective, some critics came up with reconstructions of biblical thought and ethic that are amazingly like some species of dispensationalism—which always made its points by taking apocalyptic passages literally. Yet, again, there was no friendly commerce between the Fundamentalists of Dallas and Moody and the critics of Strassburg and Göttingen, even though they were saying rather similar things.

This seems to indicate again that there is nothing inherently repellent in the opinions held by Fundamentalist biblical scholars. The problem lies in the belligerent attitude in which opinions are put forward, with the apparent claim to hold critical positions as matters of revealed dogma, and with the willingness to unchurch those who disagree. The positions themselves might get a respectful hearing if they were presented on their merits alone. However, this involves such a confidence in one's faith and its moorings that one can venture freely and courteously into the give-and-take of the critical movement. This is a realm where God has been at work disclosing a truer picture of the relationship between revelation and its human matrix, the Word and the community, himself and his children. Such a concern for the truth is required for entry into the scholarly brotherhood that one respects all others who share this concern. In a community of learning, one must be willing to be taught by anyone; in order to be listened to, one must listen. No one can appear to say, "I have all the answers before the questions are even put. If you fellows want them, you can come to me." God who has providentially given his Word to his people is not absent from the discussions in which devout and highly trained minds are seeking to understand it. The withdrawal of Fundamentalists from the critical conversation marks their refusal of wise old John Robinson's advice—that the Lord has "more truth and light yet to break forth out of his Holy Word."[3]

To turn to another field in which truth goes unrecognized, I observe that Fundamentalism seems to be a fairly popular religious expression among people with some technical, scientific training. These victims of the worst heresies of modern scientism seem to like a religion which has something of the methodology of an electronic computer. But in neither science nor religion are such persons at home when fundamental questions are raised. They become uneasy when confronted with a new breakthrough on the frontiers of science. For so long defensive tactics have relegated God to the portions of life and the universe that are still a mystery that when the area of the known expands, the conservative is inclined to feel threatened. The Fundamentalist apologist seizes too eagerly on the principle of indeterminacy as giving him an open universe for miracle; he turns the threat and moral responsibility from nuclear physics by relating it to biblical prophecy; he holds hurried conferences on the carbon 14 technique which seems to challenge his views on the antiquity of man. Despite notable liberalizing work, Fundamentalism still has not come to terms with our scientific, technological era. Though it has accommodated the activist, professional sides of scientific training, it keeps its distance from anything that might be called a substantive, philosophical, theological engagement with the sciences. This, as I say, is just an observation on my part, based necessarily on limited contacts. But I include it because it seems so generally to hold true.

Another field in which Fundamentalists fail to see God at work is social advance. The term "social gospel" has for so long been spoken with a sneer that any attempt to apply the implications of the Gospel to the social order finds little support from Fundamentalists. If part of the Christian community's stewardship is to declare the Lordship of Christ in all of life, the creaking, weary social structure needs this witness. If the basic disease of mankind is sin, this diagnosis needs to be made explicit in terms of the conflicting relationships, communities, and power situations, large and small, in which people actually do their sinning. And if the remedy is Christ, this too needs to be applied specifically in the organized world where he must be served if our faith is not to be just an escape from responsibility. A merely individual piety can be "the opiate of the people." In this realm the Christian realists have done much searching thinking in the past few decades. But again this is a realm from which Fundamentalists have been missing.

The Spirit of God is speaking today to our nation and to the world at large in terms of international co-operation through the United Nations, interracial desegregation, and interchurch ecumenicity. Such causes have been spoken of as God's incognitos. The choice before us is not whether we shall regard the work now being done in these causes as perfect or not and withhold our efforts until it is—and meanwhile go about converting individual souls. The choice before us is whether we shall have enough Christian imagination to seize these causes as limited but real instruments through which to express our obedience; or whether we shall, by default, let their alternatives—international fratricide, interracial injustice, and interchurch competitiveness—go on unprotested. Yet, in general, to these three challenging movements of our time, most Fundamentalists respond with opposition and scorn, some with indifference, few with responsible concern.

I do not wish to suggest that the church should, as the church, identify herself with specific programs or organizations and, by doing so, appear to invest them with supernatural sanctions. Only with the greatest caution should the church say, "The Bible (or Jesus, or the Gospel, or some other ultimate religious authority) leads us to commit the church to such and such a specific social or political course." The church has her primary business with her Lord in the Word and the sacraments, and the "salt of the earth" retains its savor in ministering on the Godward side of life. But, in the long run, the church must be concerned with anything that concerns man. One writer recently observed:

> The Church exists to proclaim the Gospel. The Church is interested in the price of bread, in the purity of the water supply, the loneliness of the aged, the prosperity of the garment industry, the development of antibiotics, and the probation and parole system, because the Gospel is about these things.[4]

If the church's life is to answer to the call of God and the call of man, it should be possible, without absolutizing a given piece of social legislation or a step in foreign policy, to work out a body of "middle axioms" that translates the great divine imperative that God's people be holy into guiding lines for a particular social context. The Bible says nothing about civil rights bills, the open shop, reciprocal trade, or Red China; but it does say something about man, and it implies something about specific possibilities and goals for the good society. Responsible Christian concern for the human community has occupied the skilled and devoted thought of some of the church's best thinkers for more than a generation. Fundamentalists, however, have neither made a parallel development nor contributed to the work of others. The reactions they do show on social, political, and economic matters are usually immediate, moralistic, shrill, dogmatic, and always oriented to the right. The production of a profound and practicable social ethics is a field of thought from which they have been almost entirely absent.

To cite yet another area of neglect, counseling and psychiatry have gotten scant attention from Fundamentalists. It is widely assumed that if a person will "accept the Lord Jesus Christ as his own personal Savior" his complexes, anxieties, family conflicts, and paralyzing frustrations will automatically vanish. If he finds they do not, he must suppose that he is not sufficiently "yielded" —that there is some grave defect in his spiritual life. So a new dimension of guilt is added to his already burdened mind, in the name of him who came to "set at liberty them that are bruised." If only mental health were as simple as that! No repetition of pious formulas will exorcise these demons.

Surely much of psychiatry needs what vital religion can give— and some of it is learning to co-operate with the church. It is also true, however, that many a deeply sincere believer needs what psychiatry can give—and, among Fundamentalists, this lesson is yet to be learned. No casual religious perfectionism will reach the depths of the torment of a sick soul. No mere adoption of devotional practice will heal a family in which destructive patterns of personal relationships are deeply established. In fact, piety, unrelated to psychological insight, can often add a factor of delusion to unhealthy situations. It can be used to sanctify human relationships which need instead to be judged and redirected.

A new and sensitive healing tool has, by God's providence, been put at the disposal of the church. In the Christian community we had forgotten how one person really helps another. The relationship between the insights and the practice of the behavioral sciences and the insights and the practice of the Christian religion is one of the great frontiers for investigation in the church today. Over the past half century much fine work has been done in this field. But only a few infinitesimal beginnings have been made within Fundamentalism—and these against much suspicion.

Another field might be mentioned in which Fundamentalism seems not to recognize light as light. It either disregards or opposes the theater in general and the contemporary idiom in art and literature. If God is speaking to us today, and if we are responsibly related to our generation, we will respond in contemporary (though not faddist) terms. To be sure, since God has been speaking for a long time, we shall create as part of a great tradition. But we shall work at its "growing edge," its place of relevance to the modern sensibility. For this is the place of responsibility. Amos Wilder said a few years ago:

> Our Christian faith does not dissolve our solidarity with our age. . . . In fact, we should take it as a matter of grave concern if we find the new poets only sound and fury. If O'Neill, or D. H. Lawrence or Robinson Jeffers or W. H. Auden or T. S. Eliot seem to speak a totally different language than the one we know, we should ask ourselves if we have lived in our own time, genuinely.[5]

(His comments on literature apply, of course, equally to other arts.) Any art which is out of touch with the living frontier where its own time is meeting new problems in new ways tends inevitably to become derivative, sterile, and mannered. The arts have seldom had more to give to the churches than they have today. The rejection of falseness and the facing of the ambiguity and self-destructiveness of human life give to modern art a reality and an authenticity too often missing from the sentimental, moralistic poses struck by ecclesiastical arts. As artistic sham is characteristic to some degree in most churches, it is doubly so of "conservativism." There are few areas where Fundamentalism so needs a fresh tide of the Spirit as in her music, art, writing, architecture, and general artistic life. These are not the ornaments of life; they *are* life. Their health and reality show the health and reality of the whole spiritual fabric.

In still a further area, light has been taken for darkness. Fundamentalism has rejected the life-giving contact with other Christian groups. She insulates herself against the life of the whole church. This is a grievous sin against the Spirit. The ecumenical movement would be richer for the presence of Fundamentalists, with their passion for evangelism and missions. Fundamentalists, for their part, could benefit by contact with the churchmanship and the sense of the past, the social conscience and the sense of relevance, and the intellectual freedom of the other groups. But Fundamentalists have removed themselves from the circles where the conversations are going on.

The willful rejection of truth—whatever may be its source— shows a defect in faith, in hope, and in love. It is a fearful, defensive dodge. It betrays an unwillingness to place convictions in the open arena of public contest. What is true is true, no matter who said it. If a mountaineer snake-handler says a true thing, it is true. And it is only by God's goodness that it was said at all. It is part of the Christian faith to receive that truth with gratitude. If the Jesus Christ in whose deity the Fundamentalists so conspicuously profess to believe is really the creative Logos of the prologue to the Fourth Gospel, wherever there is light in our dark world, it is his. Rejection of it, no matter by whom it comes, is rejection of him.

We have now met the obverse side of the obscurantism of Fundamentalism—this failure to recognize, welcome, and further the work of God in all of life—or even in all the church of Christ. I might continue the list of fields which tend to be rejected as places from which to expect truth. However, though it is not exhaustive, the present list will have suggested that the mind of Fundamentalism is not adventuresome, outgoing, or expansive. It is rather like those little animals which when touched by a beam of light shrink back into their shells.

II. TWO OBSERVATIONS

Let me add two general observations on this inability to see truth and error where they are and for what they are.

For one thing, the main area of blindness seems to be in what might generally be called the human sciences. The study of man, his works, his arts, his communities, his inner problems, his yearnings, his real limitations, his real achievements—these seem to be neglected by the Fundamentalists. A kind of social, political, and cultural naïveté seems to characterize the movement and its institutions. This may be a facet of the Docetism I have mentioned before. The study of man tends to be regarded as a diversion, an optional matter, something which might better be ignored lest it interfere with the main business of studying God. It is more than a matter of study; it is a matter of concern, commitment, and trust. Humanitarian work, social service, and the like are in some quarters actually considered a snare—things that, insofar as they are not religious or evangelistic, are "second best." The "merely external" effect of such work is so loudly stressed that the few Fundamentalists who are in community work or social work in many cases find their vocations somewhat difficult to justify in their own consciences. In general, then, we have met again this inclination to make the human unreal—to overstress the claims of the divine in such a way as to deny the proper claims of the human.

If I read Calvin rightly (and he still is a weighty authority in most conservative circles), the study of man and the study of God are mutually interdependent. The true knowledge of man and the true knowledge of God grow together.[6] God is more fully known as he is known in connection with the fuller depths of the knowledge of man. So, time spent on the detailed and profound study of man does not take one away from God. In fact, if it is neglected, the knowledge of God will suffer. If God and man are not known, studied, and loved alongside each other, neither will be known as he should be. "They are," to use Berdyaev's way of putting it, "two aspects of the same faith; Christianity is the religion of the God-man and therefore demands belief in both God and man."[7]

I stand by the suggestion I made the last time we met—that all the Bible Schools should make the *New Yorker* required reading for their students! By this I am suggesting that among Fundamentalists the dove-like virtues have been highly stressed and the serpent-like virtues little valued, though Jesus gave them both a place in the life of the Kingdom. At least this observer—who wishes them nothing but good—would suggest that a little more sophistication, urbanity, lightness of touch, and social ease among Fundamentalists would be like a breath of fresh air. These qualities are not in themselves virtues. But a group which has made a virtue out of rejecting them and rejecting all who embody them has only created its own drab style of worldliness. I could wish that among Fundamentalists there were a wider distribution of the grace to see oneself through the eyes of one's satirists and critics and to smile at how right they are. I cannot but think that this kind of sympathy with the human point of view would lead to theological and spiritual gain. Whatever else he may be, a Christian is still a man. It never hurts to have religious pretensions brought to terms with the realities of the human condition.

Perhaps the *New Yorker* is not the best medicine. It has its own pose; its sophistication is exaggerated. Its depiction of the human point of view could be discounted for too many good reasons. But if the *New Yorker* would not do the trick, it would be worth searching for something else that would. I am not selling magazines; I am interested in correcting a falsely pious stance. In connection with a national mood with which he was impatient, Arthur Schlesinger, Jr., said what I want to say: "What we need . . . is a rebirth of satire, of dissent, of irreverence, of an uncompromising insistence that phoniness is phony and platitudes are platitudinous."[8]

Quite apart from the devotional value of the *New Yorker*, I have an idea that more of the pressure for liberalization and redefinition in neo-Evangelicalism is coming from the arts and the humanities than from the theological and biblical fields. My guess in such a matter is necessarily a partially informed one. But I get the decided impression that in Fundamentalist liberal arts schools the scholars in literature, social sciences, philosophy, and the like who are amateur (though often competent) theologians are out ahead of their colleagues who are professional theologians, clerics, and biblical scholars but less sensitive to the theological significance of man. Do your own observations bear this out?

For a second note, I observed earlier that any statement of the meaning of obscurantism must define itself against some standard of truth, progress, and enlightenment. So let me propose my standard. It has been implicit all along, but I have not stated it until now. It is this: Truth is to be learned (in its degree) everywhere and from everyone. Final truth is nowhere and in no one save God—Father, Son, and Holy Spirit.

Thus obscurantism errs in attributing finality to the finite. It appears where God is reduced to some human definition which shares his absoluteness. Obscurantism, having "seen" God in one place in his universe, refuses to see signs of his truth elsewhere. Obscurantism is the willful limitation of the places from which and the ways in which one permits himself to be taught.

I rather hope that such a spirit of truth-seeking begins at least to approximate that of the man that Canon Vidler would like to see as the normative theologian:

—the man who is tolerant, not because he regards all opinions as doubtful, but because he knows that God alone is true, —the man who is ready to learn from all men, not because he has no creed of his own, but because his creed assures him that God is teaching and chastening all men, —the man who has plumbed the meaning for the human intellect of the great New Testament word about having nothing and yet possessing all things, —the man who can at once rigorously doubt and sincerely believe, —in short the man who has discovered that it is not only the sinner but the doubter who is justified by faith.[9]

III. THE MORALITY OF OBSCURANTISM

There are those among the neo-Evangelicals who decry Fundamentalism's obscurantism as loudly as I do. They would say in their own behalf that, unlike an older generation of conservatives, they do not oppose ideas without giving them a hearing. They claim to listen appreciatively and understandingly to positions they cannot accept. Their rejection of certain doctrines is not until after the evidence is fairly weighed. This, they will say, absolves them from the charge of obscurantism. The charge, they maintain, does not apply to any given theological position but depends on how the position was reached.

One such sensitive scholar recently wrote to me about the attitude held by himself and many of his colleagues toward some of the very evidences of obscurantism I have discussed. He said, "We abominate these errors as much as you do." Packer is no less emphatic: "Obscurantism is always evil, and wilful error is always sin. All truth is God's truth; facts, as such, are sacred, and nothing is more un-Christian than to run away from them."[10] But the general intellectual stance of the group to which these people must relate themselves is still, despite a growing body of protest from within, pretty much as I have depicted it. And the strong tension many of the new leaders feel with their own group illuminates the nature of the problem—as I hope to make clear.

Now, even the most advanced of these neo-Evangelical thinkers still draw conclusions, with whatever modifications and purifications, that include at least some items on my foregoing bill of particulars indicating "obscurantism." Am I being unjust to them? Does obscurantism lie in one's doctrines or in one's intentions and methods? Since I maintained earlier that obscurantism was a moral or a spiritual matter, not merely academic, must it not be judged on the basis of one's motives and procedures rather than his conclusions?

First, to clarify, in my foregoing discussions, such fields as biblical inerrancy, social responsibility, and psychiatry all qualified for inclusion as "obscurantism" because of the position they fill in the method rather than the substance of Fundamentalist thinking. That is, I brought them under discussion as areas where truth is or is not sought. Some areas were included because in them truth is sought in an undiscriminating, almost idolatrous, way. Others were included because truth is ignored when it comes from these sources. I was not arguing for or against particular critical, social, aesthetic, or psychological doctrines. But I was arguing against the arbitrary limitation of the sources of truth and the apparent exemption of other authorities as sources of error. Thus I was concerned with method—how and where one goes about seeking truth—more than with specific conclusions.

Secondly, in justice to those who may think I wrongly include them in my anathemas against obscurants, I should want to recognize the real merit of the thinking of many of the newer spokesmen for conservativism. Not only do they use more temperate rhetoric and ampler footnotes than their elders; not only do they seem to have really read the sources they reject; but, undeniably, some of them are beginning to say new and valuable things. The quality of the thinking of men like Packer and Ramm and Carnell is alive and moving.

These men and a score like them are perfectly sincere when they disclaim the label "obscurantist." As far as any "doctrine of intention" may be necessary to establish the charge against them, I would like to see them cleared.

But in the case of the Fundamentalist tradition as a whole, we have something bigger than any particular thinker and his motives. We have a restricting body of attitudes and a limited point of view that leads to a kind of institutionalized obscurantism. It may not be too much to say categorically that no one working within this tradition can have the free or comprehensive sympathies that are necessary to be rid of obscurantism. The fault lies not in the corrupt motives of the thinkers but in the atmosphere they must breathe.

In examining the work and the influence of leaders of thought, one must look not only at what they profess but also at how well their professions accord with the professions of the tradition to which they stand committed. If the men sincerely want to apply the ideal of liberal scholarship in pursuit of truth for its own sake, but if the tradition as a whole is still antagonistic to such an ideal, the narrowness of the tradition cannot but restrict the achievement of the individuals.

The extent to which some of the present group of thinkers and writers have been able to overcome the oppressive heritage within which they have been taught amazes me. One must admire the courage of those who have deliberately exposed themselves to influences that previous leaders would have wanted only to filter out. At the same time these people feel a responsibility to continue to serve within conservatism. It is conceivable, of course, that such leaders may, little by little, change the general complexion of the movement—this seems to be their hope. But so far it seems to be questionable as to whom the leaders are leading —and where. The emancipation of the thinkers who are breaking what for Fundamentalism is new ground has so far had little impact. Much of the most creative discussion is still clandestine and afraid of publicity. Many of the leaders with whom I talk frankly admit that they think much of the constituency of conservatism is completely unreconstructible. Many of them cannot say publicly as much as they think. Now, I insist that any thorough conquest of obscurantism must take place not only in the minds of a few able leaders of thought but also in the community to which their work has reference. The two always interact. Obscurantism has involved both individuals and a tradition; its cure must also involve both.

Of course, any thinker works within some tradition—no one is perfectly free, universal, or "central." A limitation of some sort, a group of preferences, a body of attitudes, accompanies every thinker in every field. There is nothing culpable in a Fundamentalist's having a tradition.

In fact, a tradition is not only inevitable; it can be an asset. It is not a regrettable necessity. It provides the attachments, interests, perspectives, and passions for creative work. A measure of critical detachment is necessary for thought, of course. But the mere pursuit of "objectivity" is self-defeating. Insofar as "objectivity" points toward skepticism, it is not creative. Some kind of a personal identification with matters at issue is necessary for great achievement. And the way to find this identification is through work within a large and generous tradition.

So, while traditions of thought are inevitable, they are not all relative. Some traditions (including some that have produced worthwhile and enduring works) have proved to be short-lived and to occupy extreme and narrow positions. Some have seemed uncreative—almost suicidal—from their beginnings. Some have followed out their peculiar, one-sided ideas until they twisted beyond recognition the very shape of the Christian faith. Others have proved to be great and ever-fresh sources for the thinking of centuries following their origin. Only a broad and sympathetic acquaintance with the history of Christian thought can provide a perspective whereby one's own tradition can be evaluated. Ramm once told me that he did not know how he would be classed by contemporary labels. He felt his theology to be a part of the great tradition; he liked the Fathers, the creeds, and the Reformers, and he felt most party designations to be a restriction of the norm that this firsthand conversation with the creative giants of Christian thought had given him. I feel that, as this spirit increases, the attachment to what has been known as Fundamentalism cannot but decrease. There is a broad and richly varied tradition (broader, I might add, than even just the Fathers and the Reformers) which can provide a corrective for the one-sidedness of the lesser traditions to which we find ourselves related.

Now Fundamentalism, as a tradition, has fallen victim from its start to an isolation and a narrowness that seriously restrict any scholar who must work with reference to this background. I think that if I were to seek one word in which to summarize this restriction, I would call it "oversimplification." Vast learning can be used to serve an overly simple body of answers.

But how does such a thing happen to a tradition?

The explanation must begin at the beginning: Into our twisted human situation, God speaks, and his Word is saving judgment. Those who hear his voice live in an uneasy peace with the life of today—they are aliens inasmuch as they have heard a call to another land, but they are at home inasmuch as God is at work here, and he calls them to work with him.

God is at work. But the tracing of his hand is not an easy task. No one can presume to dictate. We can only listen, watch, and follow. Our world is tragically lost, yet potentially redeemed. We are justified, yet sinners. It is natural enough to wish for a simple answer in our uncertain situation.

But the truest answers are not simple. Hooker once pointed out that the classic heresies are attempts to find more simple and rationally appealing answers than those of the stubborn paradoxes of the full faith. The heresy seeks to be "more plain than true," but the finally satisfying answers to the human dilemma always turn out to be "more true than plain." You see, I am not attacking obscurantism in the name of scientism, rationalism, or a body of "clear and distinct ideas." This would be too narrowing and dull. I appeal for an outlook that does not do less than justice to the many-sidedness of life or the manifold dimensions of revelation. The fault in Fundamentalism is not so much that it has muddied the clear waters as that it is restless with the muddy waters which are all that Christianity encourages us to expect—and its clarity is specious.[11] Christianity, as a historical religion, resists tidiness. It is rooted in a past event, a continuing community, a present experience, and a future *eschaton*. Vitality comes from contact with all of these within the responsibilities and tensions of today.

But Fundamentalism, like many another religious movement, rejected this multi-dimensional complexity and sought certainty and security in a more simple pattern. The movement seemed to want to preserve the synthesis of the late 1800's as a bit of certainty in an increasingly complicated world. A rundown of the dates of the volumes now being so copiously reprinted by the conservative presses will show with what age the Fundamentalists feel the greatest affinity. The mention of reprints suggests the name of Wilbur M. Smith. I once, just out of perversity I suppose, made a hasty check of the dates of the books listed among his one hundred best books for Bible study. Using the dates he gives (which are not always the dates of the first editions) over half of his one hundred titles were written before 1900; one quarter were written before 1875.

In fairness I should say that the book in which this list appears, his widely-used *Profitable Bible Study*, was written twenty years ago. It is highly probable that if Smith were issuing a list for the same purpose now, some newer books would appear on it, replacing older titles, and the average of the dates would be advanced. But the theological center of gravity, even in biblical studies, remains at or before the turn of the century. I should also add that Smith's list has been of genuine help to many students. The books he suggests are reverent works of substance and scholarship. His vigorous annotations have helped readers to make many valuable purchases and avoid many stupid ones. The Fundamentalist world needed to be reminded of its roots. Much of the recovered vitality of evangelical scholarship is traceable to the rediscovery of greatness in the tradition's own past. So, while I deplore the effort to revive the 19th century—an effort which, in its bibliographical aspect, Smith has influenced greatly—I would like to acknowledge the value of his work and my own gratitude for it.

In sum, the Fundamentalist mind shows a familiarity with only one period and one set of theological issues and a wish to prejudge everything in terms of these issues.

But this fixation at a certain point in history (whether it be the Romanists' 13th century, the Calvinists' 16th, the Fundamentalists' 19th, or any other) is actually an escape. It destroys the perspective on the past event, for, by absolutizing a particular point in Christian development, it equates this point with the absoluteness of Christian origins. It reads its favorite period back into the New Testament.

By this fixation, too, a group is cut off from the whole past and is unable thereby to be conservative in the larger meaning of that word. By the loss of a sense of continuity and a reduction of the wonderful variousness of the Christian heritage, the group loses the possibility of organic growth and readjustment in its life. There is no coming to terms with the present if one is still unreconciled to his past.

But archaism cuts off from the present as well as from the past. Then, being cut off from responsible participation in the life of today, a group becomes an artificial holding action, at odds with its generation—not because of the offense of the Cross, but because of an arbitrary loss of contact.

Being cut off from one's present is a frustrating experience. In some cases, it seems to lead to an attempt to resuscitate a yesterday. In others, it seems to lead to a frenzied apocalypticism for tomorrow.

The obscurantism of Fundamentalism as a tradition, then,

lies in its perpetuation of the formulas of a particular yesterday after they have been shown to be superstitions and in rejecting the truths of today because they had the misfortune to be of today and not of a century ago.

This obscurantism, as I have contended, is more than an academic matter; it is religious. It indicates a shrinking from reality and hence a shrinking from vital trust in God and from effective service. On this basis John Oman wrote long ago, "Obscurantism is already unbelief."[12] The logic of narrowing truth is ultimately to reject God's world as he has given it to us and, in distrust, to refashion it along lines that are more comfortable and familiar. Obscurantism is a kind of intellectual irreverence.

Fundamentalists have sounded frightening warnings about the "creeping humanism" implicit in biblical criticism and the dire end of the logic of conceding anything to science. But they might beware of the "creeping idolatry" which is the logic of their absolutizing a religious formulation. They might look at the "implicit atheism" in obstructing the search for truth. Any revelation that is in peril from new discovery is self-condemned. The only thing that can suffer from new truth is not God, or revelation, but our own dear idols.

At the time of the challenge of Liberalism, the old figure of the baby and the bath water was revived. It was good that Fundamentalism sought to save the baby—some Christians seemed not to realize that they might be throwing him out, too. But, dear me, the bath water does need changing from time to time— for the health of the baby.

Cordially,
Spermologos

VI

THE
WORLD

For Christians are not distinguished from the rest of mankind in country or speech or customs. For they do not live somewhere in cities of their own or use some distinctive language or practice a peculiar manner of life. They have no learning discovered by the thought and reflection of inquisitive men, nor are they the authors of any human doctrine, like some men. Though they live in Greek and barbarian cities, as each man's lot is cast, and follow the local customs in dress and food and the rest of their living, their own way of life which they display is wonderful and admittedly strange. They live in their native lands, but like foreigners. They take part in everything like citizens, and endure everything like aliens. Every foreign country is their native land, and every native land a foreign country. Like everyone else they marry, they have children, but they do not expose their infants. They set a common table, but not a common bed. They find themselves in the flesh, but they do not live after the flesh. They remain on earth, but they are citizens of heaven. . . . To put it briefly, what the soul is to the body, Christians are to the world.

THE ADDRESS TO DIOGNETUS
(Goodspeed trans.)

THE CALL
TO BE SEPARATE

O Theophilus,

You suggest that the classification of "species Fundamentalists" is popularly made in terms of the taboos. You are probably right. I know of no easy way to verify this, but my guess would be the same as yours—that if you asked people at random "What is a Fundamentalist?" the replies would usually begin, "Oh, that's a person whose religion tells him he cannot smoke or drink or dance or go to the movies or . . . ."

Most Fundamentalists would regret this public image, I think—not because of misgivings about the taboos, but because this is not the part of their life and message they want to get first attention. They regard it as secondary to their religious beliefs. However, unfortunately, most people are not at all concerned about someone else's doctrines, but they are quick to notice behavior that is out of the ordinary. So this end of things is what is observed and therefore what defines popularly the Fundamentalist group.

The presence of such a convention-defying group in the community should raise some fundamental questions of Christian social ethics. But, actual discussion seldom rises beyond the pros and cons of some of the particular practices by which certain devout consciences are troubled—and there is a limit to how long movies or makeup can be discussed profitably.

I do not think this has to be the case. Beginning with the issues raised by the Fundamentalists' general attitude, I would like to see if this subject of "separation from the world" can be discussed deeply enough to touch the moral interior of all the particular disputes.

I think we can begin with a principle that is not in dispute. Serious Christians will agree, I am certain, on the necessity of some kind of separateness from surrounding society. The distinctiveness of the Christian revelation involves a distinctive standard of life. Some persons and groups will define this principle explicitly and aggressively; others may only occasionally be made to realize that there are situations in which Christian profession necessitates an unpopular decision. But as to the general principle, it is everywhere recognized. The fellowship which is committed to the love and service of God will often find itself at odds with the great community of men not so committed. It is possible to ignore sharp alternatives, to blur over moral contrasts, and to drift into a harmless, conventional mediocrity. But every devout person, we might be sure, knows times when he is called upon to decide. A painful wrench of separation may be asked, and in the depths of his soul he must recognize "the divine imperative." No other religion defines the holy or the sinful as penetratingly as does Christianity, and we cannot remain permanently content with our attempts to reduce them to the same thing.

Disagreement comes, then, not on acknowledgment of the demand for separation but on its proper application.

I. THE SEPARATIST SOLUTION

By and large, Fundamentalists try to define their separateness from the world by making rules against certain practices. They do not always agree as to exactly what things should be ruled against, but they do seem to agree that rule-making is the way to go about the task.

They commonly declare certain classes of things categorically evil and blacklist them. I call this "separatism." Separatism, so defined, is for many Fundamentalists a basic attitude—they speak of "the separated life." It can control their recreational life in that motion pictures, card-playing, opera, golf, dancing, and mixed swimming (the list may vary considerably according to the location) may be branded "worldly" by some group or other and then avoided altogether. It can control diet and habits in that smoking, drinking, the use of makeup, certain hair and clothing styles—or in some cases even eating pork—are proscribed. It can control cultural life in that certain subjects and activities, such as psychology, jazz, contemporary drama and fiction, are regarded with suspicion. It determines church affiliations for many in that certain denominational groups are considered "apostate," and all connection with them is severed. The separatist attitude may govern social and community relations in that affiliation with certain social sets and certain organizations —for example, service clubs, fraternal orders, the labor union, the high school Hi-Y—is held to compromise one's Christian profession. I have known some cases in which contributions to charitable efforts of a nonreligious sort were conscientiously withheld on the ground that the only proper business for a Christian is "saving souls," and since the United Fund was not in the business of soul-saving, a Christian's money should properly be held for furthering the interests of another world. Some Christian separatist groups go so far as to declare government an institution so strictly of this world that they refuse to participate in it in any way beyond the biblical injunction to pay one's taxes. In short, for "separated Christians," the classes of worldly things are plainly marked out, and any contact with them is wrong.

This separatist approach has always had its problems despite its appearance of simplicity. Inconsistency and triviality seem to be its most obvious pitfalls. It is apparent that Fundamentalists in this country vary among themselves in what they include or exclude from their list of taboos. In some sections, smoking has not been regarded as a serious offense, but golf or mixed swimming has been; elsewhere, these may be reversed. Some Reformed traditions of a sternly conservative doctrinal stance allow beer and a pipe at a theological discussion. Churches have been torn asunder over such issues. The legal approach needs lawyers to make it work. Should the young people have a party? Should dancing be permitted? Can it be in the church house or in another hall? Can it be on Sunday, or must it be on another day?

Some thoughtful Fundamentalists are seeing that since such rules all go beyond Scripture, and since sincere Christians can differ on them, the position must be modified. The Fundamentalist index of vanities is under question within Fundamentalism itself as it has not been before. (In some cases, contact with European and English Christian life seems to have been a liberating factor.) But in the atmosphere of Fundamentalism, with its fondness for absolutes, this questioning has not produced a free and relaxed goodness. There remains an almost tangible pressure to conform. I see little evidence of real emancipation.

Carl Henry has made some pungent comments about the grip of the taboos when one has learned them as enforced by the highest religious sanctions:

> The Fundamentalist catalogue of "sins" is small and specific: commercial movies, dancing, gambling, card-playing, drinking beer or wine or liquor, and smoking. No "spiritual Christian" will presumably do any of these things, and generally will have little to do with anyone who does do them. Everyone who grows up in this tradition finds that it has a vise-like grip on him. His conscience has been made sensitive to these things by the never-ending tirade against them. If he "weakens" and indulges, he is filled with guilt-feelings as automatically as Pavlov's dog salivated when the bell rang.[1]

It would be hard to improve on his statement of the matter.

You have apparently come across the same problem I have. When you bring up the matter of the taboos with one of your professedly "neo-Evangelical" friends, he may agree that they represent a wrong and mischief-making ethic, but he still gives evidence of an overscrupulous, timid conscience. The separatist theory may be under revision by the "neo" group, but, for the most part, such critics seem to lack the courage, the freedom, or the opportunity to break in practice the pattern they deplore. Any real criticism of the legalistic and puritan norms so long accepted in Fundamentalism must show the marks of its authenticity, not, of course, by a childish reaction into a uniformly opposite pattern of behavior, but by the variety of practice that indicates life, color, and the freedom for each person to be himself.

Much can be said for separatism. It bears witness to a willingness to differ from society. The separatist will carry through his convictions even at the risk of seeming odd or unconventional. In order to pursue a religious goal, he is willing to deny himself certain indulgences. He seeks to demonstrate the radical transcendence of the claims of grace over the claims of nature. For him, the unseen world is the really real. He practices a kind of life-denying ethic—a moral "way of negation." This is the ascetic way—a kind of Protestant monasticism. Surely the whole Christian community, with its drift toward worldliness, needs this witness.

Having said this, I should also say that separatism and the assumptions that seem to lie behind it in its Fundamentalist form are open to several serious criticisms.

For one thing, the separatist outlook seems to imply that evil is resident in things. The world seems to be made up of good things and bad things—as though celluloid films were inherently evil, or playing cards manufactured by Lucifer; or as though tobacco were a hellish weed and fermentation morally different from other kinds of chemical change. An article in *Christianity Today* says that Fundamentalist practice raises the question "Shall it be consistent with spirituality to . . . use oblong pieces of pasteboard that have one pattern on them and are called rook cards, but not another pattern and are called bridge cards, although the principle of the two games is the same?"[2] The feeling that an "untouchability" rightly inheres in certain objects with certain associations is hard to keep out of at least the emotions of a legalist.

Now there is nothing whatever wrong with giving up a thing for sufficient reason if the thing itself (in its proper use) is acknowledged to be a good thing. But the separatist pattern of action, followed widely, certainly invites the thought that the things which are disallowed are so because they are evil things. This inference may usually be implicit. But that it is not far from the surface is indicated by a curio from my file, an amusing, unsigned early pamphlet attacking radio. It says:

> Without here expressing any opinion as to whether the discovery of wireless communication was from God or the devil, certain it is that the latter is using it not only as a medium for propagating error but as a means of ensnaring many professing Christians.

This is, I admit, phrased equivocally and is not an authoritative opinion. Nonetheless, it indicates a thought that cannot but slip into the minds of those who act on separatist principles. The easiest way to justify such behavior is to say that I avoid certain things because they are evil of themselves. This quasi-Manichaean theology is inadequate for a sound ethic. Evil is located in the will, in the one who decides, not in things. Any other view finally questions either the goodness or the creatorship of God.

Again, to make a direct connection between being a Christian and the observing of certain taboos suggests some confused equations. A set of "do's and don't's" and being a Christian are made to be the same thing. This apparent justification by works is illustrated in the story describing some early mission work. Western missionaries were scandalized by the scantiness of native attire. So, on becoming a Christian, a native was given an outfit of European clothing prepared by the good women of the missionary's homeland. With the believers thoroughly clad and the unbelievers comparatively unclothed, an inevitable connection seemed to be established between salvation and clothing—each implied the other. Natives began asking for European clothing so that they might go to heaven. The result was confused religion and deteriorated health and morals. It is dangerous to link Christianity to any arbitrary cultural norm—even the wearing of trousers! No cultural taboo is universal, so none should be inseparably linked to a universal salvation.

Furthermore, to vilify a given group of people or class of things as categorically evil presents a false picture of the world. It implies that the world is boldly painted black and white. What is allowed is white; what is forbidden is black. Such a picture is fallacious. The world as we experience it is not black and white, sharply distinguished; we never know anything or anyone as entirely good or entirely bad. Observation should demolish the fiction of a "pure church." To be sure, there are varying degrees of gray. But the Adversary is neither so stupid as to present us with temptations which are so completely bad as to deceive no one, nor so impotent as to let anything remain uncontaminated for long. Whatever the proportion, there is always a mixture. St. Paul wisely observed to the separatists of Corinth that if one wanted to avoid evil completely, he would have to leave the world altogether.[3]

The principle that an entire category of things is to be forbidden because it is open to serious abuse and degradation has an unhappy logic. By such a principle, life would be narrowed to the vanishing point. Further, it is generally true that things have potentiality for evil in proportion to their potentiality for good. The evil thing is only a misused or perverted good thing. It cannot be made a great evil unless it had the capacity to be a great good. In the attempt to restrict life in order to avoid evil, the best things in life suffer first and suffer most.

There is no precise basis for demonstrating why one group of questioned items has passed the point of acceptance and another has not. Evil cannot be put into tubes and bottles and measured in such a way as to suggest an objective criterion for the judgments that are made in practice. Without some such demonstrable judgment, the Fundamentalist mind is in difficulty. For it is unhappy with inconsistency. It reasons that if God has given an absolute revelation of himself, this must lead to an absolute, consistent pattern of behavior—right for all.

This then is the separatist dilemma—it attempts in one way or another to impose an arbitrary map onto a territory it will not fit. The absolutes of behavior which Fundamentalists seek are true neither to the reality of the world nor to the nuances of believing persons. Every attempt to apply separatist principles is a gross oversimplification of the moral problem. We must examine more deeply and sensitively the situation of the Christian vis-à-vis the world. If no objective basis can be found that can eliminate inconsistency, we must be prepared to live with it maturely and sanely. If a restricted approach cannot provide a basis for all the subtle relation to the world, some better approach must be found.

II. A COMPLEX RELATION TO THE WORLD

I agreed earlier that the separatist position has a hold on something with which Christianity cannot dispense. It insists on a certain distinctiveness in the Christian pattern of behavior. It rightly asks what is to be the impact of Christianity on society if the secular environment dictates the standards for Christians.

Those who raise questions over "worldly" practices are sincerely wondering how the church can have anything to say to the world if the church and the world are indistinguishable. From this valid point—concern for witness—their case for the taboos takes on its significance.

However, witness is a rather complex thing. It depends for its effectiveness on enough distinctiveness from the one to whom it is addressed for it to have something to say. But it also depends on there being enough commonness for real communication. Carried out rigorously enough, the insistence on separateness which is maintained in the interest of witness can actually be the means of destroying witness. It can remove the common ground from which a successful witness arises.

A too zealous pursuit of separation errs in its mistaking one valid aspect of the Christian ethic for the whole. Complementary considerations are equally important. A Christian is a citizen of two worlds. He is a man of two loyalties. He belongs to this world and has responsibilities and a mission here. He is also a citizen of heaven, and he conducts his life, at least from one point of view, as a "stranger" here, a "colonist" of another world. These two legitimate Christian sources of claim on his actions and the relation between them make the moral world vastly complex. We must examine the polarity of allegiance to which a Christian's situation commits him.

The principle of *separation* must, if it is to be Christian, be held in tension with another seemingly contrary principle—the principle of *identification*. Both of these principles are morally decisive and profoundly biblical.

Here we find the pattern for our course in God and his relation to his creation through Jesus Christ. The incarnation means that God himself became involved in the human struggle. He entered the human lot to cleanse, renew, and restore it. He did not shun a tainted category. He identified himself fully with the condition of the ones to be helped; the Son was made "in the likeness of sinful flesh."

Further, the company our Lord kept during his ministry was a frequent source of scandal to the separatists of his time. The sick, not the well, needed a physician, he maintained, so he went among them. Jesus' critics had occasion to remark the contrast with John the Baptist. John was austere, solitary, life-denying, a messenger of judgment—an Elijah. Jesus was convivial; the Kingdom he spoke of was a banquet; and he took the glad message of this Kingdom to the joyless places where it was most needed. The charge against him was that he ate with publicans and sinners. Or, as Dorothy Sayers rephrased the accusation, "He ate too heartily, drank too freely, and kept very disreputable company, including grafters of the lowest type and ladies who were no better than they should be."[4]

At his death, Jesus was crucified between two thieves, numbered with the transgressors. He thought of his death as something done on behalf of others, a ransom for "many."

Yet he, who was without sin, associated with sinners in pursuit of his mission. While he embodied love, he embodied holiness as well. He hobnobbed with publicans and sinners, not to share their sin, but to win them to righteousness. St. Luke's stories of the lost sheep, the lost coin, and the lost son were told to justify Jesus' keeping unseemly company—he was the Father's seeking, saving love in action, so he had to go where the lost were. But he did so without compromise.

His principle is ours. Separation and identification are both important; both must be obeyed. And the end sought must be redemptive. Whether we shall succeed in adjusting them as Jesus did remains doubtful, but the demand of both—of holiness and love, judgment and compassion—cannot be ignored.

In one sense there is as much false accommodation to popular opinion in overdoing separateness as there is in giving in to society through overdoing identification. It is only a question of whom one is willing to offend. The Fundamentalist, with his nonconforming taboos, seems to be defying his environment in the name of the offense of the Cross. But his norms are such as always to place him with the most respectable elements of his community. Most of his prohibitions are in the general line of the cautious, circumspect, often smug "worldly asceticism" which distinguishes the Anglo-Saxon bourgeois mind. He risks little by his peculiar habits. He carefully removes himself from the publicans and sinners, but he joins the Pharisees. His reproach in his community is almost the opposite of that of his Lord. Someone as concerned about the principle of identification as the Fundamentalist is about separation could find himself as unpopular as any Fundamentalist. He risks, if he is faithful to his Lord, being judged severely for what seems to be his indulgence in standards that are less than proper.

Since both of these imperatives are essential to a complete witness, and since both are difficult, let us look at them more carefully.

What is the more fully stated principle of separation?

We live in a moral world. The gray of experience is gray because it is a mixture of a black and a white. Behind the ill-defined moral lights and shadows of our experience are the infinitely distinguished "light and darkness," "Christ and Belial," "believers and infidels," "the temple of God and that of idols," of the biblical outlook.[5] But no category of experience contains exclusively one or the other.

The truest separation must be thought of in terms like these: There is evil in every category and every group. No Christian should compromise himself by making into good what he is convinced is wrong. But the emphasis in this separation should be not on what reaches one's surroundings or one's senses (as though there were some refuge possible) but on what reaches his heart. It would be futile to try to keep all evil away from us, for the worst evil with which we have to deal is not the evil around us but the evil within us. It is in the heart that the real struggle with evil takes place. It is there that the deepest separation from the world must be. It is not the "world" around us that is inherently "worldly"; it is the "world" that we love, the "world" that takes possession of us, that becomes "worldliness" thereby. So the true principle of separation is not found in the monastic strategy of retreat—we take the most troublesome source of worldliness with us wherever we may go.

If worldliness is really a question of the heart and its allegiance, the matter becomes much more delicate than it would otherwise be. An inward principle of separation from the world involves the profoundest issues in Jesus' teaching. The inmost heart of a Christian must look with the "single eye";[6] it must acknowledge but one Master;[7] it must know the meaning of the sacred hate[8] for all that would displace the Kingdom.

Now, if the issue lies in the heart rather than in the environment, the heart must have the courage to apply its separation from evil to every category of life. To allow convenient blind spots of prejudice and indulgence is to slip back into the separatist error of exempting some categories of life from serious judgment and dealing too severely with others.

When we consider separateness from the world, Christian faith demands that those who love and serve God reject the false, the ugly, and the wrong of their environment. But the transcendent claim of God also separates from the true, the beautiful, and the good of the world. That is, the central thing, the Christian revelation, is beyond rationalism—at the heart of its message it affirms the paradox of a God-man; it is foolishness

to the Greeks. It is beyond aestheticism—its center is in a Cross
which remains an offense to the Greek sense of godlike propriety.
It is beyond moralism (a scandal to the Jews)—it affirms the acceptance of the sinner, not the good man; its story is of "God in
the hands of angry sinners." "The wisdom of this world is folly
with God." So the separation is searching in its judgment of the
norms of the world. They all must be broken before they can be
remade.

Let me now try to clarify the principle of *identification.*

The principle of separation as discussed above regards man
primarily as a free individual answerable to his own conscience
before God. That is, though true, only a part of the truth about
man. He is also a member, an individual in relationship, having
a responsibility to the life of the whole. This aspect of human
life underlies identification. The Christian man who has found
himself strangely separated from the good and from the evil of
the world now must recognize that he is strangely identified with
both.

The discernment and rejection in every category of life of
all that is less than God is not an end in itself. It is only a
necessary step toward the rediscovery, through God, of all that
is truly good. The negation of the world in the name of Christ
only frees one to affirm the world through Christ. Wherever
there is good, it is God's good, and it is for his children. Anything
that enriches life is a Christian thing—"if it is received with
thanksgiving"[9]—that is, with humility, communion, and responsibility. No one has seen this identification as sensitively as the
seventeenth-century "poet of felicity," Thomas Traherne:

> You never enjoy the world aright, till the Sea itself floweth in
> your veins, till you are clothed with the heavens, and crowned
> with the stars: and perceive yourself to be the sole heir of the
> whole world, and more than so, because men are in it who are
> every one sole heirs as well as you. Till you can sing and rejoice
> and delight in God, as misers do in gold, and Kings in sceptres,
> you never enjoy the world.[10]

Most of us crassly insist on being small and petty, and we fail
to enter into our inheritance. Traherne is a good tonic.

But Traherne tends to minimize the reality of evil. His
world is still Eden. Any complete statement of the Christian

principle of identification must recognize an identification with evil alongside the identification with good. Wherever there is good, it is, or may be, my good. Wherever there is evil, it, too, is mine.

Without the recognition that we are responsibly identified with evil, no struggle with it can hope to be realistic or successful. Courageous warfare begins when the cause at issue becomes my cause.

The deadly "grayness" I find in the moral universe I find in myself. I am a paradox of desire for God and revolt against him. My very virtues become contaminated with self-righteousness. My very repentance needs to be repented of. For this evil of my own heart I am terribly responsible.

I am further identified with evil and failing in my family. The limitations of the fathers are visited on the children to the third and fourth generations. My children's greatest problem in life will be how to relate themselves to their impossible elders in a way that is not self-destructive. And for this evil I am responsible.

I am identified with sin and error in my church. The wrong of others hurts me, and my wrong hurts the whole body. The church is as weak as it is because it has in it people like me. I must accept my responsibility for its wrong.

I am identified with evil and injustice in my nation. If I have closed my heart against a brother in any relationship, if I have snobbishly placed myself above him, I have proved myself the same sort of person as those who, with less respectability and finesse, destroy life and property rights, who exploit and defraud others. So I must never suppose that injustice in my country is the fault of someone else. It is mine, too.

With the whole community of mankind I am united in sin. This bond with the whole family of man—creatureliness perverted to my ends, not God's—unites men at the very point at which it turns men upon one another.[11] The world is as bad as it is because of people like me—because of me. In my measure, I must accept this identification.

"Lord, have mercy on me, the sinner."

Now these two great claims—separation and identification—must both be represented in the Christian's relation to the world. To emphasize separateness at the expense of identification raises arbitrary barriers and leads to self-righteousness. Our witness is ruined because no one can hear what we say; we end by talking to ourselves. To stress identification at the expense of separateness leads to compromise and ineffectiveness. Our witness again suffers, for though people hear what we are saying, we only tell them what they already know; we have nothing distinctive to say.

Such considerations rule out the separatist approach altogether. This approach imposes a false map on reality. It tries to mark out certain areas as evil and others as good, and then it tries to chart its roadways so as to avoid travel through the evil territories. The more sophisticated separatists may indicate on their maps some gray areas—bad enough so that one is expected to feel uncomfortable in or around them, but not yet bad enough to be categorically avoided. But all such maps are certain to be misleading. They do not describe the real world. A Christian's map of his world should show the best there is and the worst. Within his world he may well exercise his discrimination; he will be attracted by some things and repelled by others. But, within his world, such preferences as he has must be qualified by the overriding consideration that he is bound under God to say "yes" to all of it and "no" to all of it. Anything in his world can be enjoyed, claimed, redeemed, used, and offered up to the Giver of all life. But also anything in his world can corrupt, mislead, or become an idol. Our world is God's world, but it is fallen. It is fallen, but in Christ it is overcome, restored, transformed. We have a stake in it, but not a final stake in it. Our map must do justice to this ambiguity in the world.

III. VARIETIES OF CHRISTIAN CONSCIENCE

This lack of a defined body of universal rules is disconcerting to a certain type of mind. So perhaps we should inquire more deeply why persons who act with as much realism and sincerity as possible will yet act differently. Moral decisions vary as people vary. Why?

The inward claims of God address themselves to consciences. St. Paul distinguishes what he calls "weak consciences" from "strong consciences." The distinction is of permanent value.[12] Always the Christian community contains both. St. Paul's instructions for their mutual coexistence are always pertinent.

The weak conscience inclines to prefer a narrow life to a life of risk. It appeals to what I call "principles of bondage."

The strong conscience prefers a complete life even though it may not be safe. It appeals to "principles of freedom."

Each of these two sets of principles embodies a genuine Christian ethical sanction, but each needs the other.

Briefly put, the "principles of freedom" are suggested in biblical passages such as these:

> For everything created by God is good, and nothing is to be rejected if it is received with thanksgiving . . . (1 Tim. 4:4).

> I know and am persuaded in the Lord Jesus that nothing is unclean in itself . . . (Rom. 14:14).

> . . . God who richly furnishes us with everything to enjoy (1 Tim. 6:17).

> To the pure all things are pure . . . (Titus 1:15).

> "All things are lawful for me" . . . (1 Cor. 6:12; cf. 10:23).

> . . . "the earth is the Lord's, and everything in it" (1 Cor. 10:26).

> . . . for us there is one God, the Father, from whom are all things and for whom we exist, and one Lord, Jesus Christ, through whom are all things and through whom we exist (1 Cor. 8:6).

These passages suggest a great theme of biblical religion. The world is the Lord's, and we are the Lord's. We are redeemed by Christ to love God, to be ourselves in God, and to use his creation to the fullest.

The things of God's world are good. They are, of course, doubly good if they are used in obedient trusteeship according to his intention. They are not contaminated, however, if they are misused. Meat offered in an idol temple is just as good as any other when bought later at market.[13] Similarly, a piece of art that is good is good irrespective of the morals of the artist, and a piece of art that is bad is bad irrespective of the piety of its artist. Creative work, done with integrity, is a gift of God, whatever the intentions and the ethics of the workman may have been.

A person who stressed the principles of freedom might well ask just how "scriptural" are the taboos. Of course the Bible says nothing about those of them that have appeared in our culture since it was written. But about those permanent ingredients of human life—sex, wine, the dance—it does have something to say, and it is not what the Fundamentalists say. It says they are things to be used, under God, with joy. The Bible tradition on the whole is life-affirming. It blesses the Lord for "wine to gladden the heart of man."[14]

Someone who made much of these principles might also ask just how goodness is to be defined. The overscrupulous tend to give it a kind of minimal definition—they define it negatively, in terms of how many things a person does not do. Is goodness not rather a positive thing, flowing from the love of God? Is love that is timid, questioning, and self-conscious real love? Cannot the attitude of self-examination about guilt and offenses take the spontaneity from the Christian life? Are Christians slaves or sons? Is not the Christian life a life of freedom to love God and one's neighbor humbly and gladly, to live as God meant his children to live?

In affirming these principles of freedom, Christians can move from the defensive stance to the offensive. Is it not possible to witness to the world with effectiveness by demonstrating the Christian way of *things used temperately under God*? How much real witness is there in withdrawal from an area of life? Would not the spectacle of persons using to the fullest the good things of life with dignity, freedom, and joy be the most telling witness imaginable?

The principles of bondage declare that we and our world are full of the effects of sin. So our freedom must be chastened, responsible freedom, exercised in full awareness of our situation. The saintly old Evangelical Bishop Moule had his usual good phrase for it when he said:

> You are free—but as the child of a Father, and as the member of a family. And such freedom would be only the harsh parody of itself if it were not a freedom to love, to be loyal, to serve, to share.[15]

Thus our freedom works within higher relationships under which alone it can be truly free. This bondage—gladly assumed because willed by a gracious God—may be thought of under three headings according to the relationship involved.

First are the Godward limitations: These include responsible stewardship of God's gifts and the obligation to do all to the glory of God.[16] For a believing person, motive, method, action, and end must reckon on the absolute claim of the Lord of all life.

Second are the manward limitations: These grow out of the relationships with men that are to be sustained in love. St. Paul speaks, for example, of a Christian's obligation to use his liberty, "not . . . as an opportunity for the flesh, but through love [to] be servants of one another."[17] When we are mindful of a responsibility to the whole body of the church, it is important to do things which "edify" and which are "expedient"—that is, things which are a positive, constructive help to Christian life.[18] We should have special regard for the sensitivity of the "weaker brother." St. Paul cautions:

> You must be careful that your freedom to eat meat does not in any way hinder anyone whose faith is not as robust as yours. . . . Surely you would not want your superior knowledge to bring spiritual disaster to a weaker brother for whom Christ died? And when you sin like this and damage the weak consciences of your brethren you really sin against Christ. This makes me determined that, if there is any possibility of meat injuring my brother, I will have none of it as long as I live, for fear I might do him harm.[19]

St. Paul is saying that what is known to be innocent in itself can become sin by the personal relationship within which it is to be done. A further aspect of the manward limitations is the regard which St. Paul says should be had for the opinion of non-Christians. He is concerned that they be given no unnecessary cause for misunderstanding or offense.[20]

Third are the selfward limitations: Without an internalized discipline, liberty can drift into license. Again a phrase of St. Paul's puts it well: ". . . I will not be enslaved by anything."[21] This principle warns that the heart can easily fall under the wrong control, and false, enslaving gods can entreat its allegiance. We can be so readily self-deceived that we may be the last to recognize our own entrapment.

Specific ethical decisions will be made by consciences of varying degrees of strength and courage. Each decision is under the two appeals—liberty and restriction; however, the choice is not two, but one. The tension is resolved in a single act which is most free when spontaneously bound by the highest considerations.

IV. FOUR OBSERVATIONS

Several implications of these moral claims are now clear. First, let me repeat that this analysis entirely rules out uniformity and legalism. Different claims will seem paramount to different people. The man who knows he has alcoholic tendencies had better be a teetotaler—and a scrupulous one. He must apply these principles conscientiously. He may trust that others, although their behavior may differ from his, are acknowledging the same claims with the same strictness. But to suppose that because some people, for Christian reasons, must be teetotalers, all must be, is to adopt a Moslem ethic under a Christian name; it is an extension of egoism, not charity.

It is in the individual conscience as it is judged before God that decision is vindicated.[22] Each decision must be made in the particularity of its circumstances. The inwardness of the Christian's relation to his Lord is the final thing by which he stands or falls, but it is not a matter for judgment by others. The wrong in the Fundamentalist taboos is not that they prefer an abstemious course of action. The wrong lies in universalizing such a decision once one has made it for himself. It is God's business, not ours, to make laws for all mankind. We should beware of presuming to use divine prerogatives. One conscience is quite enough for one person to manage.

A second observation follows. An outlook that recognizes the legitimacy of differences can only work through Christian charity. People enter Christian life with different backgrounds and capacities, and they progress at different rates in different callings. Yet all are brothers in Christ—the point of their union is beyond common background, common interests, and common behavior. So in Christ, forbearance, patience, and understanding are called for. Love has precedence over knowledge as a basis for action; an action that may be harmless in itself becomes sinful when a brother is injured by it. An indifferent ethical matter becomes significant when it is made a party issue that divides Christians against each other. Love for persons is the primary demand. It is prior to vindication of one's own side, even if it happens to be right. It is prior to the preservation of an institution, even if it is a valuable one. Again, Henry says it well:

> The weaker brother is not to be looked down upon as narrow. He is fully a person in his own right—indeed, he is one for whom Christ died. And so he is to be respected. He is not to be engaged in "doubtful disputations" nor in debates that deal only with vain reasonings (Rom. 14:1). Nor is the weaker to be baited into protest by a deliberate course of action which the stronger pursues.
>
> Neither is the weaker believer to be offended by a false impression that the stronger is ethically indifferent or insensitive . . .[23]

Fellowship in self-giving love provides the environment within which differing ethical decisions can be followed without the divisiveness of criticism and false judgment. "Let us then pursue what makes for peace and for mutual upbuilding."[24]

A third observation is that anything can be worldly. Anything at all—the finest of things—may come between a Christian and God or may be an offense to one's brother. Love for great music can be an ennobling thing under God. But it can also make me despise my less appreciative brother; it can become a consuming thing that destroys me like a jealous god. Love for one's family can, under God, be gracious and enriching. But apart from the love taught by God, it can become possessive and destructive. Anything, when organized apart from God, can become worldly.

This being the case, it is seriously misleading to designate, as Fundamentalists do, some six or eight particular practices as constituting "worldliness." Of the consequences of this error, I would like to look at two.

For one thing, listing certain items as "worldly" implies that other things are not worldly. We all know people who are scandalized at the thought of attending the motion picture theater but who watch on their television sets films that are too poor to pay their way in the movie houses. Without some general principles instead of a list of taboos, real taste and discrimination can never develop.

For another thing, when "worldliness" is defined in terms of doing certain things and the spiritual life defined in terms of not doing them, stress is put primarily on the outward acts rather than on the personal relations and character out of which acts grow.

This seriously reverses the proper order of the Kingdom. As St. Paul observed: "For the kingdom of God does not mean food and drink but righteousness and peace and joy in the Holy

Spirit."[25] The moral theology of the great tradition, following the New Testament, stoutly maintains that sins of the spirit are more serious than sins of the flesh. Drunkenness is wrong (and rather obvious); vanity is worse (and seldom apparent). Vulgarity, intemperance, sensuality, and sometimes almost prurience can appear in the Fundamentalist attacks on the vanities of "the world."

But a legalistic principle of defining the world keeps the Fundamentalists unaware of the extent to which their life and religion have become worldly through lack of an eternal rather than an external standard of discrimination. Letter-perfect conformity to a pattern of external prohibitions may coexist with an inner life that is selfish, mean, and touchy. Anyone reared under the Fundamentalist scheme might easily suppose that a person who conforms to the prescribed pattern is inwardly white as the driven snow. Is not this an invitation to self-righteousness? For primary stress on the observance of an arbitrary set of rules can produce ethical morons—people who have never been personally challenged to discriminate good from evil. The ethos of Fundamentalism has provided a shelter. Outside this shelter, its products are weak and uncertain. The aim of the good life is not just to produce circumspect conduct but to produce good people.

A final observation is that the goal of moral living is strength! I should say at once that strength is not bravado; everyone should beware of overestimating his power. There is something to be said in some situations for erring on the side of safety. Nonetheless, to run from potential danger is weakness. It should be recognized as such. The delicate, easily offended conscience is something to be overcome. St. Paul did not write 1 Corinthians 8 in defense of or out of admiration for the weaker brother. He said that stronger Christians are to defer to a weaker one, to accept his weak standard when it will avoid offending him. But they need not admire him insofar as he is weak. They rather hope that someday, through maturing and instruction and the example of more courageous consciences in people whose Christianity he does not doubt, he will become stronger. Fundamentalists tend to make the weaker conscience the standard for all. By means of explicit or implied agreement, the most fastidious conscience is legislated on the entire group. There is no sign that such a standard is regarded as low or weak or a halfway house to something stronger; rather, it seems to be regarded as a mark of sainthood—as though a person's goodness were defined in the number of things his conscience questioned. By this standard anyone who acts on stronger principles is regarded as morally compromised. This reversal of perspective is unwholesome. Innocence and scrupulosity are not virtue. We grow strong by meeting and conquering in Christ the enemies of the spirit. One of the clear elements in faith is risk or venture. Christian life cannot look for safety without betraying itself. The negative observation made above—that "anything can be worldly" —needs to be answered by the redemptive affirmation—"anything can be Christian."

V. THE CALL NOT TO BE SEPARATE

Now let me go back to the great fundamental issue from which we started and see if this discussion has clarified it at all. The issue was: "What is the relation of the redeemed community to the world?"

Some sort of separation from the world is inescapable. It comes from the sense of divine choosing. It comes from a "calling out" that makes up the church. It represents a transcendent summons, an election in grace.

The first great word in redemption, then, is "separation." "Therefore come out from them, and be separate from them, says the Lord . . ."[26] " 'Set apart for me Barnabas and Saul for the work to which I have called them.' "[27] This is the mystery of election and calling—this one from tending sheep, this one from catching fish, this one from persecuting Christians, this one from his cobbler's bench, this one from his studies—all are called by God, who sets them over against the world. Thus set "over nations and over kingdoms," men of faith are "to pluck up and to break down, to destroy and to overthrow, to build and to plant."[28] They are to retain and to remit sins.[29] They are separated to high prerogatives.

But the last word in redemption is not "separation." By itself this sense of election is too much to bear. It seems, we being what we are, to slip inevitably into self-righteousness and an arrogant claim to privilege.

The last word in redemption is "identification." The church

is not chosen for herself but chosen for the world. The holy people is for the sake of the unholy people. If we are drawn into union with Christ, it is only so that we may learn his pattern of the assumption of evil by the good—so that our identification with him may be with his love and suffering in the travail of human redemption.

Moses' calling was not alone to privilege; it was to the heartbreak of relation with his wayward people. He was willing to be identified with them—to lose himself for them:

> So Moses returned to the LORD and said, "Alas, this people have sinned a great sin; they have made for themselves gods of gold. But now, if thou wilt forgive their sin—and if not, blot me, I pray thee, out of thy book which thou hast written."[30]

St. Paul was not only a "chosen instrument" with a lofty vocation.[31] He, too, had such Christlike identification with his people as to "wish that I myself were accursed and cut off from Christ for the sake of my brethren, my kinsmen by race."[32] And Jesus, the Suffering Servant, did not lay claim to his kingliness except through a Cross borne sacrificially, as "a ransom for many."[33] He finally felt himself forsaken by God in his oneness with his brethren.

This is the spirit of the Gospel. It is the reverse of self-righteousness. It is a purpose Jesus shares with his people: "If any man would come after me, let him deny himself and take up his cross and follow me."[34] It is not separation for its own sake. It is separation as a necessary concentration of purpose for a redemptive mission. The church should not run from the world. She is committed to conquest. She should lose herself in the world's behalf. This is the way of the prophets, the saints, and the Savior.

I wonder if the ethic of separatism practiced in Fundamentalism is even looking in that direction.

Cordially,
Spermologos

POSTSCRIPT

Is it possible that the Spirit of God may be at work, on souls and minds and institutions, in ways which are no less divine than those which are precious to you?

ARCHBISHOP RAMSAY

This is the correspondence, written over a number of years, to several different people. Putting it together and looking at it as a whole, I cannot but have some second thoughts. Does it deal justly with the movement it seeks to discuss? Does it give enough place to the frontier missionary work in which the conservative or evangelical churches continue to provide more than their share of pioneers, heroes, and martyrs? Does it recognize the kindly, gentle Christian people—men and women of prayer, deeply taught by the Spirit—to many of whom I shall always be in infinite debt? Does it give credit to the eager effort on the part of teachers and students within evangelicalism to wrestle with the meaning of Holy Scripture and to believe and to act on their findings? Does it recognize the sheer passion for Christ and the world for him which Fundamentalism at its best elicits?

Probably not. This book is not balanced. No writer sees and reports things just as they are. Everyone must say what is important to him. If, then, this is a one-sided book, I can only trust that the side it presents is one that deserves a hearing. If I have been unjust in leaving out some of the best that might have been said, I like to feel that I have also dealt gently with the worst.

These letters are not a plea for Fundamentalism to abandon anything of real value that it has. I have only tried to argue that nothing of Christian value in Fundamentalism is present simply because of Fundamentalism. What is there is there because of God and his trust of his revelation to the whole of his church. For two generations Fundamentalism has been living a derived life. It has been a kind of parasite on the life of the great church—parasitic because it denies its host. It has not recognized the extent of its debt; it has tried to isolate itself and to suppose that it is self-sufficient. I have tried only to argue in this book that there is nothing of value in Fundamentalism which could not be retained—and in fact heightened and fulfilled—by its moving into the life of the broader fellowship.

I am persuaded that the second generation is finding that what Fundamentalism promises, Fundamentalism cannot deliver. It introduces one to a genuine Christian faith, and it encourages him to learn and grow; but, as he learns and grows, the self-contradictions of his tradition become apparent to him. This moment of truth forces a decision. At this point more than one of my good friends has turned back from where his live, inquiring mind was leading him, stopped raising basic questions, and buried himself in the work of a Fundamentalist-related cause. Others are so overwhelmed by the reality of the world for which they were unprepared by a sheltered Fundamentalist education that they throw over everything. Others continue to explore and grope tentatively—unable to be content within Fundamentalism but unable to break with it altogether.

The answer to this second-generation problem is not to be found in Fundamentalism as it has been known. Some who come to share this restlessness leave Fundamentalism. Many of them find a satisfying spiritual home in the laity or clergy of the churches of the ecumenical family; and a few achieve some eminence. But others who share this discontent seek to change the character of the movement from within its informed and trusted leadership. These have taken on a difficult way of obedience, but one that may show gratifying results.

To those who find that, with all the attendant wrenches of ties, they must leave their tradition, and to those who have a mission within it, I have tried to say that they need not fear to move, to grow, to reach out. They have much now. But in moving, nothing they presently have need be lost, and there is much to gain. The voice of God is in the stir of world events. It calls the church and every Christian to be a pilgrim, and in this life there is no higher calling.

NOTES AND ACKNOWLEDGMENTS

The Internal Dialogue

1. The phrase "Fundamentalist renascence" is the title of an article in the *Christian Century*, April 30, 1958. The article is a plea for more attention to Fundamentalist thought.

   Carnell's contributions to the *Century* were in the issues of October 17, 1956, and March 30, 1960. Ramm's article appeared on March 1, 1961, and Jewett's on May 24, 1961.

   Chad Walsh's editorial was in the September 6, 1953, issue of the late-lamented *Episcopal Churchnews*.

   Fr. Hebert's book was published in this country by The Westminster Press, Philadelphia, 1957. In England it is under the title *Fundamentalism and the Church of God*, SCM Press.

   The rejoinder is J. I. Packer's *"Fundamentalism" and the Word of God*, published by Inter-Varsity Fellowship, London, 1958.

   An article by Sherman Roddy appeared in the October 1, 1959, issue of the *Christian Century*. It is an attempt to reappraise the present state of Fundamentalism in the ecumenical picture.

   In addition to these, extended notice was taken of the symposium *Contemporary Evangelical Thought* in a review article by Martin Marty in the *Christian Century*, July 3, 1957.

2. The first is published by W. A. Wilde of Boston, 1950; the second by Wm. B. Eerdmans Publishing Co. of Grand Rapids, 1957.

3. Norman F. Furniss, *The Fundamentalist Controversy, 1918-1931*, p. 49. New Haven: Yale University Press, 1954.

4. Carl F. H. Henry, *Evangelical Responsibility in Contemporary Theology*, pp. 38 f.

5. E. J. Carnell, article on "Fundamentalism" in *A Handbook of Christian Theology*, p. 143.

6. Furniss, *op. cit.*, p. 41. In this vein, Stewart G. Cole, in his *History of Fundamentalism*, p. 233, cites Riley's prediction that one of the Bible conferences early in the rise of the movement "marked the beginning of a new Protestantism, an event of more historic moment that the nailing up of Martin Luther's theses at the Wittenberg cathedral." New York: Richard R. Smith, Inc., 1931.

7. See Henry, *op. cit.*, pp. 43 ff.

8. Furniss, *op. cit.*, p. 40, documents this. Bernard Ramm, *The Christian View of Science and Scripture*, has some strong pages criticizing "hyperortho-

227

doxy." See pp. 26 ff. Grand Rapids: Wm. B. Eerdmans Publishing Company, 1954. Henry, *op. cit.*, pp. 33 f., speaks of "an uncritical antithesis between the heart and the head to which most fundamentalist educators and ministers subscribed their schools and their churches."

9. Some of the activities of this sort are discussed in Ralph Lord Roy's *Apostles of Discord*. Boston: The Beacon Press, 1953.

10. E. A. Cording, "Music Worthy of God," in *Christianity Today*, November 24, 1958, p. 18. This phrase is interesting because it is so incidental—the writer seems able to assume without needing to make a point of it that the constituency addressed is all "independent."

11. Walter Marshall Horton, *Realistic Theology*, p. 2. New York: Harper & Brothers Publishers, 1934.

12. *Christian Life*, June 1947, pp. 13-15.

13. Henry, *op. cit.*, p. 34.

The External Dialogue

1. H. Richard Niebuhr, *The Kingdom of God in America*, p. 193. Hamden, Conn.: The Shoe String Press, 1956.

2. Horton, *Realistic Theology*, p. 2.

3. Edwin Lewis, *A Christian Manifesto*, p. 142. New York: The Abingdon Press, 1934.

4. William Temple, *Christian Faith and Life*, p. 54. New York: The Macmillan Company, 1931.

5. The title of a book by T. A. Kantonen, Muhlenberg Press. The same "resurgence" is described in a masterful survey in a chapter of Edwin Lewis' *A Philosophy of the Christian Revelation*. New York: Harper & Brothers Publishers, 1940. He calls Chapter XIX "The Rising Tide of Faith." In it he gives an account of the theological awakening in Christendom. The chapter is now over twenty years old and a little out-of-date, but it is still worth reading for its information and its sense of inner excitement.

6. William Hordern, *A Layman's Guide to Protestant Theology*, p. 74. New York: The Macmillan Company, 1955.

7. Roddy, in the *Christian Century*, p. 1109.

The Diagnosis: Law

1. Packer, *"Fundamentalism" and the Word of God*, p. 47.

2. Carl F. H. Henry, "Divine Revelation and the Bible," in *Inspiration and Interpretation*, ed. John F. Walvoord, p. 261. Grand Rapids: Wm. B. Eerdmans Co., 1957.

3. John Oman, *Grace and Personality*, pp. 12 f. London: Cambridge University Press, 1919. Second edition.

4. B. B. Warfield, "The Task and Method of Systematic Theology," in *American Journal of Theology*, Vol. XIV, pp. 192-205. Chicago: The University of Chicago Press, 1910. This article was subsequently included in the collection of Warfield's papers called *Studies in Theology*. I would not have known of it if reference had not been made to it by W. M. Horton

in his article on "Systematic Theology" in the symposium *Protestant Thought in the Twentieth Century*, ed. Arnold Nash, p. 110. New York: The Macmillan Company, 1951.

5. University Sermon by the Reverend C. W. J. Bowles, Principal of Ridley Hall, *The Cambridge Review*, Vol. LXXIX, No. 1928, March 8, 1958, p. 443.

6. David Wesley Soper, *Men Who Shape Belief*, p. 158. Philadelphia: The Westminster Press, 1955.

7. I noticed with interest that this observation had also been made by Sherman Roddy in his article in the *Christian Century*.

8. 1 Corinthians 14:23-25 suggests that at least in some places and at some times in the apostolic generation it was possible that unbelieving persons would be present at a service of Christian worship and that because of their presence they might be convicted by God's Spirit. But no one familiar with the extreme caution that was general in the early church with respect to the introduction of new persons to the baptized, worshiping fellowship will argue that in the primitive church the main point of Christian worship was evangelistic. If this were a consideration at Corinth, it was a subordinate one; it was not even that for long, and it was not one at all in many other places.

   I have never heard this or any other text used in Fundamentalism to defend the "evangelistic service." I would guess that it would be defended on pragmatic grounds.

9. This is the most famous sentence in Ramsay's widely noted paper in *The Bishoprick*, February 1956, p. 25.

10. Bowles, *op. cit.*, p. 447.

The Prescription: Grace

1. This I take to be the thesis of Fr. Hebert's *Fundamentalism and the Church*.

2. Henry Clarence Thiessen, *Introduction to the New Testament*, pp. 82 ff. Grand Rapids: Wm. B. Eerdmans Publishing Company, 1943. These pages will give a sample of the line of argument. Nearly all conservative authorities use it.

3. J. K. S. Reid, *The Authority of Scripture*, p. 164. New York: Harper & Brothers Publishers, n.d.

4. Packer, *"Fundamentalism" and the Word of God*, pp. 82 ff.

5. John Baillie, *The Idea of Revelation in Recent Thought*, p. 123. New York: Columbia University Press, 1956.

6. Claude Welch, *The Reality of the Church*, p. 24. New York: Charles Scribner's Sons, 1958.

7. P. T. Forsyth, *Positive Preaching and the Modern Mind*, p. 125. New York: Eaton and Mains, n.d.

8. P. T. Forsyth, *The Principle of Authority*, p. 211. London: Independent Press, 1952. Second edition.

9. Emil Brunner, *The Divine-Human Encounter*, pp. 46 ff. Philadelphia: The Westminster Press, 1943.

10. Karl Adam, *Christ Our Brother*, p. 165. New York: The Macmillan Co., 1946.

11. H. R. Mackintosh, *Some Aspects of Christian Belief,* p. 176. New York: George H. Doran Company, 1923.
12. Oman, *Grace and Personality,* p. 167.
13. J. E. Fison, *The Blessing of the Holy Spirit,* p. 152. New York: Longmans, Green and Co., 1950.
14. Henry, *Evangelical Responsibility in Contemporary Theology,* pp. 45 f.
15. Martin E. Marty, "Fundamentalism and the Church," in the *Christian Century,* November 27, 1957, p. 1412.
16. E. J. Carnell, "Orthodoxy: Cultic vs. Classical," in the *Christian Century,* March 30, 1960, pp. 377 ff.
17. C. C. Morrison, "The Past Foreshadows the Future," in the *Christian Century,* March 5, 1958, p. 273.

In Defense of the Critics

1. Hordern, *A Layman's Guide to Protestant Theology,* p. 61.
2. *Ibid.*
3. I should qualify this sentence, if only in a footnote, to indicate that a verbal theory of inspiration is only the criterion within the Protestant family. Fundamentalism finds its neighbors among the Protestant churches to be close or distant as their view of Scripture varies. But this criterion does not establish any feeling of oneness with the Roman communion or with the sects—both of these groups share the verbal inspiration theory with Fundamentalism, but Fundamentalism does not recognize them as brothers on that account.
4. R. H. Strachen, *The Authority of Christian Experience,* pp. 15 f. Nashville: Abingdon-Cokesbury Press, 1931.
5. Quoted in James Denney, *Studies in Theology,* pp. 204 f. London: Hodder and Stoughton, 1894.
6. W. Robertson Smith, *The Old Testament in the Jewish Church,* p. 5. New York: D. Appleton and Company, 1881.
7. L. Gaussen, "*Theopneustia,*" trans. Scott, pp. 115 f. Kansas City: The Gospel Union Publishing Co., 1912.
8. This point is developed in A. G. Hebert's *The Authority of the Old Testament,* pp. 93-100. London: Faber and Faber Ltd, 1947. "The Inerrancy of the Bible, as it is understood to-day, is a new doctrine, and the modern fundamentalist is asserting something that no previous age has understood in anything like the modern sense." He charges that Fundamentalism has developed out of the materialistic philosophy of modern times. He cites a frequently quoted passage from Michael Roberts, "Fundamentalism may claim the Bible for its mother, but it has Hobbes for its father." The conviction that Fundamentalism is, in its way of arriving at religious truth, a function of materialistic thought (a conviction gained independently from reading in the 17th century) was the beginning of my own defection from the movement years ago.
9. Edward J. Young, *An Introduction to the Old Testament.* Grand Rapids: Wm. B. Eerdmans Publishing Co., 1949. This author makes extensive use of this argument. On pp. 202 f. he relies heavily on the New Testament

witness to establish the unity of Isaiah. The same writer has elaborated his contention that the witness of the New Testament "proves everything. It settles the question once and for all," in a more recent book, *Who Wrote Isaiah?*, pp. 9-15. Grand Rapids: Wm. B. Eerdmans Publishing Company, 1958.

The opening line of the Scofield Bible's introduction to the book of Jonah says, "The historical character of the man Jonah is vouched for by Jesus Christ (Mt. 12:39-41)"—as though that were the end of the matter.

10. James Orr, *The Problem of the Old Testament*, pp. 523 f. New York: Charles Scribner's Sons, 1906.

11. John Murray, "The Attestation of Holy Scripture," in *The Infallible Word*, a symposium by the members of the faculty of Westminster Theological Seminary, p. 8. Philadelphia: The Presbyterian Guardian Publishing Corporation, 1946.

12. Cornelius Van Til, *The Defense of the Faith*, p. 51. Philadelphia: The Presbyterian and Reformed Publishing Company, 1955.

13. *Ibid.*, p. 124.

14. *Ibid.*, p. 125.

15. *Ibid.*, p. 360.

16. C. H. Dodd, *The Authority of the Bible*, p. 15. London: Nisbet & Co., 1938. Second edition.

17. Thiessen, *Introduction to the New Testament*, p. 86. Thiessen depended on Evans, *Great Doctrines of the Bible*, for his statistics.

18. H. Wheeler Robinson, *Redemption and Revelation*, p. 138. New York: Harper & Brothers, 1942.

19. The correct translation of this verse used to be disputed. The construction is slightly elliptical, leaving some doubt as to whether the subject of the thought is "all scripture" or "all scripture that is inspired." The Revised Standard Version goes back to the reading of the Authorized Version, and this is the construction preferred by the conservatives, for it allows that the quality of "inspiration" inheres in all that is properly "scripture." One need not contest this translation or this idea in order to find serious fault with what the Fundamentalists do with this verse, once they have it correctly into English.

20. The I. C. C. volumes by R. H. Charles give as good a list as any. Closing warnings similar to these in the Apocalypse appear in I Enoch 104:10-11; and II Enoch 48:7-8; and in the Letter of Aristeas a severe judgment is called down on any who would alter the text of the Septuagint by adding to, changing, or omitting anything in it. Irenaeus used a similar form in one of his own controversial writings as Eusebius reports (*H. E.*, vs. 20). One ancient rabbi, writing some time between A.D. 140 and 165 appends to his thought, "My son, be careful; for it is a divine work: if thou writest, were it but a letter more or less, it is as if thou wert destroying a world."

21. Wilbur Smith, *Moody Monthly*, June 1959, p. 34.

22. The point, I find, is a recollection of some remarks by Edwin Lewis which are now in his *The Biblical Faith and Christian Freedom*, pp. 173 f. Philadelphia: The Westminster Press, 1953. He puts it this way:

There was *somebody* in the Early Church, if not Paul, who herein gave powerful expression to his faith respecting the centrality of Jesus Christ and his universal supremacy; who assumed that it was the faith of the Church itself; who was concerned about the signs that the faith was being departed from; and whose writings were so highly regarded in the Church that they were esteemed worthy of preservation, and certainly in due time of being assigned to Paul. The witness of the two epistles [Ephesians and Colossians] . . . is independent of the questions of authorship, of date, of place of origin, of destination. . . . It is a curious illusion, which we shall do well to abandon, that if any of the books of the Bible were not written by the persons whose names they bear, or to whom tradition, often for very poor reasons, assigns them, they lose their significance for the history and elucidation of revelation.

William Neil, in his Torch Commentary volume on Hebrews, p. 16, gives a similar happy twist to this matter. He ends his discussion of the authorship of this letter by saying, "Most Old Testament books are of unknown authorship, and the fact that some New Testament books which were thought at one time to be written by an apostle, turn out to be likewise anonymous, makes us rather realize how much richer the early Church was in theologians than we imagined."

The Knot in the Thread

1. Deuteronomy 6:21-23; cf. 26:1-11.
2. 1 Corinthians 15:3-5.
3. The classic study of the essential proclamation of the apostolic church is still C. H. Dodd's *The Apostolic Preaching and Its Developments*. London: Hodder & Stoughton Limited, 1936. Perhaps Dodd does not sufficiently allow for the fact that all of the sermons in Acts as they now stand owe much to Luke. Therefore, it is not too remarkable that they show a common pattern. Nevertheless, Dodd's study remains a great work.
4. The great statement of this is in William Temple's *Nature, Man and God*, Lecture XII, pp. 315 ff. He speaks of the principle of revelation as "the coincidence of event and appreciation."
5. Henry, in *Inspiration and Interpretation*, p. 256.
6. Karl Barth, *The Word of God and the Word of Man*, trans. D. Horton, p. 33. London: Hodder & Stoughton, 1928. This now famous phrase is the title of the address forming chapter two.
7. David Ewen, *Dictators of the Baton*. New York: Ziff-Davis Publishing Co., 1948. Second edition, revised. See pp. 50 f.
8. Packer, *"Fundamentalism" and the Word of God*, p. 73.
9. Some remarkable pages developing this point are in the old classic *Atonement and Personality* by R. C. Moberly, Chapters VII, VIII, and IX. New York: Longmans, Green & Co., 1910.
10. H. Wheeler Robinson, "The Christian Gospel of Redemption," in *The Christian Faith*, ed. W. R. Matthews, p. 217. London: Eyre and Spottiswoode, 1936.
11. P. T. Forsyth, *The Cruciality of the Cross*, p. 197. London: Hodder and Stoughton, 1909.
12. *Ibid.*

The Meaning of the Church

1. The long quotation is from W. H. Mallock, *The Veil of the Temple*, p. 214, quoted in Edgar P. Dickie's *Revelation and Response*, p. 128. New York: Charles Scribner's Sons, 1938.

2. Perhaps it should be said that in a sense all American religious bodies are "sectarian" and "gathered" inasmuch as none is established by law, and membership in any is a matter of choice. But there is a nonpolitical aspect to the separatist theory of the nature of the church. Theologically some churches find a particularistic theory congenial while others regard it as mistaken and combat it. This difference in attitude is probably the central point in distinguishing in our society "sect" from "church."

    The general view of the church in Fundamentalism has been influenced by the dispensationalist idea that the work of the Spirit of God in this age is to call out individuals to form the true church—which is not to be identified with any institution. The true church is a heavenly people with no earthly, institutional identity. The organized life of Christendom is apostate. In this dispensationalist notion of the church there is no solidarity.

    In a few religious bodies related to the Fundamentalist movement, the Calvinist idea of "covenant" has been a factor in thinking about the church. This view would encourage a sense of corporateness and solidarity. And where it has been held, the worst abuses of individualism have been checked. But the idea of covenant does not seem to have been very creatively developed by the conservative Calvinists nor to have had any general influence in Fundamentalist ecclesiology.

3. See, for example, a vigorous editorial in the third issue of *Christianity Today*, November 12, 1956, on "The Perils of Independency."

4. *Ecclesiastical Polity*, Introduction, VII, 7.

5. Title of a little book by Paul S. Minear. New York: Association Press, 1956.

6. Ephesians 4:15-16; 5:25-27; contrast 1 Corinthians 12:12.

7. Romans 12.

8. Ephesians 2:11-22.

9. Hebrews 11:40.

10. Romans 8:22-23.

11. F. R. Barry, *The Relevance of the Church*, p. 52. New York: Charles Scribner's Sons, 1936.

12. In his chapter "The Church" in *Foundations*, edited by Streeter, pp. 341 f. London: The Macmillan Company, 1922.

13. Quoted in Massey Shepherd, *The Worship of the Church*, p. 105. Greenwich, Conn.: Seabury Press, 1952.

14. Henry Barclay Swete, *The Holy Catholic Church: The Communion of Saints*, p. 177. London: Macmillan and Co. Limited, 1915.

15. 1 John 4:20.

16. Ephesians 4:25.

17. Temple, *Christian Faith and Life*, p. 127.

18. P. T. Forsyth, *This Life and the Next*, p. 82. Boston: Pilgrim Press, 1948.

19. Edmund Burke, "Reflections on the Revolution in France." He was speaking of the state.
20. Title of a book by J. Robert Nelson. London: The Epworth Press, 1951.
21. Bull, *"Unum Sancta"* 1302 A.D.
22. James Denney, *The Death of Christ*, p. 137. New York: A. C. Armstrong, 1902.
23. Lesslie Newbigin, *The Household of God*, pp. 80 f. New York: Friendship Press, 1954.

The Implications of Churchmanship

1. D. T. Niles, "The Evangelistic Situation," address reported in *The Union Seminary Quarterly Review*, Vol. XV, No. 2, January 1960, p. 114.
2. Reuel Howe, *Man's Need and God's Action*, Chapters IV-VIII. Greenwich, Conn.: The Seabury Press, 1953.
3. Randolph Crump Miller, *The Clue to Christian Education*, p. 6. New York: Charles Scribner's Sons, 1952.
4. Roger Hazelton, *The God We Worship*, p. 2. New York: The Macmillan Company, 1946.
5. Dietrich Bonhoeffer, *Life Together*, p. 30. New York: Harper & Brothers, 1954.
6. P. T. Forsyth, *The Church and the Sacraments*, p. 43. London: Independent Press, fourth impression, 1953.
7. Henry, *Evangelical Responsibility*, p. 77; cf. pp. 84 f.
8. Forsyth, *op. cit.*, p. 44.
9. J. Moffatt, *The Thrill of Tradition*, p. 3. New York: The Macmillan Company, 1944.

Something About Obscurantism

1. Title of a chapter in Floyd E. Hamilton's *The Basis of Christian Faith*. New York: George H. Doran Company, 1927.
2. D. R. Davies, *Secular Illusion or Christian Realism?*, p. xi. New York: The Macmillan Co., 1949.
3. Wick Bromall, *Biblical Criticism*, p. 11. Grand Rapids: Zondervan Publishing House, 1957. The same a priori argument—that it is inconceivable that a divinely inspired book might contain blemishes—appears in Roman Catholic thought on the Bible. Cf. the encyclical *Providentissimus Deus*.
4. James M. Gray, "The Inspiration of the Bible—Definition, Extent and Proof," in *The Fundamentals*, Vol. III, p. 9.
5. Packer, *"Fundamentalism" and the Word of God*, pp. 77-78.
6. Alec R. Vidler, *Essays in Liberality*, p. 36. London: SCM Press, 1957.
7. Ramm, *The Christian View of Science and Scripture*.
8. Ramm recognizes as living problems the issues which are being discussed in modern theology. What he says about these problems may be on the whole conservative. But the incisiveness of his contribution to evangelical thinking is shown in his ability to say something fresh and significant on such fundamental matters as authority, revelation and world view, and hermeneutics. His recognition of what the right questions for our day really are makes his writings, in my opinion, the most valuable body of

work addressed by the new generation of leaders to the conservative constituency.

9. Van Til, *The Defense of the Faith,* pp. 57 f. For Van Til, Kant is the ogre in the history of thought.

10. E. C. Blackman, *Biblical Interpretation,* p. 11. Philadelphia: The Westminster Press, 1957.

11. D. M. Baillie, *God Was in Christ,* p. 109. New York: Charles Scribner's Sons, 1948.

12. Warfield, in *American Journal of Theology,* pp. 204 f.

13. L. Harold DeWolf, *Present Trends in Christian Thought,* p. 46. New York: Association Press, 1960.

Something More About the Same

1. Blaise Pascal, *Pensées.* See Sections VI and VII, especially paragraphs 397-424.

2. William Temple, *The Hope of a New World,* p. 70. New York: The Macmillan Company, 1942.

3. The reference is to the well-known "Farewell Address" (reported by Winslow) in which Robinson counseled the Pilgrims, departing for the New World, that "If God should reveal anything to us by any other instrument of his, to be as ready to receive it, as ever we were to receive any truth by his ministry."

4. Peter Day, *Saints on Main Street,* p. 116. Greenwich, Conn.: The Seabury Press, 1960.

5. Amos N. Wilder, *The Spiritual Aspects of the New Poetry,* p. 6. New York: Harper & Brothers Publishers, 1940.

6. John Calvin, *The Institutes of the Christian Religion,* I, i, 1.

7. Nicholas Berdyaev, *Dostoievsky,* pp. 189 f. New York: Meridian Books, 1957.

8. Arthur Schlesinger, Jr., "Where Does the Liberal Go From Here?", in the *New York Times Magazine,* August 4, 1957, p. 38.

9. Vidler, *Essays in Liberality,* p. 28.

10. Packer, *"Fundamentalism" and the Word of God,* p. 127.

11. Perhaps here I may quote a paragraph from that wisest, most careful and conscientious of Christian thinkers, the Roman Catholic, Baron von Hügel:
    Religion is dim—in the religious temper there should be a great simplicity, and a certain amount of dimness. It is a great gift of God to have this temper. God does not make our lives all shipshape, clear and comfortable. Never try to get things too clear. Religion can't be clear. In this mixed-up life there will always be elements of unclearness. I believe God wills it so. There is always an element of tragedy. How can it be otherwise if Christianity is our ideal? . . . If I could understand religion as I understand that two and two make four, it would not be worth having. To me if I can see things through and through, I get uneasy—I feel it's a fake. I know I have left something out, I've made some mistake.
    From notes from conversations in the introduction by Gwendolen Greene to her edition of *Letters from Baron Friedrich von Hügel to a Niece,* p. 23. Chicago: Henry Regnery, 1955.

12. John Oman, *Vision and Authority*, p. 23. New York: Harper & Brothers Publishers, 1929. Revised edition.

The Call to Be Separate

1. Carl F. H. Henry, *Christian Personal Ethics*, pp. 425 f. Grand Rapids: Wm. B. Eerdmans Publishing Co., 1957.
2. L. David Cowie, "What is Christian Separation?", in *Christianity Today*, November 11, 1957, p. 14.
3. 1 Corinthians 5:10.
4. Dorothy L. Sayers, *Unpopular Opinions*, p. 3. New York: Harcourt Brace & Co., 1947.
5. 2 Corinthians 6:14-16.
6. Matthew 6:22-23.
7. Matthew 6:24.
8. Luke 14:26.
9. 1 Timothy 4:4.
10. Thomas Traherne, *Centuries of Meditations*, I, 29. London: P. J. & A. E. Dobell, 1908.
11. D. R. Davies, *Down Peacock's Feathers*, p. 2. New York: The Macmillan Company, 1944.
12. 1 Corinthians 8.
13. 1 Corinthians 8:4-6.
14. Psalm 104:15.
15. H. C. G. Moule, *Thoughts for the Sundays of the Year*, p. 128. London: The Religious Tract Society, 1901.
16. 1 Corinthians 10:31.
17. Galatians 5:13.
18. 1 Corinthians 10:23; 6:12.
19. 1 Corinthians 8:9, 10, 12, Phillips translation.
20. 1 Corinthians 10:32.
21. 1 Corinthians 6:12.
22. Romans 14:10.
23. Henry, *op. cit.*, p. 430.
24. Romans 14:19.
25. Romans 14:17. Cf. Jesus' similar priority, Matthew 15:18-20 (also Mark 7:14-22).
26. 2 Corinthians 6:17 (quoting Isaiah 52:11, a command to be separate from idolatry and false religions).
27. Acts 13:2.
28. Jeremiah 1:10.
29. John 20:23.
30. Exodus 32:31-32.
31. Acts 9:15.
32. Romans 9:2-3.
33. Mark 10:45.
34. Mark 8:34.

SELECTED READINGS

The following is a select and quite personal list of titles related to topics in the foregoing chapters:

Historical and critical studies of Fundamentalism:

Cole, S. G., *The History of Fundamentalism*
Furniss, N., *The Fundamentalist Controversy, 1918-1931*
Hebert, A. G., *Fundamentalism and the Church*
Henry, C. F. H., *Evangelical Responsibility in Contemporary Theology*
Packer, J. I., *"Fundamentalism" and the Word of God*

The best in Fundamentalist thought:

The conservative world is well represented by the work of: L. Berkhof, E. J. Carnell, S. G. Craig, Frank Gaebelein, Carl F. H. Henry, J. G. Machen, John Murray, B. Ramm, Wilbur M. Smith, Merrill E. Tenney, A. W. Tozer, C. Van Til, and E. J. Young.

One hardly knows how to classify, by American standards, some British and European writers, such as Berkhouwer, G. W. Bromiley, F. F. Bruce, and Leon Morris. They show agreement with Fundamentalism, along with evidences of more spacious traditions.

Surveys of modern religious thought:

Halverson, M. (ed.), *A Handbook of Christian Theology*
Hordern, W., *A Layman's Guide to Modern Theology*
Williams, D. D., *What Modern Theologians Are Thinking*

Bible—introduction and theology:

Anderson, B., *Rediscovering the Bible*
Anderson, B., *Understanding the Old Testament*
Blackburn, A. E., *Biblical Interpretation*
Bright, J., *The Kingdom of God*
Cullmann, O., *Christ and Time*
Dodd, C. H., *The Apostolic Preaching and Its Developments*
Dodd, C. H., *The Bible Today*
Dodd, C. H., *History and the Gospel*
Hoskyns and Davey, *The Riddle of the New Testament*
Minear, P., *Eyes of Faith*

Napier, B. D., *From Faith to Faith*
Neil, W., *The Rediscovery of the Bible*
Richardson, A., *An Introduction to the Theology of the New Testament*

Theology—method, general works, and special problems:

Aulén, G., *Christus Victor*
Baillie, D. M., *God Was in Christ*
Baillie, D. M., *The Theology of the Sacraments*
Baillie, J., *Our Knowledge of God*
Barth, K., *Dogmatics in Outline*
Bevan, E., *Symbolism and Belief*
Brown, R. M., *The Spirit of Protestantism*
Brunner, E., *The Divine-Human Encounter*
Brunner, E., *The Doctrine of God*
Buber, M., *I and Thou*
Caird, G. B., *The Truth of the Gospel*
Cherbonnier, E., *Hardness of Heart*
Denney, J., *Jesus and the Gospel*
Fison, J. E., *The Blessing of the Holy Spirit*
Forsyth, P. T., *The Person and Place of Jesus Christ*
Forsyth, P. T., *Positive Preaching and the Modern Mind*
Forsyth, P. T., *The Problem of Authority*
Hicks, F. C. N., *The Fullness of Sacrifice*
Jenkins, D., *Tradition, Freedom and the Spirit*
Kierkegaard, S., *Training in Christianity*
Mackintosh, H. R., *The Christian Experience of Forgiveness*
Maritain, J., *True Humanism*
Newbigin, J. E. L., *The Household of God*
Niebuhr, H. R., *The Meaning of Revelation*
Niebuhr, R., *The Nature and Destiny of Man*
Niebuhr, R., *The Self and the Dramas of History*
Oman, J., *Grace and Personality*
Quick, O., *Doctrines of the Creed*
Reid, J. K. S., *The Authority of Scripture*
Robinson, H. W., *Redemption and Revelation*
Robinson, J. A. T., *In the End, God*
Tillich, P., *Biblical Religion and the Search for Ultimate Reality*
Vidler, A., *Christian Belief*
Welch, C., *In This Name*
Welch, C., *The Reality of the Church*
Whale, J. S., *Christian Doctrine*
Whale, J. S., *Victor and Victim*
Williams, C., *The Descent of the Dove*

Christian life and mission:

Allan, T., *The Face of My Parish*
Bell, G. K. A., *The Kingship of Christ*
Berger, P., *The Noise of Solemn Assemblies*

Bonhoeffer, D., *Life Together*
Cave, S., *The Christian Way*
Coulson, C. A., *Science and Christian Belief*
Cullmann, O., *Early Christian Worship*
Davison, A., *Protestant Church Music in America*
Garrett, T. S., *Christian Worship*
Hammond, P., *Liturgy and Architecture*
Haselden, K., *The Racial Problem in Christian Perspective*
Herberg, W., *Protestant, Catholic, Jew*
Kraemer, H., *A Theology of the Laity*
Lee, R. (ed.), *Cities and Churches: Readings in the Urban Church*
Long, E., *Science and Christian Faith*
Miller, R. C., *Biblical Theology and Christian Education*
Neill, S., *Christian Holiness*
Neill, S., *The Unfinished Task*
Newbigin, J. E. L., *The Reunion of the Church*
Nichols, W., *Jacob's Ladder: The Meaning of Worship*
Niebuhr, H. R., *Christ and Culture*
Outler, A., *Psychotherapy and the Christian Message*
Roberts, D., *Psychotherapy and a Christian View of Man*
Robinson, J. A. T., *On Being the Church in the World*
Sherrill, L. J., *The Gift of Power*
Smart, J., *The Teaching Ministry of the Church*
Temple, W., *Christianity and the Social Order*
Tournier, P., *The Meaning of Persons*
Vidler, A., *Essays in Liberality*
Wilder, A., *Modern Poetry and the Christian Tradition*
Wylie, S., *New Patterns for Christian Action*

THE CHEMISTRY OF THE LANTHANIDES

Selected Topics in Modern Chemistry

SERIES EDITORS

Professor Harry H. Sisler
Department of Chemistry
University of Florida

Professor Calvin A. VanderWerf
Department of Chemistry
University of Kansas

Published

EYRING AND EYRING—*Modern Chemical Kinetics*
KIEFFER—*The Mole Concept in Chemistry*
MOELLER—*The Chemistry of the Lanthanides*
OVERMAN—*Basic Concepts of Nuclear Chemistry*
RYSCHKEWITSCH—*Chemical Bonding and the Geometry of Molecules*
SISLER—*Chemistry in Non-Aqueous Solvents*
VANDERWERF—*Acids, Bases, and the Chemistry of the Covalent Bond*

In Press

HILDEBRAND—*An Introduction to Molecular Kinetic Theory*
SISLER—*Structure, Properties, and the Periodic Law*

(Many additional titles are in preparation.)

When a master teacher of chemistry, known for his lucid writing, has free rein to present the area in which he is a world-renowned research expert, the result is certain to be engrossing. And when that area is one which uniquely illustrates the application of certain principles of chemistry, the product is bound to be of utmost value and usefulness.

Professor Moeller's appealing and representative vignette of modern inorganic chemistry is all this and more. The fun Dr. Moeller had in writing "The Chemistry of the Lanthanides" will be mirrored by your enjoyment as you read it. And in the reading you will acquire a clearer insight into many basic relationships between atomic structure and properties of the elements.

You will discover also that a thorough understanding of the lanthanides provides the ideal approach to the fascinating chemistry of the actinides. And, just as important, you will find completely infectious the author's spirit of research— his enthusiasm for the challenge and lure of the unsolved problem and the unanswered question.

As editors we are proud to add Professor Moeller's book, a thoroughly readable blending of fact and principle, to SELECTED TOPICS IN MODERN CHEMISTRY. We are confident that you will find it interesting, stimulating, and useful.

Harry H. Sisler
Calvin A. VanderWerf

THE CHEMISTRY OF
THE LANTHANIDES

THERALD MOELLER

Professor of Inorganic Chemistry
University of Illinois
Urbana, Illinois

New York
REINHOLD PUBLISHING CORPORATION
Chapman & Hall, Ltd., London

PREFACE

There is sufficient of the unexpected, the unpredicted, and the unusual in most chemistry to make its study and practice a fascinating experience. Each of these terms aptly describes the type of chemistry that provides the basis for this small volume. In a sense, each also describes the preparation of "The Chemistry of the Lanthanides," for little did the author realize that a seminar assignment in this area received in graduate school would both open to him an interesting region for subsequent research and provide him ultimately with the incentive to prepare this manuscript. If a perusal of this account provides the reader with both information and an appreciation of the intriguing problems that remain to be solved, the author will count the intervening years as usefully spent.

"The Chemistry of the Lanthanides" is more than a mere description of the behavior of a series of elements. It is also a presentation of the theoretical principles that can be invoked to account for this behavior and a discussion of the applications and limitations of these principles. In this sense, it is a representative fragment of modern inorganic chemistry, for inorganic chemistry in its truest sense is a balanced and reasonable combination of fact and principle where the former is used to test and support or negate the latter. The lanthanides, because of their marked similarities and generally uniform changes in properties with change in atomic number, are ideal subjects for such a presentation and serve well to introduce the beginning student to a variety of useful principles.

The past several years have witnessed a somewhat dramatic rebirth of interest in the lanthanides. In part, this has stemmed from the general renaissance that has characterized inorganic chemistry as a whole; in part, it has come from the search for new materials with new properties that are essential to solving the many problems of our expanding technology; in part, also, it has arisen from the realization that the chemistry of plutonium and the other transuranium species could best be approached by way of a thorough understanding of that of the only other truly analogous elements, the lanthanides. Our presentation, then, is a blend of traditional observation with the modern, followed by a projection to the heavy elements. If the order followed appears, on occasion, somewhat unconventional, it is the result of the author's conviction that the importance of this blend requires a logical, but not necessarily chronological, development of ideas.

To name all of those whose research contributions and whose friendly and stimulating discussions have provided the author with the background for this discussion would be impossibly difficult. The author can do no more than say "Thank you" to each, with the hope that in such a simple way he can indicate the depth of his gratitude. He is, of course, indebted particularly to the late Professor B. Smith Hopkins of the University of Illinois—that fine gentleman, able investigator, and outstanding teacher who first provided him with purified materials for research and encouraged him at the incidence of his academic career.

The author is deeply grateful to Miss Jeanne C. Hammer for her very substantial assistance in preparing the manuscript.

THERALD MOELLER

Urbana, Illinois
February, 1963

CONTENTS

INTRODUCTION—AN ERA OF DISCOVERY, CONFUSION, AND ELUCIDATION

What has developed into a fascinating realm of chemistry embracing both a series of naturally occurring elements of extraordinary similarity and a closely comparable series of synthetically produced elements of rather remarkable properties had its origin in the somewhat accidental discovery by Swedish Army Lieutenant C. A. Arrhenius in 1787 of an unusual black mineral specimen at a quarry at Ytterby, a small community not far from Stockholm. When, in 1794, Johan Gadolin, a Finnish chemist at the University of Åbo, separated from samples of this mineral about 38% of a new and previously undescribed "earth" (or *oxide*, in our more modern terminology), the basis for a series of investigations extending through the present was unwittingly laid. It remained only for A. G. Ekeberg, at Uppsala, to suggest in 1797 the name *gadolinite* for the mineral and the name *yttria* for the new earth.

Shortly thereafter (in 1803), M. H. Klaproth, a German investigator, and, independently, J. J. Berzelius, the renowned

Swedish chemist, and his collaborator Wilhelm Hisinger isolated from a heavy mineral (originally found in 1871 in a mine at Bastnäs, Sweden, by A. F. Cronstedt) another similar and yet somewhat different earth. This was named *ceria*, after the then recently discovered planetoid Ceres, and the mineral *cerite*.

It was believed at the time that both yttria and ceria were derived from single elements. Yet subsequent study showed each to be a complex mixture of oxides, the complete simplification of which required more than a century of effort. This was an era of substantially blind experimentation complicated by a lack of understanding of why these substances are so closely similar, no appreciation of even how many elemental species might be involved, and a lack of positive experimental means of absolute identification of supposedly pure samples. If errors were made—and there were many—and if confusion arose—as it did in many instances—we may and should nevertheless pay tribute to the perserverance of the host of investigators who succeeded ultimately in unraveling one of the most complicated of all chemical problems.

The Simplification of Ceria and Yttria

Proof of the ultimate complexity of both ceria and yttria was given many years after their isolation by C. G. Mosander, a Swedish surgeon, chemist, and mineralogist, who was for a time an assistant to Berzelius. During the period 1839–1841, Mosander thermally decomposed a nitrate obtained from ceria and treated the product with dilute nitric acid. From the resulting solution, he then isolated first a new earth, *lanthana*, and then later another new earth, *didymia* (the twin brother of lanthana), of similar chemical, but slightly different physical properties. Similarly, in 1843, Mosander separated from the original yttria three oxide fractions: one white (*yttria*), one yellow (old *erbia*), and one rose-colored (old *terbia*).

There was again an extensive period of intense but unproductive activity, which then culminated in the partial and finally ultimate simplification of these two complex oxides. The more significant developments, including the names of the principal investigators and the origin of the names of the numerous elements, are summarized in Tables 1.1 and 1.2. The striking parallels between the investigations of the two oxides are at once apparent, as are, of course, certain items of confusion. One of the most significant of the latter concerns the reversal of names of erbia and terbia (Table 1.2), which prompts the distinction old erbia vs. new erbia and old terbia vs. new terbia. In both of these tables, the earth names are used for mixtures and the modern names of the elements, together with their symbols, for separated and clearly identified species.

Tables 1.1 and 1.2 cannot begin to suggest the complexities of the problems encountered. There was an understandable confusion among other names, prompted of course by the poor communication among workers in the 19th and early 20th centuries. The reported discovery of elements other than those now accepted was not uncommon. Although these often proved to be mixtures, on occasion more than one worker independently isolated the same material. Cases in point include gadolinium (first isolated from yttria by the Swiss chemist de Marignac in 1880 and later, in 1885, obtained from ceria by the French investigator de Boisbaudran) and lutetium (announced in 1907 by the Frenchman Urbain but obtained nearly simultaneously by both the Austrian von Welsbach and the American James). Tables 1.1 and 1.2 do serious injustice to the countless other workers who contributed data that aided materially in making possible the discoveries outlined.

TABLE 1.1. The Simplification of Ceria*

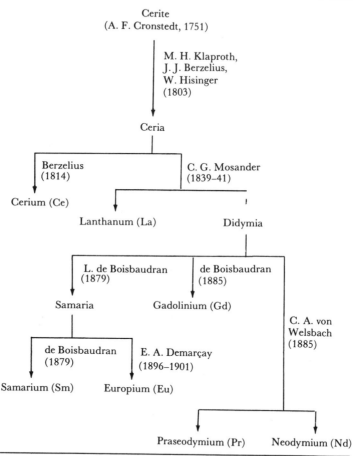

* *Origin of names:* lanthanum—to lie hidden; cerium—planetoid Ceres; praseo-dymium—green twin; neodymium—new twin; samarium—mineral samarskite; europium—Europe; gadolinium—Gadolin.

TABLE 1.2.   The Simplification of Yttria*

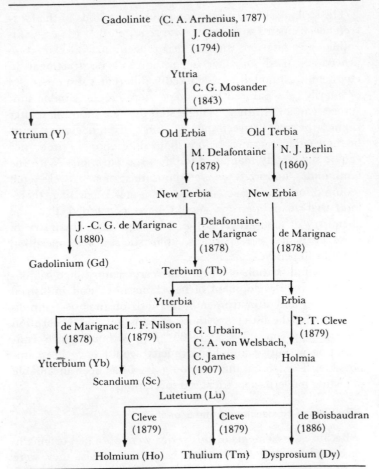

* *Origin of names:* yttrium, ytterbium, erbium, terbium—Ytterby; gadolinium—Gadolin; dysprosium—difficult of access; holmium—Stockholm; thulium—Thule (ancient name of Scandinavia); lutetium—Lutetia (ancient name of Paris); scandium—Scandinavia.

Some Consequences and Conclusions

The striking similarities among the compounds of the fourteen new elements so characterized required that the crystallization, precipitation, thermal decomposition, and extraction procedures used for their separation all be fractional in character. Although two markedly different substances can ordinarily be separated in a single step, closely similar substances cannot. Rather, a single step does no more than alter slightly the ratio between the two, and a given operation must be repeated many times before slight differences in properties can be sufficiently magnified to effect a separation. With the lanthanides, hundreds (or even thousands) of steps were often required for ultimate separation. It is not surprising, therefore, that many persons should have concluded that the chemistry of separations is the only important chemistry of these elements, nor, perhaps, that such a misconception should still persist.

The simplification of yttria and ceria contributed significantly to the development of new laboratory and industrial techniques and of instrumental methods of analysis. Prominent among the latter are those of emission and absorption spectroscopy (pp. 15, 25, 29–33, 74), without which confirmation of purity and homogeneity would have been impossible. The factual information gained has been invaluable in testing modern theoretical interpretations.

A Problem of Nomenclature and Scarcity

Because the elements of this series were obtained originally as earths (oxides) from relatively rare minerals, they were characterized as *rare earths*. Although this name is still used, it is an unfortunate one because of its implications. Crustal abundance data, as summarized in Table 1.3, indicate clearly that the lanthanides are at least as abundant as many of the commoner elements and that over-all supplies are potentially unlimited. That this is seldom appreciated is convincing proof that a scientific idea, once advanced, is never easy to dispel, regardless of its lack of merit.

TABLE 1.3. Abundances of Elements in Igneous Rocks of Crust of the Earth

Symbol	Atomic number	Abundance, g./metric ton	Symbol	Atomic number	Abundance, g./metric ton
Sc	21	5	Be	4	6
Y	39	28.1	B	5	<3
La	57	18.3	N	7	46.3
Ce	58	46.1	Co	27	23
Pr	59	5.53	Cu	29	70
Nd	60	23.9	Ga	31	15
Pm	61	ca. 0	Ge	32	7
Sm	62	6.47	As	33	5
Eu	63	1.06	Br	35	1.62
Gd	64	6.36	Mo	42	2.5–15
Tb	65	0.91	Ag	47	0.1
Dy	66	4.47	Cd	48	0.15
Ho	67	1.15	Sn	50	40
Er	68	2.47	Sb	51	1
Tm	69	0.2	I	53	0.1
Yb	70	2.66	Pb	82	16
Lu	71	0.75	Bi	83	0.2

At the present, the name *lanthanides* is preferred for these elements. This derives, of course, from lanthanum, the first of the elements of the series in order of increasing atomic number. For reasons that are discussed later (pp. 20–25), we include yttrium as a lanthanide, although it differs significantly in atomic weight (p. 37) and other properties (pp. 58–59). Other names in use are *lanthanide elements*, *lanthanons*, and *f-type transition elements*. The significance of the last of these is brought out in Chapter 2.

Element 61—Will-o'-the-Wisp or Actuality?

A comparison of the elements listed in Tables 1.1 and 1.2 with those in Table 1.3, where atomic numbers are given, shows that thus far we have given no information on element 61, i.e., the element that should appear between neodymium and samarium.

None of the investigations previously outlined gave any indication of the existence of such an element in the materials recovered. It is significant, however, that in 1902 Bohuslav Brauner, of the Bohemian University in Prague, suggested that such an element should exist. With the development of information on electronic configurations (pp. 13–16), the reasonableness of this prediction became evident, and several exhaustive searches were made, using largely neodymium-samarium fractions where this element might most logically be expected to concentrate. Although these were notably unsuccessful, in 1926, B. S. Hopkins, L. F. Yntema, and J. A. Harris, of the University of Illinois, and L. Rolla and L. Fernandes, of the Royal University in Florence, Italy, independently offered spectroscopic evidence for the existence of the element in minute quantities in various concentrates. The names *illinium* and *florentium* were proposed by these two groups, respectively. Subsequent research has failed to confirm these findings. In 1947, J. A. Marinsky, L. E. Glendenin, and C. D. Coryell reported the ion-exchange separation and identification (p. 81) of an isotope of this element, using materials obtained at Oak Ridge, Tennessee, from the fission of uranium. Subsequently, many grams of its salts have been recovered from this source. The name *promethium* (from Prometheus) is now universally accepted.

Inasmuch as small quantities of uranium are always undergoing fission, one cannot deny the absolute existence of promethium in nature. The isotopes so obtained—and, in

TABLE 1.4. Isotopes of Promethium

Mass number	Type of decay*	Half-life	Source
141	β^+	20 min.	
142	β^+	30 sec.	Daughter ^{142}Sm
143	EC, γ	270 days	
144	EC, γ	300 days	
145	β^+	16 days	
	EC, γ	18 yr.	Daughter ^{145}Sm
146	β^-	ca. 1 yr.	
147	β^-, γ	2.64 yr.	Fission ^{235}U
148	β^-, γ	42 days	
149	β^-, γ	54 hr.	Daughter ^{149}Nd
150	β^-, γ	2.7 hr.	
151	β^-, γ	27.5 hr.	Daughter ^{151}Nd

* EC = electron capture.

fact, all known isotopes of the element—decay spontaneously (Table 1.4) with such short half-lives* that it seems highly improbable that sufficient promethium could exist in nature to permit its chemical isolation. However, until it has been shown clearly that no stable or very long-lived isotope can exist, that no natural decay process (beyond fission) is continually generating a promethium isotope, and that exact repetition under carefully controlled conditions of the experiments upon which claims of isolation were based gives negative results, we cannot conclude with absolute scientific accuracy that recovery of compounds of this element from a natural source is impossible.

In any event, fission-product promethium is a true lanthanide, with properties intermediate between those of neodymium and samarium.

* Each radioactive, or spontaneously unstable, isotope has a characteristic half-life, or time necessary for one-half of the quantity present to disintegrate. Unless a species is continuously generated, it cannot occur in nature if its half-life is less than the age of the earth, i.e., about 10^9 years.

Close Relatives—The Actinides

Of all the other elements, only those with atomic numbers 89–103 (i.e., actinium through lawrencium, or the actinides) resemble the lanthanides closely in all characteristics. Only the lightest of these elements exist in nature. The others must be obtained synthetically, and such processes may yield only a few atoms of product. Fortunately, it has been possible to use the known chemistry of the lanthanides to develop the chemistry of the actinides.

Recapitulation—and Then?

We have chosen to introduce the chemistry of the lanthanides in such a fashion as to raise many questions in your mind. Among these must be at least the following:

1. Why do we have such a series of closely related elements?
2. Can we account logically for both the distinct similarities and slight differences noted among these elements and their compounds?
3. How can we classify these elements in the Periodic Table?
4. To what extent can we account for differences between these elements and other elements?
5. Why do we have another series of elements (the actinides) that resembles the lanthanides?
6. What advances have been made subsequent to those outlined above?
7. To what extent can we take practical advantage of the apparently different properties that must characterize this series?

It will be our purpose in subsequent chapters to provide answers to these and other questions. To a fair degree, this may be done by developing first some principles based largely upon atomic structures. This we do in Chapter 2.

Selected Readings

Boyd, G. E., *J. Chem. Educ.*, **36,** 3–14 (1959). (Promethium.)

Spencer, J. F., "The Metals of the Rare Earths," ch. I, Longmans, Green, London, 1919. (History.)

Vickery, R. C., "Chemistry of the Lanthanons," ch. 1, Academic Press, New York, 1953. (History.)

Weeks, M. E., "Discovery of the Elements," 6th ed., chs. 26, 31, The Journal of Chemical Education, Easton, Pa., 1956. (History.)

Yost, D. M., Russell, H., Jr., and Garner, C. S., "The Rare-Earth Elements and Their Compounds," ch. 4, John Wiley & Sons, New York, 1947. (Promethium.)

chapter two

ATOMIC STRUCTURE AND ITS CONSEQUENCES—THE DAWN OF UNDERSTANDING

If, as is suggested by the developments outlined in Chapter 1, there is an essential uniqueness in the chemistry of the lanthanides, it must, as we now know, reside in the structures of their individual atoms and ions. From modern extensions of Niels Bohr's 1913 theory of the hydrogen atom we know that as the complexity of the nucleus is increased as a result of addition of protons (and neutrons), each of the electrons needed to preserve electroneutrality seeks out not only the least energetic of the possible principal quantum levels available but also the least energetic of the several possible subsidiary levels, or *orbitals*, within that principal level. It is thus feasible to classify the elements in terms of the electronic configurations characterizing these low-energy, or *ground-state*, arrangements, and to distinguish groups of elements of potentially (and actually) similar properties in terms of observed similarities in ground-state configuration.

Electronic Configurations of the Lanthanides

The over-all properties of the lanthanides suggest that they are members of a subgroup within Periodic Group III (i.e., family IIIb). The ground-state electronic configurations

Sc $Z = 21$ $1s^2 2s^2 2p^6 3s^2 3p^6 3d^1 4s^2$
       or Ar core $+ 3d^1 4s^2$

Y $Z = 39$ $1s^2 2s^2 2p^6 3s^2 3p^6 3d^{10} 4s^2 4p^6 4d^1 5s^2$
       or Kr core $+ 4d^1 5s^2$

La $Z = 57$ $1s^2 2s^2 2p^6 3s^2 3p^6 3d^{10} 4s^2 4p^6 4d^{10} 5s^2 5p^6 5d^1 6s^2$
       or Xe core $+ 5d^1 6s^2$

Ac $Z = 89$ $1s^2 2s^2 2p^6 3s^2 3p^6 3d^{10} 4s^2 4p^6 4d^{10} 4f^{14} 5s^2 5p^6 5d^{10} 6s^2 6p^6 6d^1 7s^2$
       or Rn core $+ 6d^1 7s^2$

indicate clearly that the elements usually listed in this family are the first members of the four d-type transition series. After scandium and yttrium, the electrons required to give elements of steadily increasing atomic number are added, respectively, to the $3d$ and $4d$ levels, and the remaining elements of the first and second transition series thus result. After lanthanum, however, the energy of the $4f$ level falls below that of the $5d$, and subsequent electrons are thus added to the inner, shielded $4f$ orbitals. Inasmuch as there are seven such orbitals, each with a capacity of two electrons,[*] a total of 14 elements of this *inner* or f-type transition series may then result before the $5d$ orbitals can again fill regularly. This accounts for the elements cerium through lutetium ($Z = 58$–71) and requires that hafnium ($Z = 72$, $4f^{14} 5d^2 6s^2$) be a strict electronic analog of zirconium ($Z = 40$, $4d^2 5s^2$) and not a lanthanide. A similar situation exists after actinium (p. 99), with

[*] That each orbital can have two electrons is a consequence of the fact that two electrons may be alike in all properties except spin about their own axes. The Hund Principle of Maximum Multiplicity requires that within a given set of orbitals (here $4f$) each orbital must be occupied singly before any pairing of electrons through double occupancy can occur.

preferential occupancy of the $5f$ orbitals thus accounting for the actinides.

Although it is implied that the $4f$ orbitals are occupied regularly, the data in Table 2.1 show clearly that this is not exactly true. Instead, there is a distinct tendency for the f orbitals to be occupied in preference to maintaining the

TABLE 2.1   Ground-State Electronic Configurations of Atoms

Element	Atomic number (Z)	Configuration	
		Idealized	Observed[*]
Sc	21	$3d^1 4s^2$	$3d^1 4s^2$
Y	39	$4d^1 5s^2$	$4d^1 5s^2$
La	57	$5d^1 6s^2$	$5d^1 6s^2$
Ce	58	$4f^1\ 5d^1 6s^2$	$4f^1\ 5d^1 6s^2$
Pr	59	$4f^2\ 5d^1 6s^2$	$4f^3\quad 6s^2$
Nd	60	$4f^3\ 5d^1 6s^2$	$4f^4\quad 6s^2$
Pm	61	$4f^4\ 5d^1 6s^2$	$4f^5\quad 6s^2$
Sm	62	$4f^5\ 5d^1 6s^2$	$4f^6\quad 6s^2$
Eu	63	$4f^6\ 5d^1 6s^2$	$4f^7\quad 6s^2$
Gd	64	$4f^7\ 5d^1 6s^2$	$4f^7\ 5d^1 6s^2$
Tb	65	$4f^8\ 5d^1 6s^2$	$4f^9\quad 6s^2$
			(or $4f^8 5d^1 6s^2$)
Dy	66	$4f^9\ 5d^1 6s^2$	$4f^{10}\quad 6s^2$
Ho	67	$4f^{10} 5d^1 6s^2$	$4f^{11}\quad 6s^2$
Er	68	$4f^{11} 5d^1 6s^2$	$4f^{12}\quad 6s^2$
Tm	69	$4f^{12} 5d^1 6s^2$	$4f^{13}\quad 6s^2$
Yb	70	$4f^{13} 5d^1 6s^2$	$4f^{14}\quad 6s^2$
Lu	71	$4f^{14} 5d^1 6s^2$	$4f^{14} 5d^1 6s^2$

[*] Cunningham, B. B., "Rare Earth Research," E. V. Kleber, Ed., pp. 127–30, The Macmillan Company, New York, 1961.

$4f^n 5d^1$ arrangement that such an idealized picture would require. This tendency is a reflection of the enhanced electronic stability that is associated with complete single (here $4f^7$) or complete double (here $4f^{14}$) occupancy of any set of orbitals. Thus, the $4f^7$ and $4f^{14}$ arrangements are achieved as soon as possible (at europium and ytterbium, respectively). Gadolinium, at the exact center of the series, has the expected $4f^7 5d^1 6s^2$ ground-state configuration.

Electronic configurations are most commonly established experimentally as interpretations of observed emission spectra. This technique is based on the fact that each line in an emission spectrum reflects the energy change involved in the transition of an electron from one energy level to another. If the spectrum contains only a few lines, its interpretation is comparatively easy, and an unambiguous ground-state configuration can be established for the atom in question. If, as is true with many of the lanthanides, the spectrum is highly complex, the establishment of an absolutely correct configuration is extremely difficult. The problem with the lanthanides concerns primarily the presence or absence of a $5d$ electron. This arises, of course, from the fact that the $5d$ and $4f$ orbitals have so nearly the same energy that distinction between the two is difficult. The configurations summarized in Table 2.1 are the best available from spectroscopic and atomic beam resonance data. It is probable that no more than minor changes in them will be made as a result of future studies.

Whether the fundamental configuration is $4f^n 5d^1 6s^2$ or $4f^{n+1} 6s^2$ is of far less chemical than physical significance, since the energy differences are too small to alter many chemical properties. To some extent, lanthanum and lutetium are cases in point, since their observed chemical characteristics are nearly the same as those of the adjacent lanthanides.

That such similar electronic configurations should result in striking similarities among the chemical properties of the lanthanides is both reasonable and in keeping with experimental observation. The $4f$ electrons differentiating the several elements from one another are sufficiently well shielded by intervening electron shells as to be largely unavailable for chemical interaction, and this feature distinguishes the lanthanides from the d-type transition elements, in which the d electrons are the "outermost" or valence electrons and are involved when chemical reactions occur.

The fundamental similarity in "outer" electronic configuration between the lanthanides and scandium, yttrium, and actinium favors classification of all these elements together in the same periodic family. The physical limitations of the Periodic Table as it is usually drawn, however, result in our placing the lanthanides (and actinides) apart from the remaining elements. Neither scandium nor yttrium is properly a lanthanide, as far as electronic configuration is concerned, nor properly is lanthanum since it has no 4*f* electrons. Property-wise, as has been indicated and will be shown further in the next section, yttrium and lanthanum are better discussed with the lanthanides than with any other elements. Scandium, on the other hand, is markedly different (p. 24). Even though scandium was first isolated from yttria sources (Table 1.2), its primary mode of natural occurrence is not with the lanthanides.

Some Indirect Consequences of Electronic Configuration

Certain of the questions (1, 3, 5) raised in Chapter 1 have now been answered solely in terms of the ground-state electronic configurations of the atoms. The answers to others may be obtained on a similar basis, but somewhat less directly. Two of these relate to the marked similarities among compounds that puzzled early workers and the slight differences that enabled these workers to effect separations.

Oxidation States. It was observed even during pioneering studies that in their commonest compounds the lanthanides are uniformly *tripositive*. It is true that early investigators recognized *tetrapositive* cerium and higher-valent praseodymium and terbium as the dark-colored oxides Pr_6O_{11} and Tb_4O_7, but it was not until the 20th century that *dipositive* europium, ytterbium, and samarium were characterized.

Indeed, it was not until the 1950's that truly praseodymium(IV) and terbium(IV) compounds were described and not until the 1960's that tetrapositive neodymium and dysprosium and dipositive cerium, neodymium, and thulium were obtained. Of the nontripositive states, only tetrapositive cerium, praseodymium, and terbium and dipositive samarium, europium, and ytterbium have sufficient chemical stability to be of importance. Yttrium is always tripositive in its compounds.

That direct correlation between oxidation state and electronic configuration is the exception rather than the rule is shown by the data in Table 2.2. Inasmuch as the $6s^2$ configuration is the most generally characteristic one for the lanthanides (Table 2.1), a uniform dipositive state might be expected. Furthermore, although the removal of an additional $5d$ electron, by analogy to what occurs with d-type transition elements, might be reasonable, the cases where this is possible are obviously limited. Penetration of the $4f$ arrangement is

TABLE 2.2.   Distinguishing Electronic Configurations for Observed Oxidation States

Symbol	Configuration		
	+2	+3	+4
La		$4f^0$ (La^{3+})	
Ce	$4f^2$ $(CeCl_2)$	$4f^1$ (Ce^{3+})	$4f^0$ (Ce^{4+})
Pr		$4f^2$ (Pr^{3+})	$4f^1$ (PrO_2, Na_2PrF_6)
Nd	$4f^4$ (NdI_2)	$4f^3$ (Nd^{3+})	$4f^2$ (Cs_3NdF_7)
Pm		$4f^4$ (Pm^{3+})	
Sm	$4f^6$ (Sm^{2+})	$4f^5$ (Sm^{3+})	
Eu	$4f^7$ (Eu^{2+})	$4f^6$ (Eu^{3+})	
Gd		$4f^7$ (Gd^{3+})	
Tb		$4f^8$ (Tb^{3+})	$4f^7$ (TbO_2, TbF_4)
Dy		$4f^9$ (Dy^{3+})	$4f^8$ (Cs_3DyF_7)
Ho		$4f^{10}$ (Ho^{3+})	
Er		$4f^{11}$ (Er^{3+})	
Tm	$4f^{13}$ (TmI_2)	$4f^{12}$ (Tm^{3+})	
Yb	$4f^{14}$ (Yb^{2+})	$4f^{13}$ (Yb^{3+})	
Lu		$4f^{14}$ (Lu^{3+})	

thus essential, but why should this result preferentially in the tripositive state for all the elements?

This question can be answered only qualitatively. If the tripositive state is the preferred one in aqueous solution, then oxidation, as represented by the equation (Ln = any lanthanide)

$$Ln^{3+}(aq) + \tfrac{1}{4}O_2(g) + H^+(aq) \rightleftharpoons Ln^{4+}(aq) + \tfrac{1}{2}H_2O(l)$$

or reduction, as represented by the equation

$$Ln^{3+}(aq) + \tfrac{1}{2}H_2(g) \rightleftharpoons Ln^{2+}(aq) + H^+(aq)$$

must be unfavorable. It can be shown, although the treatment is more involved than we need consider here, that the conversion from one oxidation state to another in aqueous solution is controlled by the magnitudes of the energy required to remove an electron from the gaseous ion in its lower oxidation state (i.e., *ionization energy*) and of the energies released when the two gaseous ions combine with water to form the aquated species (*energy of hydration*). Calculation on this basis shows that in solution, all tetrapositive species (except possibly Ce^{4+}) and all dipositive species (except Eu^{2+}) must revert to the tripositive. This leads to the conclusion that the tripositive state owes its general stability to a somewhat fortuitous combination of ionization and hydration energies rather than to any particular electronic configuration.

Similarly, oxidation and reduction among solid compounds can be related to the magnitudes of the ionization energy and the energy released when the gaseous ions combine to produce crystalline solids (i.e., the *lattice* or *crystal energy*). Again, a fortuitous combination of these renders the tripositive state the most common, but the energy conditions are more favorable to the existence of nontripositive species (Table 2.2) in the solid state than in solution.

The ease of formation of the various oxidation states in solu-

TABLE 2.3. Standard Oxidation Potential Data[*] for Acidic Solutions

Symbol	E^{*}_{298}, v.	Symbol	E^{*}_{298}, v.
	Couples $Ln^0 - Ln^{III}$		
	$Ln(s) \rightleftharpoons Ln^{3+}(aq) + 3e^-$		
Y	+2.37	Gd	+2.40
La	2.52	Tb	2.39
Ce	2.48	Dy	2.35
Pr	2.47	Ho	2.32
Nd	2.44	Er	2.30
Pm	2.42	Tm	2.28
Sm	2.41	Yb	2.27
Eu	2.41	Lu	2.25
	Couples $Ln^{II} - Ln^{III}$		
	$Ln^{2+}(aq) \rightleftharpoons Ln^{3+}(aq) + e^-$		
Sm	+1.55	Yb	+1.15
Eu	0.43		
	Couples $Ln^{III} - Ln^{IV}$		
	$Ln^{3+}(aq) \rightleftharpoons Ln^{4+}(aq) + e^-$		
Ce	−1.74	Pr	−2.86

[*] Estimated, in many cases.

tion is indicated by the standard oxidation potential data summarized in Table 2.3. It is apparent that the elemental lanthanides are very powerful reducing agents and that oxidation to the tripositive state occurs readily and vigorously. The enhanced stabilities of the empty, half-filled, and completely filled $4f$ arrangements are also indicated by these data. Thus cerium(IV), with its $4f^0$ configuration, is much less readily reduced to the tripositive state than the $4f^1$ species praseodymium(IV). Furthermore, the $4f^7$ species europium(II) and the $4f^{14}$ species ytterbium(II) are the weakest reducing agents of the dipositive species. The preponderance of $4f^0$ species (La^{III}, Ce^{IV}), $4f^7$ species (Eu^{II}, Gd^{III}, Tb^{IV}), and $4f^{14}$ species (Yb^{II}, Lu^{III}) supports this general relationship.

Size Relationships. The sizes of atoms and ions are determined both by nuclear charge and by the number and degree of occupancy of electronic shells. Both of these factors are reflected in the data for atomic and crystal (ionic) radii summarized in Table 2.4. Thus, among either the metals Sc, Y, La or the ions Sc^{3+}, Y^{3+}, La^{3+} there is a steady increase in size with increase in atomic number, corresponding to the fact that addition of electrons to higher and higher energy levels overcomes increasing contractive effects that result from the enhanced attraction produced by larger nuclear charge. In the series La–Lu or La^{3+}–Lu^{3+}, however, a general decrease in size with increase in atomic number results because addition of electrons to the shielded $4f$ orbitals cannot compensate for the effect of increased nuclear charge. A similar but more limited trend characterizes the nontripositive ions. These

TABLE 2.4. Size Relationships

Symbol	Atomic number	Atomic radius,* Å.	Crystal or ionic radius, Å.		
			Ln^{2+}	Ln^{3+}	Ln^{4+}
Sc	21	1.641		0.68	
Y	39	1.801		0.88	
La	57	1.877		1.061	
Ce	58	1.82		1.034	0.92
Pr	59	1.828		1.013	0.90
Nd	60	1.821		0.995	
Pm	61	—		(0.979)	
Sm	62	1.802	1.11	0.964	
Eu	63	2.042	1.09	0.950	
Gd	64	1.802		0.938	
Tb	65	1.782		0.923	0.84
Dy	66	1.773		0.908	
Ho	67	1.766		0.894	
Er	68	1.757		0.881	
Tm	69	1.746	0.94	0.869	
Yb	70	1.940	0.93	0.858	
Lu	71	1.734		0.848	

* For structures in which each atom has 12 other atoms as nearest neighbors.

decreases are known as the *Lanthanide Contraction*. The general decrease in crystal radius from Ln^{2+} to Ln^{3+} to Ln^{4+} reflects increasing cationic charge.

As indicated in Fig. 2.1, the lanthanide contraction is essen-

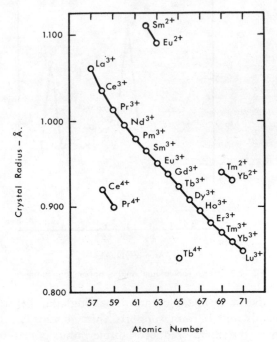

Fig. 2.1. Crystal radii of Ln^{2+}, Ln^{3+}, and Ln^{4+} ions.

tially parallel among the di-, tri-, and tetrapositive ions. A slight, but detectable, discontinuity among the tripositive ions appears at gadolinium. Fig. 2.2 shows the contraction among the metals, but indicates dramatically the large atomic radii of europium and ytterbium. It is believed that these seemingly anomalous values reflect a tendency for these two elements to

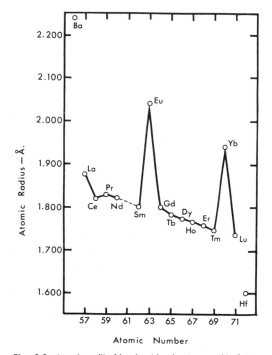

Fig. 2.2. Atomic radii of lanthanides, barium, and hafnium.

be dipositive in the metallic state. The rough parallel between these metals and barium supports this contention. Correspondingly, the slightly reduced atomic radius of cerium may suggest a tetravalent state (compare hafnium, Fig. 2.2).

Atomic and ionic radii affect those properties of the metals and their cations, respectively, that reflect attraction or lack of attraction for electrons and anions, i.e., properties of *basicity*. Broadly, basicity is a measure of the ease with which a species loses electrons or of the lack of attraction which a cation has for electrons or anions. Thus, radii are important in terms of both (1) their absolute magnitudes and (2) their change with atomic number.

1. *Consequences of Numerical Magnitude.* Both the atoms and their derived cations are comparatively large (Table 2.5). Observations that the elemental lanthanides are powerful reducing agents (Table 2.3), comparable in strength to the alkaline earth metals and greater in strength than most metals that yield tripositive ions, correlate well with the large atomic radii. Observations that compounds of the lanthanides have

TABLE 2.5. Some Comparative Atomic and Crystal Radii (Ångstrom units)

Type of radius	Lanthanides		Nonlanthanides	
Atomic	La	1.877	Al	1.248
	Gd	1.802	Fe	1.165
	Lu	1.734	Ca	1.736
	Eu	2.042	Sr	1.914
	Yb	1.940	Ba	1.981
Crystal (M^{2+})	Sm	1.11	Fe	0.74
	Eu	1.09	Ca	0.99
	Tm	0.94	Sr	1.12
	Yb	0.92	Ba	1.34
Crystal (M^{3+})	La	1.061	Al	0.51
	Gd	0.938	Cr	0.63
	Lu	0.848	Fe	0.64
			Ac	1.11
Crystal (M^{4+})	Ce	0.92	Zr	0.79
	Pr	0.90	Hf	0.78
	Tb	0.84	Th	0.99
			U	0.93

pronounced ionic character and that complex species are limited correlate with the reduced attractions for anions and polar groups resulting from large cationic radii. The close parallel suggested between the dipositive species and the heavier alkaline earth metal ions is supported by experimental observation (pp. 44–45). The large tripositive ions resemble strikingly only the comparably sized actinide ions (pp. 101, 104).

Similarly, cerium(IV) resembles tetrapositive thorium and uranium but not zirconium and hafnium.

2. *Consequences of the Lanthanide Contraction.* These include the position of yttrium, variations in properties among the lanthanides, and variations in properties among the species that follow the lanthanides in atomic number.

The magnitude of the lanthanide contraction is such that the crystal radius of the Y^{3+} ion is reached in the holmium-erbium region. The resulting similarity in size, coupled of course with equality in ionic charge, accounts reasonably for the invariable natural occurrence of yttrium with the heavier lanthanides (pp. 67–70); for the difficulties experienced in separating yttrium from these elements (Chapter 1); and for the marked similarities in crystal structure, solubility, and chemical properties between yttrium compounds and those of the heavier lanthanides that make yttrium a practical member of this series. Indeed, the behavior of the more abundant yttrium (Table 1.3) is considered to be so characteristic of these elements that they are referred to as *yttrium earths*. The rather marked differences observed between the chemistry of scandium and that of the lanthanides are consistent with the fact that the Sc^{3+} ion is much smaller than even the Lu^{3+} ion.

The lanthanide contraction is responsible for the small variations in properties that permit separation of the lanthanides by fractional means (pp. 75–91). In terms of crystal radius, basicity may be expected to decrease in the order

$$La^{3+} > Ce^{3+} > Pr^{3+} > Nd^{3+} > Pm^{3+} > Sm^{3+} > Eu^{3+} > Gd^{3+} > Tb^{3+} >$$

$$Dy^{3+} > Ho^{3+} > Y^{3+} > Er^{3+} > Tm^{3+} > Yb^{3+} > Lu^{3+} > Sc^{3+}$$

with the more highly charged Ce^{4+} ion being less basic than any tripositive ion. Basicity differences are reflected in the hydrolysis of ions, the solubilities of salts, the thermal decomposition of oxy salts, and the formation of complex species (Chapter 3). The lanthanide contraction may be related also to the decreasing ease of oxidation of the metals with increasing atomic number, as shown by oxidation potential (Table 2.3) and ionization energy (Table 3.1) data.

Certain of these effects· continue beyond the lanthanides. Thus, although titanium and zirconium (Periodic Group IVb) differ substantially, hafnium resembles zirconium so closely that the separation of their compounds is at least as difficult as separation of those of adjacent lanthanides. Further striking similarities are noted between niobium and tantalum (Group Vb), molybdenum and tungsten (Group VIb), and technetium and rhenium (Group VIIb). Indeed, these similarities between members of the second and third d-type transition series continue through the platinum metals to at least silver and gold. They result, of course, from the lanthanide-induced reductions in crystal radii in the third series, as indicated by the values (in Ångstrom units):

Group IVb: Ti^{4+} 0.68, Zr^{4+} 0.79, Hf^{4+} 0.78

Group Vb: V^{5+} 0.59, Nb^{5+} 0.69, Ta^{5+} 0.68

Group VIb: Cr^{6+} 0.52, Mo^{6+} 0.62, W^{6+} 0.62

Group VIIb: Mn^{7+} 0.46, Tc^{7+} 0.56, Re^{7+} 0.56

Some Direct Consequences of Electronic Configuration

The indirect consequences are largely chemical; the direct ones substantially physical. Although the most obvious of the latter, the emission spectra, are of extreme importance, we can do no more in this treatment than indicate their utility in measuring purity. On the other hand, the $4f$ electrons are directly responsible for both the magnetic and light absorption properties of the cationic species, and these properties are more amenable to interpretation. Both such characteristics are related to the presence of unpaired electrons. For this reason, the preferential single occupancy of the seven $4f$ orbitals before pairing can occur (p. 13) is of importance.

Magnetic Characteristics. The major magnetic properties of chemical substances result from the fact that each moving electron is itself a micromagnet. Since an electron has both *spin* and *orbital* motion, it may contribute to magnetic behavior in two ways. The observed magnetic properties of a substance then represent the combined contributions of all of the electrons present. When a substance is placed in a magnetic field, it is observed to align itself either in opposition to the field (*diamagnetic behavior*) or parallel to the field (*paramagnetic behavior*). Diamagnetism results when pairing of all electrons nullifies their individual contributions. The ions Y^{3+}, La^{3+}, Lu^{3+}, Yb^{2+}, and Ce^{4+} are diamagnetic. Paramagnetism results when unpaired electrons are present to prevent such compensation. All of the other lanthanide ions are paramagnetic.

Magnetic character is described in terms of the molar magnetic susceptibility, χ_M. Molar diamagnetic susceptibility has a magnitude of ca. 10^{-6} c.g.s. units; molar paramagnetic susceptibility a magnitude in the range 10^{-3} to 10^{-2} c.g.s. units. The molar susceptibility is related empirically to the Kelvin temperature, T, by the Langevin expression

$$\chi_M = N\mu_B^2/3kT \qquad (2.1)$$

where N is Avogadro's number, k is the Boltzmann constant, and μ_B is the permanent magnetic moment of the species in question. Each paramagnetic substance has its own characteristic permanent magnetic moment (expressed in Bohr magnetons). The underlying diamagnetism of a paramagnetic species is normally so small that it can be neglected unless the greatest accuracy is required. Contrary to what one might expect on these bases, however, the most strongly paramagnetic species is not the Gd^{3+} ion with seven unpaired $4f$ electrons (Table 2.6). Rather, the ions Dy^{3+} and Ho^{3+} have

TABLE 2.6.   Permanent Magnetic Moments of Tripositive Cations

Ion	Unpaired electrons	μ_B, Bohr magnetons		
		Theoretical (Van Vleck)	Observed ($Ln_2(SO_4)_3 \cdot 8H_2O$)	Observed ($Ln(C_5H_5)_3$)
La^{3+}	0	0	*	0
Ce^{3+}	1	2.56	—	2.46
Pr^{3+}	2	3.62	3.47	3.61
Nd^{3+}	3	3.68	3.52	3.63
Pm^{3+}	4	2.83	—	—
Sm^{3+}	5	1.55–1.65	1.58	1.54
Eu^{3+}	6	3.40–3.51	3.54	—
Gd^{3+}	7	7.94	7.9	7.98
Tb^{3+}	6	9.7	9.6	—
Dy^{3+}	5	10.6	10.3	10.0
Ho^{3+}	4	10.6	10.4	—
Er^{3+}	3	9.6	9.4	9.45
Tm^{3+}	2	7.6	7.0	—
Yb^{3+}	1	4.5	4.3	4.00
Lu^{3+}	0	0	—	—
Y^{3+}	0	0	0	

* Does not give such a salt.

maximum permanent moment, and a second, but less pronounced, maximum characterizes the Nd^{3+} ion.

The American physicist J. H. Van Vleck has shown that
although Eq. 2.1 is generally valid, the properties of paramagnetic substances can be better described by the relationship

$$\chi_M = N\bar{\mu}_B^2/3kT + N\bar{\alpha} \qquad (2.2)$$

where $\bar{\mu}_B$ is a low-frequency part of the magnetic moment and
$\bar{\alpha}$ is a combination high-frequency component and diamagnetic contribution. Because the $4f$ electrons are shielded, both
their orbital and spin motions contribute, and the observed
permanent moment results from appropriate coupling of these
components. Its magnitude is determined by the magnitudes
of separation between the energy levels so produced and the
term kT. In practice, it is found that only with the Gd^{3+} ion

are these separations sufficiently small in comparison with kT to allow one to neglect the last term in Eq. 2.2. For all other tripositive ions except Sm^{3+} and Eu^{3+}, they are large enough so that both terms must be considered. For the ions Sm^{3+} and Eu^{3+}, they are of about the same order of magnitude as kT, and again both terms must be considered but in a different way. The net result is that the permanent magnetic moment of only the Gd^{3+} ion depends directly upon the number of unpaired electrons or, most specifically, upon electron spin. In all other cases, the value observed reflects a combination of spin and orbital effects. The validity of these considerations is shown by the agreement between theoretically calculated and experimentally measured values (Table 2.6).

It is pertinent to recall that the magnetic moments of the cations of the first d-type transition series are determined largely by the number of unpaired d electrons. Inasmuch as these electrons also participate in bond formation, their orbital contributions are quenched by the bonded groups, and observed moment is only a function of electron spin. Thus, the magnetic moments of such ions are markedly affected by complexing ligands. It is observed, however, that complexing groups—or, indeed, anions of any type—have little effect upon the magnetic moments of the lanthanide ions, as long as the resulting structure is such that each paramagnetic ion can remain far enough from the others to behave independently (i.e., a magnetically dilute structure). Thus, as a result of shielding, the f orbitals differ somewhat from the d orbitals.

The electronic configurations suggested for the nontripositive species (Table 2.2) are in agreement with magnetic data. Thus, cerium(IV) and ytterbium(II) are diamagnetic, corresponding to $4f^0$ and $4f^{14}$ configurations; samarium(II) and europium(III) are magnetically similar (both $4f^6$); and europium(II) gives values very nearly the same as those for gadolinium(III) (both $4f^7$).

Color and Light Absorption. The striking colors characteristic of crystalline salts of a number of the tripositive ions persist in aqueous and nonaqueous solutions and are unaffected by alteration of the anion present or addition of colorless complexing groups. They are apparently characteristic of the cations themselves. Interestingly, the colors of the ions from La^{3+} through Gd^{3+} repeat themselves, at least qualitatively, from Lu^{3+} back through Gd^{3+} (Table 2.7). It is tempt-

TABLE 2.7.   Color Sequence for Tripositive Cations

Ion	Unpaired electrons	Color	Unpaired electrons	Ion
La^{3+}	0	Colorless	0	Lu^{3+}
Ce^{3+}	1	Colorless	1	Yb^{3+}
Pr^{3+}	2	Green	2	Tm^{3+}
Nd^{3+}	3	Reddish	3	Er^{3+}
Pm^{3+}	4	Pink; yellow	4	Ho^{3+}
Sm^{3+}	5	Yellow	5	Dy^{3+}
Eu^{3+}	6	Pale pink (?)	6	Tb^{3+}
Gd^{3+}	7	Colorless	7	Gd^{3+}

ing to conclude, then, that a given color is related to a given number of unpaired electrons, but the divergence in color between the tripositive species and isoelectronic nontripositive ions (Table 2.8) suggests that the situation is somewhat more complex. Furthermore, the ions Ce^{3+}, Gd^{3+}, and Yb^{3+}, all of which contain unpaired electrons, are colorless.

TABLE 2.8.   Colors of Isoelectronic Ions

Tripositive Ion	Color	Unpaired electrons	Color	Nontripositive Ion
La^{3+}	Colorless	0	Orange-red	Ce^{4+}
Eu^{3+}	Pale pink	6	Reddish	Sm^{2+}
Gd^{3+}	Colorless	7	Straw yellow	Eu^{2+}
Lu^{3+}	Colorless	0	Green	Yb^{2+}

Inasmuch as color has no quantitative significance, it is more fundamental to measure the amounts of light of different wavelengths absorbed by each species. This is reasonable since the color one sees is the result of absorption of light of certain wavelengths and transmission of light of other wavelengths. With such measurements, it is observed that all the tripositive ions except Y^{3+}, La^{3+}, and Lu^{3+} absorb somewhere in the wavelength range 2000–10000 Å.* The colored ions absorb in the visible region, and on occasion in the ultraviolet. The colorless species absorb either in the ultraviolet (Ce^{3+}, Gd^{3+}) or the infrared (Yb^{3+}). The dipositive ions absorb strongly in the ultraviolet. The only tetrapositive ion stable in aqueous solution, the Ce^{4+} ion, absorbs in the blue and ultraviolet regions.

The absorption spectrum of each of the tripositive ions (except Ce^{3+} and Yb^{3+}) contains several very sharply defined bands, as indicated by the typical spectra in Fig. 2.3 and the data in Table 2.9. These bands, although not intense, peak at wavelengths that can often be measured to an Ångstrom unit

TABLE 2.9.   Principal Absorption Bands

Ion	Wavelength, Å.	Ion	Wavelength, Å.
La^{3+}	None	Tb^{3+}	3694, 3780, 4875
Ce^{3+}	2105, 2220, 2380, 2520	Dy^{3+}	3504, 3650, 9100
Pr^{3+}	4445, 4690, 4822, 5885	Ho^{3+}	2870, 3611, 4508, 5370, 6404
Nd^{3+}	3540, 5218, 5745, 7395, 7420, 7975, 8030, 8680	Er^{3+}	3642, 3792, 4870, 5228, 6525
		Tm^{3+}	3600, 6825, 7800
Pm^{3+}	5485, 5680, 7025, 7355	Yb^{3+}	9750
Sm^{3+}	3625, 3745, 4020	Lu^{3+}	None
Eu^{3+}	3755, 3941		
Gd^{3+}	2729, 2733, 2754, 2756	Y^{3+}	None

* The eye is sensitive to radiation in the region 4000–7000 Å. This is the *visible* region. The region below 4000 Å. is the *ultraviolet;* that above 7000 Å. the *infrared*. The energy associated with radiation increases as wavelength decreases.

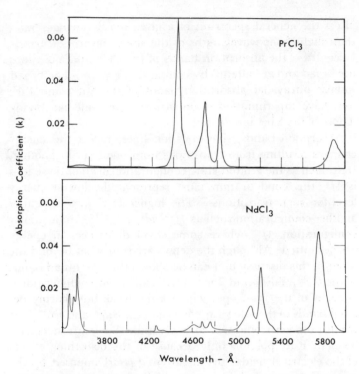

Fig. 2.3. Portions of absorption spectra of aqueous PrCl₃ and NdCl₃ solutions. (Redrawn from Moeller, T., and Brantley, J. C., *Anal. Chem.* **22,** 433 (1950).)

or less. As such, they resemble the lines of emission spectra more closely than the broad absorption bands of *d*-type transition metal ions (e.g., Ti^{3+}, Ni^{2+}, Pt^{4+}). Indeed, such line-like absorption spectra are characteristic of no other ionic species except the related actinides. These bands are even more sharply defined for crystalline solids than for solutions. Decreasing the temperature and adding strongly complexing ligands also have a sharpening effect. However, neither changing from solution to solid nor introducing complexing groups alters the general spectrum of a given ion or changes more than slightly the wavelengths of the sharp absorption bands. In contrast, the absorption bands of the Ce^{3+} and Yb^{3+} ions are broad and are altered by complexing groups. The broad, intense ultraviolet absorption bands of the Sm^{2+} and Eu^{2+} ions have superimposed upon them weaker, line-like bands. Those of the Yb^{2+} ion do not.

Absorption bands, like emission lines, reflect the energy changes resulting from transitions from one level to another. Inasmuch as the ground-state configuration of all of these ions is $4f^n$, this configuration must represent the lowest energy level for such transitions. The higher level may be either another configuration such as $4f^{n-1}5d^1$ or $4f^{n-1}5g^1$ or a similar configuration, $4f^{n'}$, where some small differences in energy are permitted. Although the details are somewhat beyond the scope of this discussion, it can be shown that the broad bands of the Ce^{3+}, Yb^{3+}, and Lu^{2+} ions result from configurational changes of the first type, whereas the weak but sharply defined bands of the other Ln^{3+} ions and the Sm^{2+} and Eu^{2+} ions result from electronic transitions within the $4f$ arrangement. The latter are possible only because of the disturbing effects of the electrical fields (so-called *crystal fields*) imposed by the anions that surround these cations. Such transitions prove to be impossible with $4f^1$ (Ce^{3+}), $4f^{13}$ (Yb^{3+}), or $4f^{14}$ (Yb^{2+}) configurations. Inasmuch as the $4f$ electrons are so well shielded, it is not surprising that neither the nature nor the environment of the compound being studied has much effect upon the sharply defined bands.

The almost unique absorptions associated with the f electrons make certain of the ions of the lanthanides particularly useful in light filters. Glass containing neodymium and praseodymium ions (so-called didymium glass) absorbs yellow sodium light so specifically and so strongly that it is used extensively in glass blowers' goggles. Indeed, standard filters that take advantage of the sharpness of the absorption bands are used uniformly for wavelength calibration in optical devices. The absorption spectra of the tripositive ions are also used extensively for both the qualitative detection and the quantitative determination of the lanthanides in mixtures (p. 74).

Again, Recapitulation—and Then?

The ease and logic with which we have been able to answer many of the questions raised in Chapter 1 may suggest to us that a complete understanding of the chemistry of the lanthanides should result from mere consideration of their electronic configurations. Certainly, we have in this way accounted for many early experimental observations that would otherwise remain as confusing as they were when they were first recorded. Although in principle an extension of these considerations should give us this understanding, our enthusiasm for the purely theoretical approach must certainly be tempered by the fact that we still do not have sufficient factual information in mind to judge its validity and scope. It is essential, therefore, for us to summarize in some detail the chemical behaviors of the metals and their ions by bringing together in the next chapter in a logical manner the wealth of data accumulated during a century and a half of experimental observation.

When we do this, we shall find that there are certain facts, relating in particular to yttrium chemistry but also encompassing that of the heavier members of the series, that are unexplained by the approach we have developed. The imperfections and weaknesses of these concepts may help convince us of the danger of accepting any theoretical approach without first examining it in the light of *all* pertinent factual information. If the theory is fundamentally sound, it can by slight alteration accommodate apparent exceptions; if it is unsound it cannot accommodate these and thus must be rejected. Fortunately, the former applies to the lanthanides.

Selected Readings

Asprey, L. B., and Cunningham, B. B., "Progress in Inorganic Chemistry," F. A. Cotton, Ed., Vol. II, pp. 267–86, Interscience Publishers, New York, 1960. (Oxidation states).

Moeller, T., "The Rare Earths," F. H. Spedding and A. H. Daane, Eds. ch. 2, John Wiley & Sons, New York, 1961. (Electronic configuration and general properties.)

Moeller, T., and Kremers, H. E., *Chem. Rev.* **37**, 98–159 (1945). (Size relationships and basicity.)

Selwood, P. W., "Magnetochemistry," 2nd ed., pp. 140–57, Interscience Publishers, New York, 1956. (Magnetic properties.)

Yost, D. M., Russell, H., Jr., and Garner, C. S., "The Rare-Earth Elements and Their Compounds," chs. 1–3, John Wiley & Sons, New York, 1947. (Electronic configurations, oxidation states, magnetic properties, absorption spectra.)

THE OXIDATION STATES— A COMBINATION OF THE COMMONPLACE AND THE UNUSUAL

It is now appropriate that we supplement the small amount of chemical information already presented, implement the approaches outlined in Chapter 2, and add to our fund of knowledge by discussing in some detail the general chemistry of the lanthanides. This is conveniently done in terms of the several oxidation states already mentioned.

Oxidation State Zero—The Metals

Yttrium and the elemental lanthanides are all metals, as might be expected from their electronic configurations (Table 2.1), their large atomic radii (Table 2.4), and their position in the Periodic Table. As metals of commerce and for laboratory usage, most of them are comparative newcomers. This stems from a combination of unavailability of pure compounds from which they can be prepared and of difficulty of preparation. The successful solution of these problems in the years since around 1950 is described in detail in subsequent sections (pp. 41–43, 80–92).

Physical Characteristics.   Important physical constants supplementing those already given (Tables 2.3 and 2.4) are listed in Table 3.1. Many of these values are more meaningful when they are compared with those for more familiar elements, as presented in Table 3.2. The wide ranges of density, melting point, boiling point, and cross section for thermal (slow) neutron capture encompassed by these elements are apparent. As is characteristic of any periodic family, density increases in general with atomic weight. The exceptions at europium and ytterbium probably reflect differences in crystal structure (Table 3.1). In fusibility and volatility, europium and ytterbium resemble calcium more closely than they do the neighboring lanthanides. This may again suggest a difference in inherent oxidation state (p. 22), for the melting point and boiling point are measures of the strength of bonding in the solid and liquid states, respectively.

Inasmuch as neutron absorption is a nuclear property, it bears no direct relationship to atomic number. Cerium compares with our weaker neutron absorbers (Table 3.2), but samarium, europium, and gadolinium are more effective than boron or cadmium, the substances normally used in neutron-control devices (p. 94). Europium is of particular interest because its isotopes undergo series of n,γ reactions, each of which gives a europium isotope of large absorption cross section.[*]

The metals are soft, malleable, and ductile. When freshly

---

[*] In an n,γ reaction, a nucleus absorbs a neutron, thereby undergoing an increase in mass, and emits *gamma* (very short wavelength) radiation. There is no change in nuclear charge.

TABLE 3.1. Numerical Constants for the Elements

Symbol	Atomic weight ($^{12}C = 12.0000$)	Density,* g./cm.^{3}	Ionization energy,[†] e.v./g. atom	Melting point, °C.	Boiling point (approx.), °C.	Cross section for thermal neutron capture,[‡] barns/atom
Sc	44.956	2.992	6.56	1539	2727	24
Y	88.905	4.478	6.6	1509	2927	1.31
La	138.91	6.174	5.61	920	3469	9.3
Ce	140.12	6.771	6.91	795	3468	0.73
Pr	140.907	6.782	5.76	935	3127	11.6
Nd	144.24	7.004	6.31	1024	3027	46
Pm	(147)	—	—	—	—	—
Sm	150.35	7.536	5.6	1072	1900	5600
Eu	151.96	5.259	5.67	826	1439	4300
Gd	157.25	7.895	6.16	1312	3000	46000
Tb	158.924	8.272	6.74	1356	2800	46
Dy	162.50	8.536	6.82	1407	2600	950
Ho	164.930	8.803	—	1461	2600	65
Er	167.26	9.051	—	1497	2900	173
Tm	168.934	9.332	—	1545	1727	127
Yb	173.04	6.977	6.2	824	1427	37
Lu	174.97	9.842	5.0	1652	3327	115

* For stable modification at room temperature—all hexagonal close-packed except Sm (rhombohedral), Eu (body-centered cubic), Yb (face-centered cubic).
[†] For one electron.
[‡] For neutrons of velocity 2200 m./sec. Natural isotopic mixtures.

TABLE 3.2. Some Numerical Constants[*] for Comparison

Symbol	Density, g/cm³	Symbol	Melting point, °C	Symbol	Boiling point (approx.), °C	Symbol	Neutron capture, barns/atom
Al	2.7	Sr	770	K	1400	Zr	0.18
Ba	3.5	As	814	Cd	1413	Rb	0.73
Ti	4.54	Ca	851	Sb	1440	Sr	1.21
Ge	5.32	Ge	936	Ca	1482	Pt	8.8
V	6.11	Ag	960.5	Te	1814	Se	12.3
Zr	6.45	Au	1063	In	2075	Ta	21
Sb	6.68	Cu	1083	Mn	2097	Cs	29
Zn	7.13	Be	1284	Cr	2199	Co	37
Mn	7.44	Ni	1452	Cu	2595	Ag	63
Fe	7.87	Co	1493	Ge	2700	Hf	105
Nb	8.57	Fe	1535	Ni	2900	Rh	156
Cd	8.65	Pd	1552	Au	2966	In	196
Cu	8.94	Ti	1668	Fe	3000	B	755
Bi	9.08			Co	3100	Cd	2450
				Ti	3260		
				Zr	3580		

[*] Data from Hampel, C. A., "Rare Metals Handbook," 2nd ed., ch. 35, Reinhold Publishing Corp., New York, 1961.

cut, they have a silvery luster. In electrical conductivity, they cover the same range that cesium and mercury do. Except for yttrium, which is only mildly so, the metals are appreciably paramagnetic (p. 26). Terbium is very strongly paramagnetic, and gadolinium is unique in being ferromagnetic* up to 16°C.

Chemical Characteristics. The oxidation potentials for the couples Ln^0–Ln^{III} in acidic solution (Table 2.3) suggest that these metals are comparable to magnesium in electropositive character and ease of oxidation. The same is true under alkaline conditions, although the potential data (La, ca. 2.90 v., and Lu, ca. 2.72 v.; vs. Mg, 2.69 v.) are even less well established. Inasmuch as these potentials measure displacement of equilibria of the types[†]

$$Ln(s) + xH_2O \rightleftharpoons Ln(H_2O)_x{}^{3+} + 3e^- \quad \text{(acidic medium)}$$

and

$$Ln(s) + 3OH^- \rightleftharpoons Ln(OH)_3(s) + 3e^- \quad \text{(alkaline medium)}$$

they indicate ease of oxidation under aqueous conditions. That the metals are strong reducing agents under these conditions follows from the large amounts of energy released in the hydration or hydrolysis of their gaseous tripositive ions as compared with the smaller quantities of energy needed to form these ions (p. 18). We may wonder, therefore, whether or not comparable ease of oxidation is noted in the absence of

---

* Ferromagnetism ($\chi_M = \infty$) differs from paramagnetism in that it results from the parallel orientation of molecular magnets over microscopic regions of a crystalline solid. A ferromagnetic substance becomes paramagnetic when the temperature is raised above a characteristic critical value (the Curie temperature or point). Typical Curie points are: Gd, 16°C.; Dy, −168°C. Common ferromagnetic materials include iron and certain of its alloys (especially with cobalt and nickel).

[†] Inasmuch as x is not known with certainty, we may also formulate these ions Ln^{3+}(aq), as was done in Table 2.3.

water. It is observed that although reactions under these conditions are strongly exothermic, they are normally slow at room temperature and take place rapidly and vigorously only when the temperature is raised.

Reactions of the metals with typical reagents are summarized in Table 3.3. The large concentration of hydronium ion in dilute aqueous acids promotes vigorous oxidation to the tripositive cation in each instance. Water, with its reduced hydronium ion content, reacts more slowly at room temperature to give the insoluble hydrous oxide or hydroxide, but reasonably rapidly at elevated temperatures. Europium is attacked much more rapidly than the other metals, forming first the soluble, yellowish $Eu(OH)_2 \cdot H_2O$ (compare alkaline

TABLE 3.3.   Typical Chemical Reactions of the Elemental Lanthanides

Reagent(s)	Product(s)	Conditions
X_2 ($= F_2, Cl_2, Br_2, I_2$)	LnX_3	Slow at room temperature; burn above 200°C.
O_2	Ln_2O_3	Slow at room temperature; burn above 150–180°C.
S	Ln_2S_3	At boiling point of sulfur
N_2	LnN	Above 1000°C.
C	LnC_2, Ln_2C_3 (also LnC, $Ln_2C, Ln_3C,$ Ln_4C)	At high temperature
B	LnB_4, LnB_6	At high temperature
H_2	LnH_2, LnH_3	Rapid above 300°C.
H^+ (dil. HCl, H_2SO_4, $HClO_4$, $HC_2H_3O_2$, etc.)	$Ln^{3+} + H_2$	Rapid at room temperature
H_2O	Ln_2O_3 or $Ln(OH)_3$ $+ H_2$	Slow at room temperature; more rapid at higher temperature
$H_2O + O_2$	Ln_2O_3 or $Ln(OH)_3$	Rapid with Eu; slower with others
Metal oxides	Metal	At high temperatures (except CaO, MgO, Ln_2O_3 in general)

earth metals) and then hydrous Eu_2O_3. Dry oxygen (air) attacks the pure metals very slowly at room temperature, but at higher temperatures the metals ignite and burn. Moist air attacks europium very rapidly, and lanthanum, cerium, praseodymium, and neodymium quite rapidly. The resulting hydrous oxide is always so voluminous that any protective oxide coating is ruptured, and a new metal surface is continually exposed. The impure metals and alloys rich in cerium (e.g., mischmetal, p. 92) are pyrophoric. Other reactions require no additional comment.

Europium and ytterbium, like the alkaline earth and alkali metals, dissolve in liquid ammonia to yield the dark blue, strongly reducing solutions that are believed to contain the ammonated electron, $e(NH_3)_y^-$. This behavior emphasizes the ease with which these metals lose electrons.

Preparation. The ease of oxidation of the metals suggests that reduction of ions to the metallic state is difficult. In aqueous systems, neither electrolytic nor chemical reduction is effective; rather, hydrogen is the preferential reduction product. Decrease in ease of oxidation upon alloying with mercury, however, permits amalgam formation when buffered acetic acid solutions are treated with sodium amalgam or when alkaline citrate solutions are electrolyzed with a lithium-amalgam cathode. Electrolysis or displacement is effective in nonaqueous media (e.g., in alcohols) only if amalgams can result. Thermal decomposition of such amalgams gives the finely divided metals, but complete removal of mercury is difficult. Under any circumstance, europium, ytterbium, and samarium (and in this order) give amalgams most readily.

Two more generally successful reduction systems involve electrolysis of molten halides and metallothermic treatment of anhydrous salts. Electrolysis is complicated both by the high melting points of the useful anhydrous salts (Table 3.4) and by the reactivity of the liberated metals with gases and cell refractories. Lower temperatures are achieved with lower-melting mixtures of salts. Thus pure cerium is obtained by electrolyzing molten CeF_3–LiF–BaF_2 at temperatures near the melting point of that metal and adding cerium(IV) oxide to replenish the bath, and yttrium is obtained in high purity from a KCl–YCl_3 melt.

Metallothermic reduction of the anhydrous fluorides with calcium in tantalum apparatus at ca. 800–1000°C., as developed at Iowa State University by A. H. Daane, H. A. Wilhelm, and F. H. Spedding,

$$2LnF_3 + 3Ca \rightarrow 2Ln + 3CaF_2$$

is generally considered more convenient. Alternative but comparable procedures use the anhydrous chlorides and magnesium, lithium, or sodium, but the fluorides are preferred

TABLE 3.4.   Melting Points[*] of Some Typical Anhydrous Lanthanide(III) Compounds

Cation	Melting point, °C.			
	Fluoride	Chloride	Bromide	Iodide
Sc^{3+}	1515	960	960	945
Y^{3+}	1152	700	904	1000
La^{3+}	1493	852	783	761
Ce^{3+}	1430	802	732	752
Pr^{3+}	1395	776	693	733
Nd^{3+}	1374	760	684	775
Pm^{3+}	—	—	—	—
Sm^{3+}	1306	678	664	816–824
Eu^{3+}	1276	623	(702)	(877)
Gd^{3+}	1231	609	765	926
Tb^{3+}	1172	588	(827)	952
Dy^{3+}	1154	654	881	955
Ho^{3+}	1143	718	914	1010
Er^{3+}	1140	774	950	1020
Tm^{3+}	1158	821	(952)	1015
Yb^{3+}	1157	854	940	(1027)
Lu^{3+}	1182	892	(957)	1045

[*] Estimated values in parentheses.

because they are not hygroscopic. The trifluorides of samarium, europium, and ytterbium are reduced only to the difluorides. However, the fact that these metals are more volatile than lanthanum permits their preparation *in vacuo* from the oxides, as

$$Ln_2O_3 + 2La \rightarrow La_2O_3 + 2Ln(g)$$

The metals are best purified by distillation in tantalum apparatus with a vacuum of at least 10^{-5}mm. of Hg.

Oxidation State +2—A So-Called "Anomalous" State

Although C. Matignon and E. Cazes obtained samarium(II) chloride in 1906 by reducing the trichloride at elevated temperatures with hydrogen, ammonia, or aluminum, and G. Urbain and F. Bourion prepared europium(II) chloride in 1911 by a comparable reduction involving hydrogen, the true significance and possible utility of these observations were not realized until about 1930. In 1929, W. Klemm and W. Schuth obtained ytterbium(II) chloride by hydrogen reduction, and the following year, L. F. Yntema and R. Ball, working in the laboratory of the University of Illinois, obtained the Eu^{2+} and Yb^{2+} ions in aqueous solution by electrolytic reduction. Subsequent work has shown that a number of other dipositive species can be prepared (Table 2.2). Proposals that all of the lanthanides can be dipositive, however, lack complete experimental verification.

Chemical Stability and Stabilization. It is convenient to discuss samarium(II), europium(II), and ytterbium(II) separately because only these dipositive species exist in aqueous solution and form series of compounds. Standard oxidation potential data (Table 2.3) indicate that in aqueous solution these three cations are all strong reducing agents, with reducing strength decreasing as

$$Sm^{2+} >> Yb^{2+} >> Eu^{2+}$$

Thus the Eu^{2+} ion lies between elemental iron and cadmium, the Yb^{2+} ion just below elemental manganese, and the Sm^{2+} ion just below elemental aluminum. Both the Sm^{2+} and Yb^{2+} ions are rapidly oxidized by hydronium ion

$$2Ln^{2+} + 2H_3O^+ \rightarrow 2Ln^{3+} + 2H_2O + H_2(g)$$

but the Eu^{2+} ion is oxidized only very slowly. In the presence of oxygen, all ions are oxidized rapidly

$$4Ln^{2+} + 4H_3O^+ + O_2 \rightarrow 4Ln^{3+} + 6H_2O$$

At reduced acidity, either reaction path may give difficultly soluble basic salts, LnOX. The general instability of the dipositive species with respect to oxidation has been discussed in Chapter 2 (pp. 18, 19).

Although some stabilization with respect to oxidation may be expected in less strongly solvating media (e.g., the alcohols), it is best achieved by including these ions in solid compounds. Hydrated water-soluble samarium(II) and ytterbium(II) salts are oxidized by their water, but those of europium(II), particularly the chloride $EuCl_2 \cdot 2H_2O$, are comparatively stable. Water-insoluble compounds (e.g., the sulfates, carbonates, fluorides) resist oxidation even in the presence of water. The sulfates are most useful for recovery and preservation of these ions. More extensive stabilization is noted when the ions are trapped in an inert solid matrix (e.g., EuO in SrO, Ln^{2+} in silicate glasses, LnF_2 in LnF_3).

The other dipositive species are known only as solid halides. All are immediately oxidized upon contact with water. The observed isomorphism between the compounds TmI_2 and YbI_2 suggests that the ion Tm^{2+} exists. However, some of the other dihalides show the metallic properties associated with "free" electrons and are perhaps better formulated as $Ln^{3+}(e^-)(X^-)_2$.

General Physical and Chemical Properties. Properties of the Sm^{2+}, Eu^{2+}, and Yb^{2+} ions related to electronic configuration have been discussed in Chapter 2. As the crystal radii (Table 2.4) suggest and as we imply in previous discussions, there are striking similarities in solubility and crystal structure between compounds of these ions and those of the alkaline earth metal ions (especially Sr^{2+} and Ba^{2+}). For this reason, the Sr^{2+} and Ba^{2+} ions are commonly used to carry the dipositive lanthanides in separations (p. 92). Cases in point include both the sulfates (above) and the chloride $EuCl_2 \cdot 2H_2O$. The latter, like its barium analog, is difficultly soluble in concentrated hydrochloric acid.

The dipositive fluorides are all isomorphous and have the cubic fluorite (CaF_2) structure (p. 64). Anhydrous samarium(II) chloride is isostructural with the strontium and barium compounds, but europium(II) and ytterbium(II) chlorides are not. Of the dipositive bromides, only the ytterbium compound is not isostructural with strontium bromide. None of the iodides is isomorphous with either strontium or barium iodide. The oxides, sulfides, selenides, and tellurides, insofar as they have been examined, have the cubic sodium chloride-type structure of their strontium and barium analogs. The carbonates are isomorphous with barium carbonate. Only samarium(II) and europium(II) sulfates have the barium sulfate structure. It is apparent that some structures can better tolerate small variations in crystal radii than others.

Although it is known that one or two europium(II) aminepolycarboxylate complex ions (p. 55) have essentially the same solution stability as their strontium counterparts, detailed information on complex species is lacking.

Preparation. General methods of obtaining the dipositive lanthanides include

1. *Reduction of anhydrous compounds at elevated temperatures.* Typical procedures include reduction of the anhydrous fluo-

rides or chlorides as previously described (p. 43) and reduction of fused trihalides (e.g., NdX_3, TmI_3) or of oxides (e.g., Eu_2O_3, Sm_2O_3) with the corresponding metal.

2. *Chemical reduction in solution.* Amalgamated zinc (e.g., as a Jones reductor) reduces europium(III) quantitatively to europium(II), but samarium(III) and ytterbium(III) are unaffected. The observation that magnesium reduces samarium(III) chloride to insoluble samarium(II) chloride in anhydrous ethanol suggests that a variety of procedures involving nonaqueous systems may be feasible.

3. *Electrolytic reduction in solution.* Both aqueous europium(III) and ytterbium(III) solutions yield the dipositive ions at a mercury cathode (p. 43), but the samarium(II) ion is too strongly reducing to be so prepared.

4. *Thermal decomposition of anhydrous iodides.* Ease of reduction at elevated temperatures as

$$2LnX_3(s) \longrightarrow 2LnX_2(s) + X_2(g)$$

increases in the series $Sm^{3+}-Yb^{3+}-Eu^{3+}$ and $Cl^--Br^--I^-$.

5. *Chemical oxidation.* Samarium, europium, and ytterbium amalgams, when treated with acid, apparently give the dipositive ions as intermediate oxidation products. Mercury(II) iodide oxidizes elemental thulium to the diiodide.

Oxidation State +3—The "Characteristic" State

It is apparent from previous discussions (Chapters 1 and 2) that the properties of this state very largely determine the chemistry of the lanthanides. For completeness, however, it is necessary to consider in more detail the properties of specific compounds and complex ion formation. These are important both to our understanding of the nature of bonding and to our appreciation of the practical chemistry discussed in Chapter 4.

Properties—Some Specific and General Considerations. The tripositive species are found in generally crystalline compounds containing essentially all known anionic species. Where these anions can be decomposed thermally (e.g., $OH^-, CO_3^{2-}, SO_4^{2-}, C_2O_4^{2-}, NO_3^-$), the corresponding compounds are converted to basic derivatives and ultimately to oxides when heated. Hydrated salts, as a consequence of hydrolysis at elevated temperatures, often give similar products. Anhydrous compounds containing thermally stable anions (e.g., $O^{2-}, F^-, Cl^-, Br^-, PO_4^{3-}$) melt without decomposition. Both their high melting points (e.g., Table 3.4) and excellent electrical conductivities in the fused state indicate a high degree of ionic bonding. Available crystal structure data show the presence of Ln^{3+} ions.

Conductance, transference number,[*] and activity coefficient[†] data, of which those given for the chlorides in Table 3.5 are typical, indicate that salts containing weakly basic anions (e.g., $Cl^-, Br^-, I^-, NO_3^-, ClO_4^-$) are strong electrolytes in aqueous solution. Indeed, such solutions are often used as standards of comparison for electrolyte behavior since solutions derived from other tripositive species (e.g., $Cr^{3+}, Fe^{3+}, Al^{3+}, In^{3+}$) are those of weaker electrolytes as a consequence of enhanced covalence, solvation, and complex ion formation. The influence of the lanthanide contraction is apparent in the general decrease in ionic character from lanthanum to lutetium.

A similar trend is noted in the slight increase in degree of

---

[*] The transference number of an ion is the fraction of the total current carried by that ion in a conductance experiment.

[†] The activity coefficient of an ion is the correction factor γ needed to convert observed molality (m) to effective (thermodynamic) concentration or activity (a) in the relationship $a = \gamma m$. For a salt $M_x A_y$, the mean activity coefficient ($\gamma_{\pm}$) is equal to $\gamma_+^x \gamma_-^y$.

TABLE 3.5. Some Physical Properties of Aqueous $LnCl_3$ Solutions at 25° C.[*]

Ion	Normality	Equivalent conductance, mho/cm.	Normality	Transference number of Ln^{3+}	Molality	Mean activity coefficient, $\gamma_\pm$
La^{3+}	0.0010	137.4	—	—	0.00125	0.7661
	0.0100	122.1	0.00903	0.4629	0.01247	0.5318
	0.1000	99.0	0.0933	0.4389	—	—
Gd^{3+}	0.0010	134.9	—	—	0.00171	0.7728
	0.0100	120.2	0.0117	0.4602	0.0171	0.5345
	0.1000	98.4	0.1051	0.4315	—	—
Yb^{3+}	0.0010	132.8	—	—	0.00114	0.7732
	0.0100	118.1	0.0104	0.4495	0.01144	0.5385
	0.1000	96.4	0.1038	0.4224	—	—

[*] Adapted from Spedding, F. H., et al., J. Am. Chem. Soc., **74**, 2055, 2778, 2781, 4751 (1952); **76**, 879 (1954).

hydrolysis in solution from the La^{3+} ion to the Lu^{3+} ion. However, unlike the more common tripositive ions, these cations are never extensively hydrolyzed. Thus solutions containing weakly basic anions are only mildly acidic. Strongly basic anions (e.g., CN^-, S^{2-}, NO_2^-, OCN^-, N_3^-) are themselves so strongly hydrolyzed to hydroxyl ion that they precipitate basic salts or hydrous oxides. Under such circumstances, ease of precipitation decreases from the Lu^{3+} ion to the La^{3+} ion.

We see in these observations indications of the basicity order previously mentioned (p. 24). The yttrium ion usually occupies the position among the heavy lanthanides that its crystal radius suggests (see p. 20).

We have discussed the ease of formation of the tripositive ions in aqueous solution in terms of oxidation potential data (pp. 18, 19). The ease of formation and, therefore, the thermal stability of typical solid compounds containing these ions are indicated by the thermodynamic data in Table 3.6.[*] That these values are uniformly larger than those for comparable aluminum compounds is undoubtedly again an indication of increased ionic character. The effects of the lanthanide contraction are also apparent.

As may be expected from the crystal radii (Table 2.4), there are many cases of isomorphism. These include a num-

---

[*] The standard heat of formation, $\Delta H°$, is the energy associated with the formation at 25°C. of the compound from its elements. It is related to the standard free energy of formation, $\Delta F°$, and the standard entropy of formation, $\Delta S°$, by the relationship

$$\Delta H° = \Delta F° - T\Delta S°$$

The strength of a bond is measured by the magnitude of $\Delta H°$, the tendency for a reaction to take place as written by the magnitude of $\Delta F°$, and the alteration in the randomness of the system by the magnitude of $\Delta S°$. *Negative* quantities signify energy release. All spontaneous reactions have *negative* $\Delta F°$ values.

ber (but not all) of the individual halides; the oxides (within each of the three crystal types, p. 62); the hydrated sulfates, $Ln_2(SO_4)_3 \cdot 8H_2O$; the bromates, $Ln(BrO_3)_3 \cdot 9H_2O$; the many double nitrates, $2Ln(NO_3)_3 \cdot 3M^{II}(NO_3)_2 \cdot 24H_2O$ (M = Mg, Zn, Ni, Mn) and $Ln(NO_3)_3 \cdot 2NH_4NO_3 \cdot 4H_2O$; the ethyl sulfates, $Ln(C_2H_5SO_4)_3 \cdot 9H_2O$; and a host of others. Separations by fractional crystallization depend upon isomorphism. Unfortunately, the crystal structures of only a few compound types have been determined. Unlike many other tripositive ions, these cations do not form alums.

TABLE 3.6. Some Thermodynamic Data for Formation of Typical Compounds[*]

Compound	$\Delta H°$, kcal./g. mole	$\Delta F°$, kcal./g. mole	$\Delta S°$, e.u./g. mole
La_2O_3	−428.6	(−408)	(−72)
Gd_2O_3	−434.0	(−412)	(−76)
Yb_2O_3	−433.6	(−410)	(−76)
Y_2O_3	−455.4	(−434)	(−72)
Al_2O_3	−399.9	−376.8	−12.2
$LaCl_3$	−255.9	−238	−59
$GdCl_3$	−240.1	−222	−61
$YbCl_3$	(−224)	(−206)	(−62)
YCl_3	−232.7	−215	−59
$AlCl_3$	−166.2	−152.2	−40
LaI_3	−160	(−159)	(− 4)
GdI_3	−142	(−140)	(− 6)
YbI_3	(−130)	(−128)	(− 7)
YI_3	−137	(−136)	(− 4)
AlI_3	− 75.2	− 75.0	—

[*] Data for lanthanides from Montgomery, R. L., *U. S. Bur. Mines, Rept. Invest.* **5468** (1959). Estimated values in parentheses.

Solubilities. Water-soluble compounds include the chlorides, bromides, iodides, nitrates, acetates, perchlorates, and bromates and a number of double nitrates. Water-insoluble compounds include the fluorides, hydroxides, oxides, carbonates, chromates, phosphates, and oxalates, and indeed the salts of most di- or trinegative anions. The normal sulfates vary from very soluble to difficultly soluble.

Although it is tempting to conclude that solubility should be directly related to crystal radius, experimental observation shows that this is not the case since, depending upon the salt, solubility may decrease with decreasing radius (e.g., dimethyl phosphate, OH^-), increase with decreasing radius (e.g., double magnesium nitrates), or change irregularly (e.g., SO_4^{2-}, BrO_3^-). Such trends are shown by the data in Table 3.7. No explanation for these variations has been offered.

Very broadly, there are sufficient differences between the solubilities of many specific salts of the lighter lanthanides and those of the heavier lanthanides to justify a subdivision into so-called cerium and yttrium groups (Table 3.8). This is

TABLE 3.7. Solubilities of Typical Salts in Water

Cation	Solubility, g./100 g. H_2O			
	$Ln_2(SO_4)_3 \cdot$ $8H_2O$ $(20°C.)$	$Ln(BrO_3)_3 \cdot$ $9H_2O$ $(25°C.)$	$Ln[(CH_3)_2PO_4]_3 \cdot$ nH_2O $(25°C.)$	$LnCl_3 \cdot$ $6H_2O$ $(20°C.)$
Y^{3+}	9.76	—	2.8	217.0
La^{3+}	—	462.1	103.7	—
Ce^{3+}	9.43[*]	—	79.6	—
Pr^{3+}	12.74	196.1	64.1	—
Nd^{3+}	7.00	151.3	56.1	243.0
Pm^{3+}	—	—	—	—
Sm^{3+}	2.67	117.3	35.2	218.4
Eu^{3+}	2.56	—	—	—
Gd^{3+}	2.89	110.5	23.0	—
Tb^{3+}	3.56	133.2	12.6	—
Dy^{3+}	5.07	—	8.24	—
Ho^{3+}	8.18	—	—	—
Er^{3+}	16.00	—	1.78	—
Tm^{3+}	—	—	—	—
Yb^{3+}	34.78	—	1.2	—
Lu^{3+}	47.27	—	—	—

[*] Calculated as anhydrous salt.

most striking with the double sodium, potassium, or thallium(I) sulfates, $Ln_2(SO_4)_3 \cdot M^I_2SO_4 \cdot nH_2O$. However, none of these differences is completely clean-cut, and one group shades into the other.

TABLE 3.8.   General Trends in Solubility in Water

Anion	Cerium group ($Z = 57$–62)	Yttrium group ($Z = 39, 63$–71)
Cl^-, Br^-, I^-, NO_3^-, ClO_4^-, BrO_3^-, $C_2H_3O_2^-$	Soluble	Soluble
F^-	Insoluble	Insoluble
OH^-	Insoluble	Insoluble
HCO_2^-	Slightly soluble	Moderately soluble
$C_2O_4^{2-}$	Insoluble; insoluble in $C_2O_4^{2-}$	Insoluble; soluble in $C_2O_4^{2-}$
CO_3^{2-}	Insoluble; insoluble in CO_3^{2-}	Insoluble; soluble in CO_3^{2-}
Basic NO_3^-	Moderately soluble	Slightly soluble
PO_4^{3-}	Insoluble	Insoluble
Double M^I sulfate	Insoluble in M_2SO_4 solution	Soluble in M_2SO_4 solution

The insolubility of the oxalates, even in dilute acids (pH 4 or less), is both striking and important. Precipitation with oxalic acid under these conditions may be used to separate the tripositive lanthanides from all other cationic species except the tri- and tetrapositive actinides.

Although the oxides and hydroxides are nearly quantitatively insoluble in water, they are sufficiently basic to dissolve readily in acids. Even the ignited oxides dissolve rapidly. Unlike the analogous compounds of common tripositive species (e.g., Al^{3+}, Cr^{3+}, Ga^{3+}), these substances are almost completely unreactive with aqueous alkalies and with basic oxides at elevated temperatures. That the hydrous oxides and hydroxides precipitate at steadily decreasing pH values from the light to the heavy end of the series (e.g., La^{3+}, 7.82; Gd^{3+},

6.83; Lu^{3+}, 6.30—all from nitrate solutions at 25°C.) is an important confirmation of the basicity order.

Complex Species. The importance of these species in the chemistry of the lanthanides may be expected from their importance in that of the *d*-type transition metals. It is observed experimentally, however, that except for the common aquated ions, $[Ln(H_2O)_n]^{3+}$, complex species are limited in number and notably stable only when derived from the strongest chelating agents. Indeed, there is a much greater similarity in behavior to the alkaline earth metal ions than to the *d*-type transition metal ions. This is perhaps not unreasonable when we realize that the transition metal species owe their properties to interaction between the *d* electrons of the valence shell and the ligands. The *f* electrons of the lanthanides are too well shielded to interact similarly, as pointed out in our earlier discussions of magnetic and light absorption properties (pp. 28, 32). The result is that each lanthanide ion is effectively an inert gas-type ion, like those of the alkaline earth metals, that attracts ligands only by over-all electrostatic forces. On this basis, we would expect—and indeed we do observe—a general decrease in case of complex ion formation with a specific ligand in the series $Ln^{4+} > Ln^{3+} > Ln^{2+}$.

Known types of complex species, together with appropriate illustrative examples, are summarized in Table 3.9. Those indicated as ion pair associations exist in solution, where their presence can be inferred from the changes in conductance, transference number, ion migration, or solvent extraction behavior that follow addition of the complexing group. They do not, in general, carry through series of reactions without change, and they are not distinguishable in solid compounds. Of the isolable nonchelated species, only the antipyrene derivatives are stable in contact with water; the others yield hydroxides, indicating that ammonia or the amine is only weakly held.

TABLE 3.9. A Classification of Typical Complex Species Derived from Ln^{3+}

Type	Examples*
Ion pair associations	Halo-LnF^{2+}
	Sulfito-$LnSO_3^+$
	Sulfato-$LnSO_4^+$
	Thiosulfato-$LnS_2O_3^+$
	Oxalato-$LnC_2O_4^+$
	Acetato-$LnC_2H_3O_2^{2+}$
Isolable nonchelated species,	Ammines: $LnCl_3 \cdot xNH_3$
	Amine adducts: $LnX_3 \cdot yRNH_2$
	Antipyrine adducts:
	$[Ln(ap)_6]X_3(X = I, ClO_4, NCS)$
Isolable chelated species	
1. Nonionic	8-Quinolinols: $[Ln(On)_3] \cdot nH_2O$
	1,3-Diketones: $[Ln(diket)_3] \cdot H_2O$
2. Ionic	Citrates: $[Ln(C_6H_5O_7)_2]^{3-}$
	α-Hydroxycarboxylates:
	$[Ln(R{-}CHOHCO_2)_6]^{3-}$
	Aminepolycarboxylates:
	$[Ln(EDTA)]^-, [Ln(NTA)_2]^{3-}$

$$* \quad ap = \begin{matrix} CH_3 \ CH_3 \\ | \quad | \\ C{-}N \\ \| \quad\ \ NC_6H_5 \\ C{-}C \\ | \quad \| \\ H \quad O \end{matrix}
\qquad
diket = HC\begin{matrix} R \\ \diagdown \\ C{-}O^- \\ \diagup \\ C{=}O \\ R \end{matrix}$$

On =

For EDTA and NTA see Table 3.10.

The chelated species are much more stable with respect to their components. The nonionic, or *inner complex*, species are difficultly soluble in water but quite soluble in organic solvents such as benzene or chloroform. They are ordinarily obtained by precipitation from aqueous solutions of carefully controlled pH. The 1,3-diketone chelates have the same colors as the aquated tripositive ions, and there are only slight modifications in the absorption bands. The 8-quinolinol chelates are uniformly yellow, as a result of the organic group present, but their absorption spectra consist of sharply defined, weak bands at the wavelengths of those for the aquated ions superimposed on the broad, intense bands of the 8-quinolinol grouping.

The other chelated species mentioned are usually soluble in water, so soluble in fact that crystallization of their salts may be extremely difficult. The formation of such chelated species in aqueous solution involves stepwise equilibria of the type

$$Ln^{3+} + AA \rightleftharpoons Ln(AA) \qquad (3\text{-}I)$$

$$Ln(AA) + AA \rightleftharpoons Ln(AA)_2 \qquad (3\text{-}II)$$

$$Ln(AA)_2 + (n - 2)AA \rightleftharpoons Ln(AA)_n \qquad (3\text{-}III)$$

or, for the final substance, the over-all equilibrium

$$Ln^{3+} + nAA \rightleftharpoons Ln(AA)_n \qquad (3\text{-}IV)$$

where AA is the chelating group and both aquation and the charges of the chelated species are neglected. The displacement of each such equilibrium, and therefore the stability of the species in question with respect to its components, is measured quantitatively by the magnitude of the appropriate equilibrium constant. Thus for equilibrium 3-IV this would be

$$K_{Ln(AA)_n} = c_{Ln(AA)_n}/c_{Ln^{3+}}c_{AA}^n \qquad (3.1)$$

Constants of this type are called *formation* or *stability constants*. For convenience, $\log_{10} K$ values (see Table 3.11), rather than the formation constants themselves, are usually used.

Undeniably, the most stable, and at the same time the most interesting and useful, chelated species of the lanthanides are those derived from the aminepolycarboxylic acids. As is indicated by the graphic formulas given in Table 3.10, the

TABLE 3.10. Aminepolycarboxylic Acids

Name	Formula	Possible chelate rings
Nitrilotriacetic acid (H$_3$NTA)	$N{\Large\langle}\begin{array}{l}CH_2COOH\\CH_2COOH\\CH_2COOH\end{array}$	3
N-Hydroxyethylethylenediamine-triacetic acid (H$_3$HEDTA)	$\begin{array}{l}HOCH_2CH_2{\Large\rangle}NCH_2CH_2N{\Large\langle}\begin{array}{l}CH_2COOH\\CH_2COOH\end{array}\\HOOCCH_2\end{array}$	4
Ethylenediaminetetraacetic acid (H$_4$EDTA)	$\begin{array}{l}HOOCCH_2{\Large\rangle}NCH_2CH_2N{\Large\langle}\begin{array}{l}CH_2COOH\\CH_2COOH\end{array}\\HOOCCH_2\end{array}$	5
1,2-Diaminocyclohexanetetraacetic acid (H$_4$DCTA)	$\begin{array}{l}\quad CH_2\text{—}CHN{\Large\langle}\begin{array}{l}CH_2COOH\\CH_2COOH\end{array}\\CH_2\\\quad CH_2\text{—}CHN{\Large\langle}\begin{array}{l}CH_2COOH\\CH_2COOH\end{array}\end{array}$	5
Diethylenetriaminepentaacetic acid (H$_5$DTPA)	$\begin{array}{l}HOOCCH_2{\Large\rangle}NCH_2CH_2NCH_2CH_2N{\Large\langle}\begin{array}{l}CH_2COOH\\CH_2COOH\end{array}\\HOOCCH_2\qquad\qquad\;\;|\\\qquad\qquad\qquad\quad CH_2\\\qquad\qquad\qquad\quad |\\\qquad\qquad\qquad\quad COOH\end{array}$	7

56

anions of these acids are each capable of forming more than one chelate ring by utilizing the several oxygen and nitrogen donors that are available. Indeed, in every instance there are sufficient donors present that 1:1 species result (e.g., $Ln(EDTA)^-$, $Ln(DTPA)^{2-}$). Formation constant data for a number of these systems are summarized in Table 3.11 and Fig. 3.1.

It is apparent that an increase in the number of like chelate rings in which a given cation can simultaneously participate increases the formation constant or stability. This is a general observation and principle. For a given ligand, the general increase in stability with decrease in crystal radius that we have predicted is observed. However, a closer examination of these and other data shows that although this increase is invariable

TABLE 3.11. Stabilities of Some Aminepolycarboxylic Acid Chelates at 25°C.

Cation	$\log_{10} K_{Ln(AA)}$				
	AA = NTA	AA = HEDTA	AA = EDTA[*]	AA = DCTA	AA = DTPA
Y^{3+}	11.48	14.65	18.09	19.41	22.05
La^{3+}	10.36	13.46	15.50	16.35	19.48
Ce^{3+}	10.83	14.11	15.98	—	20.5
Pr^{3+}	11.07	14.61	16.40	17.23	21.07
Nd^{3+}	11.26	14.86	16.61	17.69	21.60
Pm^{3+}	—	—	—	—	—
Sm^{3+}	11.53	15.28	17.14	18.63	22.34
Eu^{3+}	11.52	15.35	17.35	18.77	22.39
Gd^{3+}	11.54	15.22	17.37	18.80	22.46
Tb^{3+}	11.59	15.32	17.93	19.30	22.71
Dy^{3+}	11.74	15.30	18.30	19.69	22.82
Ho^{3+}	11.90	15.32	—	19.89	22.78
Er^{3+}	12.03	15.42	18.85	20.20	22.74
Tm^{3+}	12.22	15.59	19.32	20.46	22.72
Yb^{3+}	12.40	15.88	19.51	20.80	22.62
Lu^{3+}	12.49	15.88	19.83	20.91	22.44
Al^{3+}	—	—	16.13	17.63[*]	—
Fe^{3+}	15.87[*]	—	25.1	—	28.6
Co^{3+}	—	—	36	—	—

[*] At 20°C.

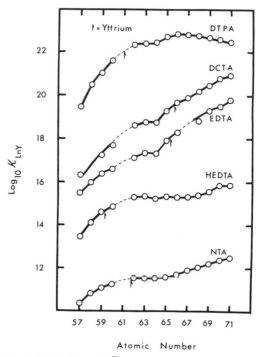

Fig. 3.1. Stabilities of Ln^{III}-aminepolycarboxylate chelates.

in the region La^{3+} through Eu^{3+}, with something of a break or discontinuity at the Gd^{3+} ion, two different behaviors characterize the region Gd^{3+} through Lu^{3+}, namely:

1. A continuing and rather regular increase in stability, with the yttrium chelate occupying the position expected from the crystal radius of the Y^{3+} ion (e.g., with NTA, EDTA, DCTA).

2. An increase in stability, followed by a decrease or a leveling off to essential constancy, with the yttrium chelate occupying a position in the Nd^{3+}–Sm^{3+} region and completely

out of line with that expected on a size basis (e.g., with HEDTA, DTPA).

Thus the concept of an electrostatic attraction between cation and ligand that increases as crystal radius decreases appears reasonable for the lighter lanthanides, but it is apparent that additional factors are also of importance among the heavier lanthanides. What these factors are and how they operate are not presently understood. It is probable that they reflect the fact that the formation constant really measures the displacement of an equilibrium of the type

$$[Ln(H_2O)_n]^{3+} + EDTA^{4-} \rightleftharpoons [Ln(EDTA)(H_2O)_m]^- +$$

$$(n - m) H_2O$$

where EDTA is cited as typical, rather than the reaction of the anhydrous cation. The smoothing effect of hydration on crystal radii, the rupture of Ln—OH_2 bonds, the formation of new bonds, and the retention of water in the product are undoubtedly important in determining the measured stability.

It is tempting to associate the *gadolinium break* (Fig. 3.1) with the corresponding break in crystal radii (Fig. 2.1), but the latter is insufficient alone to account for the former. Furthermore, the nomadic behavior of yttrium is not limited to chelated species. Thus, in fractional precipitation, yttrium may concentrate with either the lighter (using $Fe(CN)_6^{3-}$ or $Fe(CN)_6^{4-}$) or the heavier (using OH^-) lanthanides. Clearly, we have here both an indication that our simple approach to basicity is not completely adequate and a warning that what is observed for the lighter cations cannot always be extrapolated to the heavier. The fundamental value of experimental observation cannot be overemphasized (p. 33).

Differences in formation constant between adjacent cations are somewhat larger for the aminepolycarboxylates than for other known ligands, except possibly some of the α-hydroxycarboxylates. These differences are used to advantage in both laboratory and practical separations (pp. 80–88). As indicated by the comparison data in Table 3.11, the formation constants associated with similar chelates of more familiar tripositive ions are larger. This probably reflects the greater importance of covalent bonding.

The compositions of some of the species mentioned suggest a *coordination number* of *six* for each of the Ln^{3+} ions. This coordination number has been assumed for many years. However, facts such as the invariable presence of bound water in 1,3-diketone and aminepolycarboxylate complex species and the ability of [Ln(NTA)] compounds to form readily $[Ln(NTA)_2]^{3-}$ ions suggest a larger coordination number than six, at least *seven* but perhaps even *eight* or *nine*. Thus far, we do not know with certainty.

Unlike the *d*-type transition metal ions, the lanthanides do not form π-type complex species with unsaturated hydrocarbons (e.g., olefins, cyclopentadiene).* Indeed, a complete study of the cyclopentadienides, $Ln(C_5H_5)_3$ (Table 2.6), indicates that these compounds are salts rather than complex compounds.

Oxidation State +4—Another "Anomalous" State

Inasmuch as cerium(IV) oxide is formed when an alkaline suspension of cerium(III) hydroxide is exposed to the atmosphere or treated with chlorine or hydrogen peroxide or when many cerium(III) salts containing oxy anions are heated in the air, it is probable that tetrapositive cerium was recognized even in early studies of the lanthanides. Indeed, under the conditions outlined, the tetrapositive state is so readily formed at the expense of the tripositive that it has often been regarded

---

*Doubly occupied *p*-type atomic orbitals of carbon atoms in such hydrocarbons may interact by a sidewise overlap with vacant orbitals of cations to give so-called π bonds.

as the more completely characteristic oxidation state. The other tetrapositive lanthanides, however, are encountered only in solid compounds (Table 2.2) that undergo reduction when dissolved.

Chemical Stability and Stabilization. It is thus convenient to discuss cerium separately. The listed standard oxidation potential (Table 2.3) describes the equilibrium

$$Ce(aq)^{3+} \rightleftharpoons Ce(aq)^{4+} + e$$

when neither complexing by the anion nor hydrolysis occurs. However, experimentally measured potentials vary widely as these reactions become important (e.g., for solutions $1N$ in the acid indicated: $HClO_4$, -1.70 v.; HNO_3, -1.61 v.; H_2SO_4, -1.44 v.). Correction for these effects gives the listed value.

In acidic media, cerium(IV) is slightly stronger as an oxidizing agent than lead(IV) oxide and slightly weaker than hydrogen peroxide. It can be formed from cerium(III) by only a few chemical oxidizing agents (e.g., $S_2O_8^{2-}$, O_3) and is best prepared by electrolytic oxidation. On the other hand, reduction is readily effected by many reagents (e.g., Fe^{2+}, Sn^{2+}, I^-, H_2O_2, organic compounds). That the change is a completely reversible, one-electron change makes cerium(IV) a particularly useful analytical oxidant. Although no potential data are available for alkaline systems, experiment shows that there cerium(IV) is a much weaker oxidizing agent.

Hydrated cerium(IV) oxide dissolves without reduction in nitric, perchloric, or sulfuric acid. Such solutions readily hydrolyze and deposit basic salts as the acidity is reduced, but if the acidity is kept sufficiently high they can yield hydrated cerium(IV) salts. In the presence of ammonium nitrate, the orange-red double salt $Ce(NO_3)_4 \cdot 2NH_4NO_3$ is easily crystallized. This is a common water-soluble source of cerium(IV). A comparable double sulfate, $Ce(SO_4)_2 \cdot 2(NH_4)_2SO_4 \cdot 2H_2O$, can be prepared also. In the solid state, cerium(IV) is substantially stabilized as the oxide (CeO_2) or fluoride (CeF_4).

The other tetrapositive species (Pr^{IV}, Nd^{IV}, Tb^{IV}, Dy^{IV}) apparently require trapping in a suitable crystal lattice for their stabilization. The estimated potential of -2.86 v. for the Pr^{III}–Pr^{IV} couple suggests that praseodymium(IV) is comparable to elemental fluorine in oxidizing strength in acidic solution. It is probable that the other tetrapositive species are at least as strongly oxidizing.

Stabilization in the Solid State. Except for cerium(IV), where any preparable solid resists reduction, only oxide and fluoride systems are known to stabilize tetrapositive species.

1. *Oxide Systems.* The common compounds are off-white to brownish CeO_2, black Pr_6O_{11}, and dark brown Tb_4O_7, although both PrO_2 and TbO_2 have been prepared. The formulations Pr_6O_{11} and Tb_4O_7 represent average analytical compositions, rather than true compounds, but they suggest that compounds intermediate in analysis between $LnO_{1.5}$ (i.e., Ln_2O_3) and LnO_2 can be obtained. This is experimentally true. As is shown by Fig. 3.2, there is a continuous decrease in the lattice dimension a as one increases the mole ratio of oxygen to lanthanide in both the praseodymium–oxygen and the terbium–oxygen systems. This includes those of the oxides Pr_6O_{11} and Tb_4O_7. Since this suggests continuous alteration in composition without substantial change in crystal structure, we must ask how this can be possible.

The three distinguishable forms of the sesquioxides (Ln_2O_3) have the broad regions of existence noted in Fig. 3.3. The A type (hexagonal, with seven oxide ions surrounding each Ln^{3+} ion) and the B type (monoclinic, with some Ln^{3+} ions surrounded by six oxide ions and others by seven) are less important in this connection than the C type (cubic), the

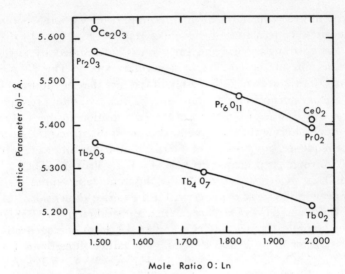

Fig. 3.2. Variation in lattice parameter with O:Ln ratio. (Redrawn from Gruen, D. M., Koehler, W. C., and Katz, J. J., *J. Am. Chem. Soc.* **73**, 1475 (1951).)

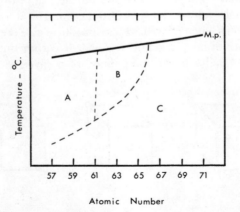

Fig. 3.3. Regions of existence of crystal modifications of Ln_2O_3 (not drawn to scale).

structure of which is shown in comparison with the cubic fluorite-type structure of the oxides LnO_2 in Fig. 3.4. In the fluorite arrangement, each Ln^{4+} ion is surrounded by eight oxide ions at the corners of a regular cube. The C-type Ln_2O_3 arrangement differs only in the fact that one-fourth of these oxygen positions are not used. Thus, by adding oxygen one can transfer from the $LnO_{1.50}$ composition to the LnO_2 without altering the fundamental nature of the structure. As a consequence, any number of intermediate compositions might be distinguished, e.g., $PrO_{1.71}$, $PrO_{1.77}$, $PrO_{1.66}$, $TbO_{1.71}$, $TbO_{1.81}$. Correspondingly, two different lanthanides can appear in the same oxide crystal if the lattice dimensions (a) of $LnO_{2.00}$ and C-$LnO_{1.50}$ are not markedly different ($\pm 2.25\%$). For example, the oxides CeO_2 and Ln_2O_3 form homogeneous crystals for $Ln = Y$ and Pm–Lu. The lattice dimensions (a) of the LnO_2 oxides are CeO_2, 5.411 Å.; PrO_2, 5.395 Å.; TbO_2, 5.213 Å. Again the lanthanide contraction is apparent.

These relationships provide an explanation for the observations that oxidation of cerium(III) hydroxide or oxide gives products that are green, blue, and purple before the final off-white to pale yellow CeO_2 is obtained and that cerium(IV) oxide darkens when heated. These products owe their color to the presence of both tri- and tetravalent cerium in the same crystal. Mixed-valence compounds of a given element are

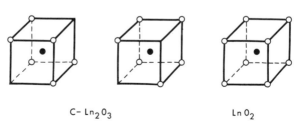

C– Ln_2O_3 Ln O_2

Fig. 3.4. Comparison of crystal structures of C-type Ln_2O_3 and LnO_2 ($\circ = O^{2-}$; $\bullet = Ln^{3+}$ or Ln^{4+}).

often deeply colored, even though color is absent when but a single oxidation state is present.

2. *Fluoride Systems.* Although the compound CeF_4 was prepared many years ago, the terbium analog was not obtained until 1954. It is colorless and isostructural with the cerium(IV) compound. Pure praseodymium(IV) fluoride has not been prepared. However, the complex compounds $Na[PrF_5]$ and $M_2[PrF_6]$ (M = Na, K, Rb, Cs) have been obtained and have been shown to contain praseodymium(IV) by analysis, magnetic measurements, absorption spectra, and X-ray evaluation of structure. Analogous terbium compounds $M_2[TbF_6]$ (M = K, Rb, Cs) have been prepared. Both neodymium and dysprosium yield the apparently isomorphous compounds $Cs_3[LnF_7]$ (Ln = Nd, Dy).

Preparation. General methods of obtaining the tetrapositive species include

1. *Oxidation with oxygen at elevated temperatures.* Ignition in air of salts containing thermally decomposable oxy anions (e.g., OH^-, CO_3^{2-}, $C_2O_4^{2-}$) or of the sesquioxides gives the oxides CeO_2, Pr_6O_{11}, and Tb_4O_7. The stoichiometric oxide PrO_2 results when the sesquioxide is heated in oxygen at 100 atmospheres of pressure at 500°C. Heating the sesquioxide with atomic oxygen at 450°C. gives the oxide TbO_2.

2. *Oxidation with fluorine at elevated temperatures.* Elemental fluorine at 300–500°C. converts the trifluorides to CeF_4 and TbF_4. Treating mixtures of alkali metal chlorides and the trichlorides of praseodymium, neodymium, and dysprosium with elemental fluorine at 300–500°C. yields the solids $Na[PrF_5]$, $M_2[PrF_6]$, $Cs_3[NdF_7]$, and $Cs_3[DyF_7]$.

3. *Chemical oxidation at ordinary temperatures.* Cerium(III) oxide or the hydrous hydroxide slowly absorbs atmospheric oxygen and ultimately yields the dioxide. This oxidation is more rapid with alkaline hydrogen peroxide or sodium hypochlorite. Both bromate ion and permanganate ion oxidize

cerium(III) ion to the dioxide in suitably buffered solutions. Peroxydisulfate yields cerium(IV) ion under acidic conditions.

In Conclusion

The general chemistry of the lanthanides, as just presented, both implements the conceptual approach followed in Chapter 2 and provides the background essential to understanding the problems of recovery, separation, and application to be discussed in Chapter 4. We see that in the main experimental observation is in accord with the broad theoretical background that has been developed but that there are instances of difference where modification of this background is essential. We shall see that a combination of this background with the factual information given has done much to reduce the complex problems of separation to logical routine.

Selected Readings

Asprey, L. B., and Cunningham, B. B., "Progress in Inorganic Chemistry," F. A. Cotton, Ed., Vol. II, pp. 267–86, Interscience Publishers, New York, 1960. (Anomalous oxidation states.)

Daane, A. H., "The Rare Earths," F. H. Spedding and A. H. Daane, Eds., ch. 13, John Wiley & Sons, New York, 1961. (Metals.)

Daane, A. H., "Rare Metals Handbook," C. A. Hampel, Ed., ch. 33, Reinhold Publishing Corp., New York, 1961. (Yttrium metal.)

Kremers, H. E., "Rare Metals Handbook," C. A. Hampel, Ed., ch. 19, Reinhold Publishing Corp., New York, 1961. (Metals.)

Pearce, D. W., *Chem. Rev.* **16,** 121–47 (1935). (Anomalous oxidation states.)

Pearce, D. W., and Selwood, P. W., *J. Chem. Educ.* **13,** 224–230 (1936). (Anomalous oxidation states.)

Vickery, R. C., "Chemistry of the Lanthanons," ch. 8, 13, 14, Academic Press, New York, 1953. (General chemistry.)

Yost, D. M., Russell, H., Jr., and Garner, C. S., "The Rare-Earth Elements and Their Compounds," ch. 6, John Wiley & Sons, New York, 1947. (General chemistry.)

chapter four

OCCURRENCE, RECOVERY, SEPARATION, APPLICATION— THE REALM OF THE PRACTICAL

Thus far, we have obviously—and indeed very deliberately—assigned the practical aspects of the chemistry of the lanthanides to a subordinate role. The wisdom of this somewhat unconventional procedure lies in the extreme difficulty of considering the practical in any ordered or logical fashion without some prior knowledge of why these substances behave as they do, of what similarities and differences among them can be exploited, and of what commonplace and unusual properties they have. This background permits us to systematize our discussion and to make the practical a unified part of the whole.

Occurrence in Nature

The abundance data already cited (Table 1.3) indicate only that as a group and, in certain instances as individuals, the lanthanides are potentially available in unlimited quantities. A complete picture of availability, however, must include also data on concentrations of these species in economically interesting deposits. Here, the nature of the minerals available, the ease with which such minerals can be cracked and thus the cost of processing, the geographical location of ore bodies, and the markets for products are all of importance.

As may be expected from similarities in crystal radii, oxidation state, and general properties (Chapters 2 and 3), each known lanthanide mineral contains all members of the series (except, presumably, promethium). This is true of even cerite or gadolinite, although the historical developments outlined in Chapter 1 might suggest otherwise. It is observed, of course, that natural processes of geochemical concentration have given us certain minerals rich in the cerium group (p. 51) and others rich in the yttrium group. This tendency for cations of closely similar radii to concentrate in particular minerals accounts also for the natural occurrence of yttrium in association with the heavier lanthanides.

Important cerium and yttrium group minerals, together with their compositions and the geographical locations of their most important deposits, are summarized in Table 4.1.

Monazite, both because of its availability and substantial thorium content, is the most important of the mineral sources. Although massive monazite crystals are found in many pegmatites, in only a few instances (notably in South Africa) are they present in sufficient quantity to permit vein mining. Natural weathering and gravity concentration processes (sp. gr. of monazite = 5.2), however, have produced sizable placer deposits of monazite sands. The most notable of these are in Travancore, where the beach deposits are seemingly limitless and regenerate with each crest of tide. Commercial mining of monazite sands in the United States has centered in Florida and the Carolinas, the substantial Idaho deposits being diffi-

TABLE 4.1. Important Minerals

Name	Composition* Idealized	Composition* Generalized	Location of significant deposits

1. *Cerium Group Minerals*

Name	Idealized	Generalized	Location of significant deposits
Monazite	$(Ce)PO_4$	49–74% Ce earths 1–4% Y earths 5–9% ThO_2 1–2% SiO_2 tr. U	Travancore, India; Brazil; Union of South Africa; Florida, North and South Carolina, Idaho
Bastnaesite	$(Ce)FCO_3$	65–70% Ce earths < 1% Y earths	California, New Mexico; Sweden
Cerite	$(Ce)_3M^{II}H_3Si_3O_{13}$ $(M = Ca, Fe)$	51–72% Ce earths tr.–7.6% Y earths tr. Th, U, Zr	Sweden; Caucausus

2. *Yttrium Group Minerals*

Name	Idealized	Generalized	Location of significant deposits
Euxenite†	$(Y)(Nb,Ta)TiO_6 \cdot$ xH_2O	13–35% Y earths 2–8% Ce earths 20–23% TiO_2 25–35% $(Nb,Ta)_2O_5$	Australia; Idaho
Xenotime	$(Y)PO_4$	54–65% Y earths ca. 0.1% Ce earths up to 3% ThO_2 up to 3.5% U_3O_8 2–3% ZrO_2	Norway; Brazil
Gadolinite	$(Y)_2M^{II}_3Si_2O_{10}$ $(M = Fe, Be)$	35–48% Y earths 2–17% Ce earths up to 11.6% BeO tr. Th	Sweden; Norway; Texas, Colorado

* The symbols (Ce) and (Y) represent the cerium and yttrium group lanthanides, respectively.

† Name used when $(Nb,Ta)_2O_5/TiO_2 = 1:4$ or more; when this ratio is 1:3 or less, the mineral is polycrase.

cultly accessible. Other heavy minerals such as zircon, ilmenite, garnet, and rutile are common contaminants in monazite deposits. The large bastnaesite deposits at Mountain Pass, California, represent a potentially competitive mineral source of negligible thorium content. Cerite is only of historical interest.

The yttrium group lanthanides are recovered commercially from monazite concentrates, even though their over-all concentration is low. Both gadolinite and euxenite are sufficiently abundant to be of potential commercial interest. Commercial processing of the latter (e.g., from Idaho) for niobium and tantalum gives the mixed lanthanides as by-products. Xenotime is found in small quantities in monazite sands.

Gross Recovery from Mineral Sources

Similarities between laboratory and technical approaches make it impractical, either here or later, to distinguish between them. Processing amounts to cracking the mineral, recovering the lanthanides (and thorium), removing thorium if it is present, and separating the lanthanides. It is ordinarily most convenient to remove cerium before fractionating the other lanthanides.

Cracking and Recovery Procedures. The chemical treatment used depends upon the composition of the mineral. The silicate minerals are conveniently decomposed to insoluble silica and the soluble chlorides by digestion with hydrochloric acid. Euxenite may be treated with hydrofluoric acid to solubilize the niobium, tantalum, and titanium values and leave the insoluble lanthanide fluorides. Monazite (or xenotime) is decomposed by digestion with either concentrated sulfuric acid or sodium hydroxide solution. Bastnaesite is converted by concentrated sulfuric acid to the water-soluble sulfates, with the loss of gaseous carbon dioxide and hydrogen fluoride.

The sulfuric acid treatment of monazite sand may be summarized as shown in Scheme 4.1. From the resulting solution, thorium can be precipitated as a phosphate by diluting to the proper acidity or as the fluoride by adding hydrofluoric acid and taking advantage of the greater solubility of the LnF_3 compounds in strongly acidic solutions. In either procedure, the lanthanides must be separated from phosphate species by precipitation as hydrous hydroxides or oxalates. Alternatively, both the thorium and the lanthanides can be freed of phosphate by precipitation as oxalates and conversion to the more reactive hydrous oxides or hydroxides with caustic soda.

The sodium hydroxide treatment of monazite sand may be summarized as in Scheme 4.2. This procedure has the advantage of removing phosphate more readily than the sulfuric acid procedure, but its higher cost has limited its adoption.

Removal of Thorium. In addition to the procedures mentioned, the following have been used:

1. *Selective precipitation* as ThO_2 (with sodium hydroxide at pH 5.8, or with reagents such as $S_2O_3^{2-}$ or $(CH_2)_6N_4$ that control pH appropriately by hydrolysis); as $Th(IO_3)_4$ from concentrated HNO_3 solution); or as ThP_2O_6 (from strongly acidic solution). None of these procedures is completely specific, since each depends only on the lower solubility of the thorium compound under optimum conditions.

2. *Selective extraction into nonaqueous solvents*, such as tri-*n*-butyl phosphate or certain higher amines, whereby thorium is more readily transferred to the nonaqueous phase than the lanthanides. Tri-*n*-butyl phosphate systems are discussed later (pp. 88, 90) with specific reference to the lanthanides. The amines function best with sulfate solution, from which thorium is removed as the amine salt of a sulfato complex (e.g., $(amine \cdot H)_2[Th(SO_4)_3]$) completely and in a high state of purity.

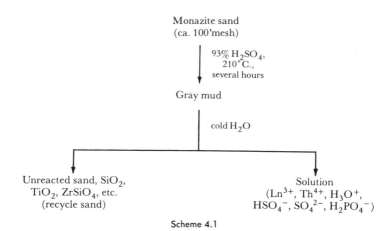

Monazite sand
(ca. 100'mesh)

93% H_2SO_4,
210°C.,
several hours

Gray mud

cold H_2O

Unreacted sand, SiO_2,
TiO_2, $ZrSiO_4$, etc.
(recycle sand)

Solution
(Ln^{3+}, Th^{4+}, H_3O^+,
HSO_4^-, SO_4^{2-}, $H_2PO_4^-$)

Scheme 4.1

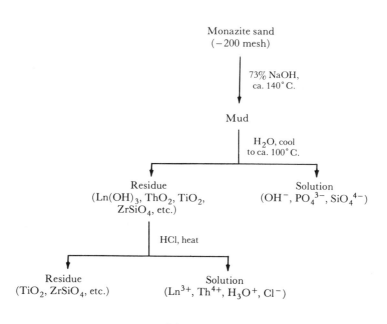

Monazite sand
(−200 mesh)

73% NaOH,
ca. 140°C.

Mud

H_2O, cool
to ca. 100°C.

Residue
($Ln(OH)_3$, ThO_2, TiO_2,
$ZrSiO_4$, etc.)

Solution
(OH^-, PO_4^{3-}, SiO_4^{4-})

HCl, heat

Residue
(TiO_2, $ZrSiO_4$, etc.)

Solution
(Ln^{3+}, Th^{4+}, H_3O^+, Cl^-)

Scheme 4.2

3. *Selective anion exchange*, whereby an amine-type exchanger removes thorium as a nitrato or sulfato complex ion. The separation is rapid and complete.

Removal of Cerium. Useful procedures are based upon reduced basicity in the tetrapositive state. They include:

1. *Selective reaction of the mixed oxides with nitric acid (pH 3–4)*, in which the reduced solubility of cerium(IV) results in its concentration in the residues, but not in its complete separation.

2. *Selective hydrolysis* to a basic nitrate or sulfate as a result of diluting and boiling a concentrated solution containing Ce^{4+} and Ln^{3+} ions. Although some three-fourths of the cerium is obtained in a high state of purity, complete separation cannot be achieved.

3. *Selective oxidation*, anodically or chemically with bromate or permanganate, followed by *nearly* complete precipitation of cerium(IV) from the buffered solution.

4. *Selective crystallization* of the double ammonium nitrate (p. 61) from nitric acid solutions. Separation from the tripositive species is complete, but recovery is not quantitative.

5. *Selective extraction into nonaqueous solvents*, especially tri-*n*-butyl phosphate, where cerium(IV) parallels thorium in behavior. Reduction with aqueous sodium nitrite returns cerium (as Ce^{3+}) to the aqueous phase, but leaves thorium in the nonaqueous.

Separation of the Lanthanides

Separation may be effected by one or another or some combination of the following general procedures involving
1. Fractional crystallization of isomorphous salts
2. Basicity differences
   a. Fractional precipitation from solution
   b. Fractional thermal decomposition of salts
   c. Ion exchange

d. Solvent extraction
3. Selective oxidation or reduction
4. Physical differences

All procedures, except certain of those involving oxidation or reduction, are fractional in character. Thus in each step there is a concentration of one species at the expense of the other, but separation results only if that step is repeated many times.

The efficiency of a fractionation procedure is given by the magnitude of its *separation factor*. For two lanthanides, Ln and Ln′, being changed from an initial concentration condition (1) to a final one (2), the separation factor (α) may be defined as

$$\alpha = \frac{c_{\text{Ln}(2)}/c_{\text{Ln}'(2)}}{c_{\text{Ln}(1)}/c_{\text{Ln}'(1)}} = \frac{c_{\text{Ln}(2)}c_{\text{Ln}'(1)}}{c_{\text{Ln}(1)}c_{\text{Ln}'(2)}} \tag{4.1}$$

No separation results if $\alpha = 1$, but the greater the departure from unity, the more efficient the process is.

Methods of Following Separations. It is important that the path taken by each component be followed analytically as fractionation proceeds, preferably by a rapid procedure that is specific for each cation and does not destroy or alter the sample. Spectrophotometric procedures are the most generally useful. Each absorbing tripositive species has bands (Table 2.9) free from interference by other cations that adhere to the Beer-Lambert relationship

$$\log_{10} I_0/I = kcl \tag{4.2}$$

where I_0 and I are the intensities of the incident and transmitted light, c is concentration, l is the light path, and k is a constant. Secondary X-ray fluorescence is also useful, but emission spectrographic procedures are best applied only to the detection and determination of small quantities of contaminants in highly purified samples.

Magnetic susceptibility data (pp. 26, 28) are of analytical significance only for binary mixtures of paramagnetic sub-

stances of known moments or of a paramagnetic and a diamagnetic substance. Average atomic weight, based usually
upon the results of analyses of the mixed oxalates for both
lanthanide and oxalate content, although of historical importance, is of quantitative significance only for a binary
mixture or a sample containing yttrium. The lower atomic
weight of yttrium (88.905) compared with those of the lanthanides (138.91–174.97) permits one to follow it by this
means.

Inasmuch as little of the early work on separations could be
followed quantitatively, it is impossible to judge the efficiencies
of many of the procedures described.

Fractional Crystallization. The quantity of work reported
and the amount of information accumulated relating to this
classical procedure (Chapter 1) are truly overwhelming. It is
probable that every anion found to form soluble salts with the
tripositive ions has been investigated in the hope of developing
an efficient crystallization separation. Inasmuch as only those
anions yielding truly isomorphous salts that are easy to crystallize, have reasonable and temperature-dependent solubilities, and possess measurable solubility differences as the Ln^{3+}
ion changes can be effective, the number of really successful
systems must be limited.

Both fractional crystallization and fractional precipitation
involve the formation of a solid phase from a solution phase
and can thus be described similarly in terms of separation
factor. Separation factors for several procedures of this type,
as calculated from Eq. 4.1, are summarized in Table 4.2.
These can be criticized on the ground that the slow equilibration necessary to produce the completely homogeneous solid
phase required by Eq. 4.1 is seldom realized in practice.
Rather, the true equilibrium is normally between the solution
and an infinitesimally thin layer at the crystal surface. Under

TABLE 4.2. Separation Factors for Fractional Crystallization and Precipitation Processes[*]

Procedure	Ion pair	α
Double ammonium nitrate crystallization	$La^{3+}-Nd^{3+}$	3.1
Dimethyl oxalate precipitation	$La^{3+}-Pr^{3+}$	4.9
Alkali carbonate precipitation	$La^{3+}-Nd^{3+}$	4.9
Magnesium oxide precipitation	$La^{3+}-Nd^{3+}$	5.6

[*] Data from Weaver, B., *Anal. Chem.* **26**, 474 (1954).

these conditions, the separation factor is given more exactly by the logarithmic expression

$$\alpha' = \log_{10}(c_{Ln(2)}/c_{Ln(1)})/\log_{10}(c_{Ln'(2)}/c_{Ln'(1)}) \qquad (4.3)$$

The data in Table 4.3 suggest that for a given separation α' is more nearly constant than α. Although qualitatively either α or α' could be used to compare the efficiencies of two procedures, very few of the data available on fractional crystallization can be used to evaluate either factor.

TABLE 4.3. Comparison of Homogeneous (α) and Logarithmic (α') Separation Factors for Precipitation by Hydrolysis of Methyl Oxalate[*]

Cerium(III) precipitated, %	Neodymium(III) coprecipitated, %	α	α'
15.0	24.6	1.85	1.74
21.1	35.4	1.93	1.74
34.2	53.9	2.25	1.85
56.0	76.7	2.53	1.75
62.7	82.7	2.85	1.78
74.4	90.2	3.17	1.71
83.9	95.9	4.49	1.75
92.0	99.0	8.26	1.80

[*] Feibush, A. M., Rowley, K., and Gordon, L., *Anal. Chem.* **30**, 1605 (1958). See also Salutsky, M. L., and Gordon, L., *Anal. Chem.* **28**, 138 (1956).

Among the more effective compounds are

1. The double ammonium nitrates, $Ln(NO_3)_3 \cdot 2NH_4NO_3 \cdot 4H_2O$, for the removal of lanthanum and the separation of praseodymium from neodymium (pp. 4, 78).

2. The double manganese nitrates, $2Ln(NO_3)_3 \cdot 3Mn(NO_3)_2 \cdot 24H_2O$, for the separation of members of the cerium group but not the yttrium group.

3. The bromates, $Ln(BrO_3)_3 \cdot 9H_2O$, and the ethyl sulfates, $Ln(C_2H_5SO_4)_3 \cdot 9H_2O$, for the separation of members of the yttrium group.

Crystallization in each instance is from water. The procedure followed with the double ammonium nitrates is typical. The appropriate solution containing the mixed cations is evaporated until about half of the salts present will crystallize upon cooling to room temperature. The crystals are separated from the mother liquor. Each fraction is then recrystallized, the initial crystals by dissolving in water and evaporating until half the material deposits and the mother liquor by evaporating directly. Four fractions result. The mother liquor from the first crystals in this step is then combined with the second crystals, and the operation repeated. In this way, the triangular scheme shown in Fig. 4.1 is developed, with the least soluble double ammonium nitrate (that of La^{3+}) concentrating at the *head* (crystal end) of the series, the moderately soluble ones (Pr^{3+}, Nd^{3+}) at the center, and the most soluble one (Sm^{3+}) at the *tail* (solution end).

It is apparent that a triangular scheme of this type can expand into a large number of fractions of steadily decreasing content of lanthanides unless some means of control is used. In practice, it is found desirable to omit certain portions of the scheme, thus permitting removal of one lanthanide in a state of purity and treatment of remaining mixed species as a single species. It is found that if the same weight fraction of a

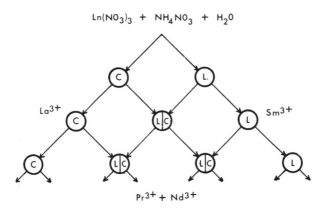

Fig. 4.1. Triangular fractional crystallization scheme for cerium earth double ammonium nitrates.

given component is allowed to crystallize in each step, fractions of repeating total composition result. These may be removed and combined, and more of the original mixture may be added when a fraction that repeats its composition is obtained.

Fractional crystallization is normally most effective at the lanthanum end of the series where solubilities differ the most. Pure lanthanum is quite readily separated as the double ammonium nitrate, but no other fractional crystallization procedure is now of commercial importance. Generally, separations in the samarium-europium-gadolinium region and within the yttrium group are particularly tedious and inefficient; pioneering studies often involved hundreds or even thousands of crystallizations.

If bismuth(III) nitrate is added to a mixture of cerium group nitrates containing magnesium ion, its double magnesium nitrate crystallizes between the isomorphous ones of samarium and europium. From the resulting Sm^{3+}–Bi^{3+} and

Bi^{3+}–Eu^{3+} mixtures, bismuth can be removed readily with hydrogen sulfide. Bismuth(III) is apparently unique among the nonlanthanides as a separating ion, but easily removable lanthanides (e.g., Ce^{3+} between La^{3+} and Pr^{3+} in the double ammonium nitrates or Pr^{3+} between Er^{3+} and Tm^{3+} in the bromates) may function similarly.

Fractional Precipitation. This is somewhat more limited in practicality than fractional crystallization because of the added tedium of removing and redissolving precipitates. Although fractional precipitation reflects the basicity order more nearly exactly than fractional crystallization, yttrium is much more migratory in behavior during precipitation than during crystallization (p. 59).

All separations by fractional precipitation depend fundamentally upon basicity differences. However, these differences can be operative only when equilibration between solution and solid phases is complete. This condition seldom pertains in practice, for addition of a precipitating anion to the mixed lanthanides results in a localized excess of reagent and precipitation of all the species present. Redissolution may then be too slow or too far from complete to permit true equilibration before more reagent is added.

For the specific case of a gaseous reagent such as ammonia, this problem is avoided by introducing the gas extensively diluted with unreactive nitrogen. More generally, it is solved by generating the precipitating ion slowly and homogeneously throughout the solution. Cases in point include hydroxyl ion generated by the cathodic decomposition of water; carbonate and hydroxyl ions formed by adding urea and heating; carbonate ion produced by thermally hydrolyzing trichloroacetate ion; and oxalate ion produced by thermally hydrolyzing dimethyl oxalate. Precipitates so formed are commonly granular and easy to handle. Control of the precipitating reagent by addition of another species that may give a complex species has the same effect. This is exemplified by the use of zinc or cadmium ion with ammonia. Similarly, addition of solid oxides (e.g., MgO, Ln_2O_3) or carbonates (e.g., $PbCO_3$, $ZnCO_3$) provides a slowly increasing and controlled source of hydroxyl ion.

True basicity effects are also achieved by adding a weak complexing agent or insufficient complexing agent (e.g., $EDTA^{4-}$ or NTA^{3-}) to tie up all of the lanthanide ions before adding the precipitant. In either case, the least readily complexed cation is the most available for precipitation.

Although fractional precipitation was once of particular importance in separating yttrium from the heavier lanthanons, it is now of little practical importance.

Fractional Thermal Decomposition of Salts. The temperature at which an oxy salt (e.g., nitrate, sulfate, acetate) is converted to an oxide or basic salt of lower solubility decreases with decreasing basicity of the tripositive cation. Fusion of the mixed nitrates followed by leaching with water rapidly concentrates yttrium in the more basic fractions and effects its separation from the heavier lanthanides. The procedure is effective where oxidation can occur (e.g., with Ce or Pr, p. 65) but not in most other cases.

Ion Exchange. The exchange of metal ions in solution with protons on a solid ion exchanger is an equilibrium process

$$M^{n+} + nHR\ (s) \rightleftharpoons M\ (R)_n(s) + nH^+$$

where HR represents an exchange point on a hydrogen-cycle resin. Similarly, one metal ion may exchange for another

$$M'^{n+} + M(R)_n(s) \rightleftharpoons M'(R)_n(s) + M^{n+}$$

This process is familiar in the exchange of calcium ion for sodium ion in water softening.

Observation that the tenacity with which a cation is held by an ion exchanger decreases with its crystal radius and charge, as

$$Th^{4+} > La^{3+} > Ce^{3+} > Y^{3+} > Lu^{3+} > Ba^{2+} >$$
$$Ca^{2+} > K^+ > NH_4^+ > H^+$$

suggested separation of the lanthanides by an exchange process. However, the pioneering studies of D. W. Pearce and R. G. Russell at Purdue University showed that when several tripositive lanthanides were adsorbed on an exchanger, their removal by adding sodium chloride effected no greater degree of separation than conventional fractional crystallization or precipitation. On the other hand, observation at Oak Ridge, Tennessee, that niobium and zirconium could be removed selectively from an ion exchange column with oxalic acid solution suggested that separation of the lanthanides might be similarly effected by elution with appropriate complexing agents.

Extensive tracer-scale experiments, carried out largely under the supervision of G. E. Boyd and E. R. Tompkins at Oak Ridge and first reported publicly in 1947, showed that if the mixed tripositive lanthanides are adsorbed as a band at the top of a cation exchange column and then eluted with a suitable complexing agent (e.g., buffered citric acid solution), separation of the cations into individual bands occurs on the column, and the species ultimately leave the column in reverse order of their atomic numbers. This is shown in Fig. 4.2, where the fractionation of 0.01–0.1 mg. quantities shows an elution peak for each ion in question. The use of such data in establishing the existence of element 61 (Pm) has been discussed in Chapter 1 (p. 8).

1. *Ion Exchange Equilibria and the Significance of Complexing Agents.* In order that subsequent developments may be both understandable and logical, we must now show why the

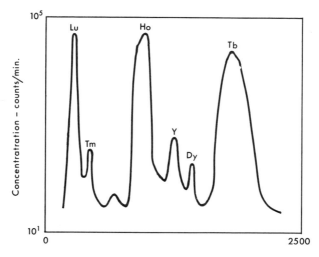

Fig. 4.2. Tracer-scale elution with 5% citrate at pH 3.20.   (Redrawn from Ketelle, B. H., and Boyd, G. E., *J. Am. Chem. Soc.* **69**, 2800 (1947).)

fractionating ability of an exchanger is enhanced by a complexing agent.

The distribution of a lanthanide between a solid exchanger (r) and an aqueous phase (aq) in terms of the equilibrium (p. 80).

$$\mathrm{Ln^{3+}(aq) + 3HR(s) \rightleftharpoons Ln(R)_3(s) + 3H^+(aq)}$$

is described as

$$\lambda_0 = c_{\mathrm{Ln^{3+}(r)}} / c_{\mathrm{Ln^{3+}(aq)}} \qquad (4.4)$$

where λ_0 is a distribution coefficient. Neglecting ionic charges for convenience gives

$$\lambda_0 = c_{\mathrm{Ln(r)}} / c_{\mathrm{Ln(aq)}} \qquad (4.5)$$

For a second lanthanide (Ln′), we have similarly

$$\lambda'_0 = c_{Ln'(r)} / c_{Ln'(aq)} \tag{4.6}$$

and the separation factor (p. 74) then becomes

$$\alpha = \lambda'_0 / \lambda_0 = c_{Ln'(r)} c_{Ln(aq)} / c_{Ln(r)} c_{Ln'(aq)} \tag{4.7}$$

Under the conditions described, the value of α seldom departs significantly from unity.

If now a chelating agent (p. 54) is introduced, the additional equilibria (p. 55)

$$Ln + n(AA) \rightleftharpoons Ln(AA)_n$$

and

$$Ln' + n(AA) \rightleftharpoons Ln'(AA)_n$$

are established in solution. Inasmuch as the total concentration of either lanthanide in solution is the sum of the complexed and uncomplexed material, the distribution between resin and solution (for Ln as typical) is modified to

$$\lambda = c_{Ln(r)} / (c_{Ln(aq)} + c_{Ln(AA)_n(aq)}) \tag{4.8}$$

The expression for the formation constant for the chelated species (Eq. 3.1, p. 55) can be solved to give

$$c_{Ln(AA)_n(aq)} = K_{Ln(AA)_n} c_{Ln(aq)} c^n_{AA(aq)} \tag{4.9}$$

which upon substitution in Eq. 4.8 yields

$$\lambda = c_{Ln(r)} / c_{Ln(aq)} (1 + K_{Ln(AA)_n} c^n_{AA(aq)}) \tag{4.10}$$

Then substitution of the relationship in Eq. 4.4 gives

$$\lambda = \lambda_0 / (1 + K_{Ln(AA)_n} c^n_{AA(aq)}) \tag{4.11}$$

which, if the formation constant is sufficiently large, reduces to

$$\lambda = \lambda_0 / K_{Ln(AA)_n} c^n_{AA(aq)} \tag{4.12}$$

Equation 4.12 indicates how distribution between resin and solution phases is affected by the stability of the complex species. Quite obviously, the behavior of Ln′ would be similarly described in terms of $K'_{Ln'(AA)_n}$.

Under these circumstances, we may then define a new separation factor as

$$\alpha = \lambda'/\lambda \qquad (4.13)$$

which in terms of Eq. 4.12 and its equivalent for Ln′ and simplification becomes

$$\alpha = \lambda'_0 K_{Ln(AA)_n}/\lambda_0 K'_{Ln'(AA)_n} \qquad (4.14)$$

Thus if the chelating agent gives complex species of different stability with two (or more) cations, the ability of a resin to separate these ions is markedly enhanced. The feasibility of separating the lanthanides in this way is apparent from the trends in stability of complex species already discussed (pp. 57, 60).

These considerations are simplest when but a single complex species formed as a result of reaction of the cation with the ligand in a 1:1 mole ratio results. Although this is generally true of the amine polycarboxylates (pp. 57, 60), it is not true of the citrates, where several compositions, depending upon pH, are possible. It is assumed in these discussions, of course, that the chelated species are of sufficient stability that the concentration of an uncomplexed cation in solution is negligible in comparison with that of the complex species and that the pH is sufficiently high that equilibria of the type

$$Ln(AA)_n^{m-} + H^+ \rightleftharpoons HLn(AA)_n^{(m-)+1}$$

can be neglected.

Elution of adsorbed ions thus involves the successive steps of removal from the resin as the complexed species and redeposition from that species further down the column. Inasmuch as both equilibria are controlled by the stability of the chelated species, separation of the cations into individual bands ultimately occurs. The ideal requirements that each band be sharply defined and that overlap between adjacent bands be minimized necessitate rapid and essentially complete constraining reactions at

a. The front of the band, where the *retaining ion* on the unused exchanger must permit redeposition of the Ln^{3+} ion from solution and simultaneous removal of the chelating agent in soluble form. The retaining ion may be hydrogen ion or a metal ion that gives more stable chelated species than the lanthanides (p. 57).

b. The rear of the band, where the complexing agent must remove the lanthanides from the exchanger.

2. *Macro Separations by Ion Exchange.* Adaptation of these techniques to a macro scale was due largely to the work of F. H. Spedding, J. E. Powell, and their collaborators at the Iowa State University laboratories. It was found that the 5% ammonium citrate system at pH 2.5–3.2 which proved effective on a tracer scale so spread each lanthanide throughout a macro column that extensive overlapping of the characteristic bell-shaped elution curves (Fig. 4.2) could be avoided only by excessive increase in column length. Use of 0.1% ammonium citrate at pH 5.0–8.0, where only the species $[Ln(cit)_2]^{3-}$ is significant, however, effected rapid separation with the development of sharply defined rectangular bands of minimum overlap (Fig. 4.3). Both constraining reactions were rapid and complete, and hydrogen ion proved to be a suitable retaining ion. This system was used to separate kilogram quantities of lanthanides of better than 99.99% purity, but its low total capacity renders it commercially unattractive.

Experimental observations that the aminepolycarboxylates give over wide pH ranges 1:1 chelates of both greater stability and larger differences in stability between adjacent lantha-

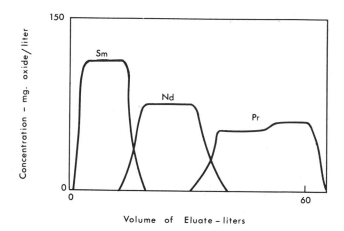

Fig. 4.3. Macro-scale elution with 0.1% citrate at pH 5.30. (Redrawn from Spedding, F. H., Fulmer, E. I., Powell, J. E., and Butler, T. A., *J. Am. Chem. Soc.* **72,** 2354 (1950).)

nides (Table 3.11) and are useful at larger concentrations directed attention to these reagents. All of the early investigations and much of the current practice have involved ethylenediaminetetraacetate (p. 56). For this chelating agent, an average separation factor of 2.38 for adjacent lanthanides is observed.

Initially it was shown that when a binary mixture (e.g., Nd^{3+} and Er^{3+}) was treated with insufficient ethylenediaminetetraacetate to tie up all the ions and then passed through an ammonium-cycle exchanger, the more basic cation (Nd^{3+}) was retained, and the less basic (Er^{3+}) passed through. This *differential filter* behavior of the exchanger resulted in gross separations but direct substitution of ethylenediaminetetraacetate for citrate in elution procedures involving hydrogen ion as a retaining species resulted in precipitation of the free acid H_4EDTA and certain of the hydrogen chelates $H[Ln(EDTA)] \cdot xH_2O$. However, use of a suitable metal ion as a retainer obviates this problem. Copper(II) ion has been used most successfully. It does not yield precipitates under optimum pH conditions, and it elutes with the Yb^{3+} and Lu^{3+} ions. The latter is a consequence of the fact that although the formation constant of the copper(II)–EDTA chelate is less than that of the erbium chelate, the more highly charged lanthanides are held more tenaciously by the exchanger. The lanthanides separate in the order of their formation constants (Table 3.11), with yttrium appearing between terbium and dysprosium.

Data for a typical Cu^{2+}–$EDTA^{4-}$ system are summarized in Table 4.4. In practice, columns several feet in diameter and many feet in height and with capacities of hundreds of pounds are used routinely by all large-scale producers.

Other chelating agents may be used to advantage. Both the acids H_3HEDTA and H_5DTPA (Table 3.10) permit the rapid recovery of yttrium by concentrating this element with

TABLE 4.4. Ion Exchange Separation of Neodymium from Praseodymium with EDTA and Cu^{2+} Retaining Ion at pH 7.97[*]

Sample		Ln_2O_3 recovered, g.	Pr_6O_{11}, %	Nd_2O_3, %
Original		11.6194	50	50
Fraction	1	0.4126	<0.08	>99.9
	2	0.9584	<0.08	>99.9
	3	0.9519	<0.08	>99.9
	4	0.9867	<0.08	>99.9
	5	0.9575	<0.08	>99.9
	6	0.9453	11	88
	7	0.9400	64	34
	8	0.9283	96	4
	9	0.9213	>99.9	0.1
	10	0.9156	>99.9	<0.06
	11	0.9122	>99.9	<0.06
	12	0.9167	>99.9	<0.06
	13	0.6265	>99.9	<0.06

[*] Data from Spedding, F. H., Powell, J. E., and Wheelwright, E. J., *J. Am. Chem. Soc.* **76,** 2557 (1954)

the cerium group. Inasmuch as neither reagent is precipitated by acid, the proton is a useful retaining ion in these systems. The α-hydroxycarboxylates (lactate, hydroxybutyrate) are also efficient for macro separations. The reagent H_4DCTA is similar to H_4EDTA, but the enhanced stabilities of its chelates increase the time necessary for separations. Increased temperatures result in more rapid separations.

3. *Anion Exchange.* At the present, this approach is useful only for the removal of thorium (p. 73).

Solvent Extraction. The pioneering work of W. Fischer and his associates at Hannover (reported in 1937) showing small differences in distribution of the trichlorides between water and partially miscible alcohols, ketones, or ethers gave little promise for easy separations but established a foundation for future success. Highly significant was J. C. Warf's observation (1949) that cerium(IV) can be readily and completely separated from the tripositive cations by extraction from an aqueous nitric acid solution into tri-*n*-butyl phosphate (p. 73). The importance of this type of system for the separation of the tripositive species from each other was first emphasized in 1953 by D. F. Peppard and his collaborators at the Argonne National Laboratory. This was followed in the same year by the isolation of the "first kilogram" of pure gadolinium by B. Weaver and his co-workers at the Oak Ridge National Laboratory using the same procedure. Subsequently the method has been used on both tracer and macro scales.

1. *Tri-n-butyl Phosphate Extractions.* It is generally agreed that in nitrate medium, where extractions with tri-*n*-butyl phosphate (TBP) are most effective, an equilibrium of the type

$$Ln^{3+}(aq) + 3NO_3^-(aq) + 3TBP(org) \rightleftharpoons$$
$$Ln(NO_3)_3(TBP)_3(org)$$

where (org) represents the nonaqueous phase, is established. Distribution between the two phases is then described as

$$\lambda = c_{Ln(NO_3)_3(TBP)_3(org)} / c_{Ln^{3+}(aq)} \qquad (4.15)$$

and for two lanthanides, the separation factor becomes

$$\alpha = \lambda' / \lambda$$
$$= c_{Ln'(NO_3)_3(TBP)_3(org)} c_{Ln^{3+}(aq)} / c_{Ln(NO_3)_3(TBP)_3(org)} c_{Ln'^{3+}(aq)} \qquad (4.16)$$

Peppard reported an average separation factor of ca. 1.5 for adjacent lanthanides for $15.8M$ nitric acid–100% TBP systems.

Such a distribution equilibrium is described as

$$K = c_{Ln(NO_3)_3(TBP)_3(org)} / c_{Ln^{3+}(aq)} c^3_{NO_3^-(aq)} c^3_{TBP(org)} \qquad (4.17)$$

Combination of this expression with Eq. 4.15 and simplification gives

$$\lambda = K c^3_{NO_3^-(aq)} c^3_{TBP(org)} \qquad (4.18)$$

If this equilibrium is the correct one, a plot of $\log_{10}\lambda$ vs. $c_{NO_3^-}$ at constant c_{TBP} should be a straight line with slope 3. That this is indeed the case above nitric acid concentrations of ca. $10M$ is shown in Fig. 4.4. This figure also indicates that, as we might expect, extent of extraction increases with decreasing crystal radius. Yttrium appears at $Z = 67$–68. The regularity is such that Eq. 4.16 can be reduced to

$$\log_{10}\lambda = Z \log \alpha + \text{constant} \qquad (4.19)$$

2. *Di(2-ethylhexyl)phosphoric Acid Extractions.* This reagent is both more resistant to hydrolytic decomposition in contact with aqueous nitric acid than TBP and a more efficient extractant. An average separation factor of 2.5 for adjacent lanthanides has been reported.

Esters of this type (HDGP) exist as dimers in the non-aqueous phase. Extraction apparently involves the equilibrium

$$Ln^{3+}(aq) + 3(HDGP)_2(org) \rightleftharpoons$$
$$Ln[H(DGP)_2]_3(org) + 3H^+(aq)$$

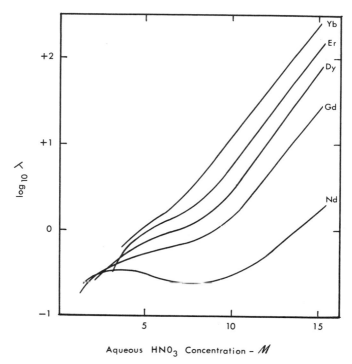

Aqueous HNO₃ Concentration – M

Fig. 4.4. Extraction of tripositive ions with 100% TBP.   (Redrawn in part from Hesford, E., Jackson, E. E., and McKay, H. A. C., *J. Inorg. Nucl. Chem.* **9,** 279 (1950).)

from which a distribution ratio

$$\lambda \; = \; K c^3_{(\mathrm{HDGP})_2(\mathrm{org})} \big/ c^3_{\mathrm{H}^+(\mathrm{aq})} \qquad (4.20)$$

can be derived.   The experimentally determined distribution ratio for a given lanthanide does indeed depend upon $c^3_{(\mathrm{HDGP})_2(\mathrm{org})}$ and $1/c^3_{\mathrm{H}^+(\mathrm{aq})}$. It is believed that esters of this type form chelates in which units of the type

$$\begin{array}{c} \text{RO} \\ \text{RO} \end{array} \text{P} \begin{array}{c} \text{O--H--O} \\ \text{O} \end{array} \text{P} \begin{array}{c} \text{OR} \\ \text{OR} \end{array}$$

$$\text{Ln/3}$$

where R is an alkyl group, exist.

3. *Other Extractions.* Less success has been achieved with monoalkylphosphoric acids, $RP(O)(OH)_2$; pyrophosphate esters, $(RO)_2 P(O)—O—P(O)(OR)_2$; phosphonates, $(RO)_2(R)PO$ and $(RO)(R)P(O)(OH)$; 1,3-diketones; or 8-quinolinols. Amines (p. 71) are not useful.

4. *Present Status of Solvent Extraction.* Although solvent extraction is promising as a general method and lends itself to continuous operation with a minimum of attention, it is not yet competitive with ion exchange as a general method for separation. Its major uses are in the purification of cerium (p. 73), thorium (p. 71), and lanthanum. Lanthanum is somewhat less readily extracted than the other tripositive ions and can thus be freed from them rather readily. Scandium is easily separated and purified by solvent extraction with tri-*n*-butyl phosphate or diethyl ether.

Selective Oxidation or Reduction. Previous discussions of the nontripositive oxidation states (pp. 17–19, 43–46, 60–66, 80) have provided sufficient information so that only a few additional comments are necessary. Inasmuch as change of oxidation state is accompanied by a profound change in properties, selective oxidation or reduction provides a remarkably clean and efficient way of separating specific lanthanides.

1. *Oxidation to the Tetrapositive State.* Practical separations are limited to the removal of cerium after oxidation (p. 73).

2. *Reduction to the Dipositive State.* Only the reduction of europium(III) with zinc, followed by its recovery as the divalent sulfate or chloride, is useful. In practice, it is possible to recover europium from mixtures containing only trace

quantities by adding zinc dust, barium chloride, and sulfuric acid and oxidizing the mixed barium–europium(II) sulfate precipitate (procedure of· H. N. McCoy). This is often a better approach than ion exchange.

3. *Reduction to Amalgams.* Europium, samarium, and ytterbium are readily removed from mixtures either by extracting a buffered acidic solution with liquid sodium amalgam (J. K. Marsh) or by electrolyzing an alkaline citrate solution with a lithium amalgam cathode (E. I. Onstott). Other lanthanides can be separated less readily in this way. The sodium amalgam procedure is convenient·and rapid; the electrolytic one can be operated continuously and on a large scale. Modification of each permits separation of the individual elements.

Physical Methods. Differences in volatility of the anhydrous halides at elevated temperature, in speed of ionic migration in solution, in thermal or other types of diffusion in solution, or in attraction by a strong magnetic field have all been suggested as bases for separation. None of these has proved practical, although the first is promising.

Applications of the Lanthanides

Quite arbitrarily, these may be classified as (1) metals and alloys, (2) nonnuclear uses of compounds, and (3) nuclear applications.

Metals and Alloys. Roughly one-fourth of the production of lanthanides is used in this way. The pure metals have little use in their own right, but alloys (known as mischmetals) containing predominantly cerium (30–50%), together with smaller quantities of the other cerium group metals·and non-lanthanide impurities,* have sufficiently strong reducing power for metallurgical applications. Mischmetal is an excellent scavenger for oxygen or sulfur in many metal systems.

---

* A typical mischmetal contains 45–50% Ce, 22–25% La, 18% Nd, 5% Pr, 1% Sm, and smaller amounts of other lanthanides.

Magnesium alloys containing ca. 3% mischmetal and 1% zirconium have sufficiently high strength and creep resistance at 450–600°F. to be useful in jet engine parts. Mischmetal imparts high-temperature strength to aluminum, oxidation resistance to nickel alloys, hardness to copper, and workability to stainless steel and vanadium. When alloyed with ca. 30% iron, it is sufficiently pyrophoric to be useful in lighter flints. Both mischmetal and yttrium have a marked nodulizing effect upon graphite and thus enhance the malleability of cast iron.

Compounds—Nonnuclear Applications. Ceramic and related applications consume about one-fourth of the lanthanides produced. Another fourth, as fluorides, appears in cored carbons for improvement of intensity and color balance in arc lights.

1. *Ceramic Applications.* These include cerium(IV) oxide and cerium-rich (> 40% CeO_2) oxide mixtures as highly efficient glass-polishing compositions; neodymium and praseodymium oxides as coloring agents for glass and in the production of standard filters (p. 32); lanthanum oxide in the preparation of low-dispersion, high-refraction optical glass; cerium(IV) oxide to improve the stability and discoloration resistance of glass to gamma or electron-beam radiation; cerium(IV) and neodymium oxides to counteract the iron(II)-produced green in glass; ca. 3% praseodymium oxide in combination with zirconium(IV) oxide to give a yellow ceramic glaze; and cerium(IV) oxide to opacify in enamels. The high melting points of the oxides, certain sulfides (e.g., CeS), borides, carbides, and nitrides suggest their use as refractories, although at least some of these are reactive at high temperatures.

2. *Catalytic Applications.* Known uses of these compounds as catalysts include the oxides in the hydrogenation, dehydrogenation, and oxidation of various organic compounds;

the anhydrous chlorides in polyesterification processes; and the chlorides and cerium phosphate in petroleum cracking. In the sense that heterogeneous catalysts are commonly characterized by unpaired electrons, paramagnetism, defect structures, or variability in oxidation state, catalysis is a promising practical area.

3. *Magnetic and Electronic Applications.* Industry has been slow in taking advantage of the para- and ferromagnetic properties of the lanthanides. The low electrical and eddy-current losses of the ferrimagnetic garnets, $3Ln_2O_3 \cdot 5Fe_2O_3$, make these substances useful in microwave devices and as magnetic core materials. The yttrium compound (so-called "yig") is particularly important. Certain compounds (e.g., selenides, tellurides) are of potential interest as semiconductors or thermoelectrics. The titanates and stannates, as a consequence of large dielectric constants and small temperature coefficients of capacitance, are useful ceramic capacitors.

Nuclear Applications. These include actual and potential uses of high-cross-section metals or compounds (p. 37) in control, shielding, and flux-suppressing devices; of hydrides (especially of yttrium) as hydrogen-moderator carriers; of oxides as diluents in nuclear fuels; of metals for structural components (e.g., yttrium pipe that is not attacked by molten 5% Cr–95% U at 1000°C.) or structural-alloy-modifying components (e.g., scavengers) of reactors; of coprecipitants of fission-product poisons (e.g., high-cross-section [149]Sm) in molten fluoride fuels; and of suitably irradiated materials as portable X-ray sources (e.g., Tm) or as radiation sources (e.g., Eu).

The Possibilities. Extensive uses of the lanthanides have always been limited by commercial scarcity and high cost. The problems of availability have not been solved completely, but they have been reduced substantially. Costs have decreased almost exponentially since the development of ion exchange techniques. As continuing research reveals new and unique potentialities, costs may be expected to decrease until ultimately they will reach levels where the lanthanides can become competitive with some of the more common elements.

And Now, What Remains?

Thus we conclude our treatment of the chemistry of the lanthanides. If, in presenting this account, we have both answered some of your questions about this interesting series of elements and simultaneously raised some additional ones in your mind, we shall consider our efforts useful. One task remains—to clarify some of our allusions to the actinides as another series of closely related elements, the chemistry of which has rendered that of the lanthanides no longer completely unique. This we do, but with apologies for necessary brevity, in the next chapter.

Selected Readings

Kremers, H. E., "Rare Metals Handbook," C. A. Hampel, Ed., ch. 19, Reinhold Publishing Corp., New York, 1961. (Technology, applications.)

Little, H. F. V., "A Text-book of Inorganic Chemistry," J. N. Friend, Ed., Vol. IV., 2nd ed., ch. X, Charles Griffin and Co., London, 1921. (Occurrence, recovery, classical separations.)

Spedding, F. H., and Daane, A. H., Eds., "The Rare Earths," John Wiley & Sons, New York, 1961. (Fractional crystallization, ch. 3; solvent extraction, ch. 4; ion exchange, ch. 5; applications, chs. 19–22; analysis, chs. 23, 24.)

Vickery, R. C., "Chemistry of the Lanthanons," Academic Press, New York, 1953. (Occurrence, recovery, separations, uses.)

Vickery, R. C., "Analytical Chemistry of the Rare Earths," Pergamon Press, London, 1961.

Yost, D. M., Russell, H., Jr., and Garner, C. S., "The Rare-Earth Elements and Their Compounds," ch. 5, John Wiley & Sons, New York, 1947. (Separations.)

chapter five

THE ACTINIDES—
A RELATED SERIES FOR
SCIENTIFIC PIONEERING

Prior to 1940, there was apparently every reason to believe that electronic configurations based upon f orbitals were unique to the lanthanides. No element heavier than uranium had been positively identified, and the properties of the heaviest of the known elements (Ac, Th, Pa, U) seemed to resemble those of the d-type transition metals of Periodic Groups IIIb–VIb (i.e., La, Hf, Ta, W) sufficiently to permit classification in these groups. Although it is true that some apparent anomalies in magnetic and spectroscopic properties, particularly of uranium compounds, had prompted theoretical speculation as to the possible existence of a second lanthanide-type, or $5f$, series, experimental support was lacking. Indeed, what seemed to be the only support of this type—namely, the postulation by E. Fermi that the multiplicity of β^- activities obtained when uranium is bombarded with slow neutrons indicates the formation of transuranium species—vanished when, in 1939, O. Hahn and F. Strassmann associated these activities with well-known lighter elements produced by neutron-induced fission.

In 1940, E. M. McMillan and P. Abelson proved conclusively that a nuclide with a half-life of 2.3 days, which remained in natural uranium after fission of the 235 isotope, was not a lanthanide. Rather, it was a new species resembling the lanthanides in a lower oxidation state and uranium (as UO_2^{2+} ion) in a higher state but differing significantly from each. This was neptunium (from the planet Neptune), the first of the true transuranium elements, formed as a consequence of the reaction sequence[*]

$$^{238}_{92}U + ^1_0n \longrightarrow ^{239}_{92}U + \gamma$$

$$^{239}_{92}U \underset{23 \text{ min.}}{\longrightarrow} ^{239}_{93}Np + \beta^-$$

The discovery of plutonium (from Pluto) by G. T. Seaborg, E. M. McMillan, J. W. Kennedy, and A. C. Wahl later in 1940 as a result of the sequence

$$^{238}_{92}U(d, 2n)\,^{238}_{93}Np \xrightarrow[2.1 \text{ days}]{-\beta^-} ^{238}_{94}Pu$$

and the subsequent identification of the important 239 isotope in 1941 by the same group in collaboration with E. Segrè as the decay product of neptunium-239 laid the basis for work that has now given us elements with atomic numbers through 103 (Lw). Much of this work was done at the University of California under the able direction of G. T. Seaborg.

---

[*] These nuclear reactions are described more concisely by the notation

$$^{238}_{92}U(n,\gamma)\,^{239}_{92}U \xrightarrow[23 \text{ min.}]{-\beta^-} ^{239}_{93}Np$$

The Actinide Hypothesis

Intensive chemical studies involving both the newly isolated transuranium species and the elements Ac–U revealed many similarities to the lanthanides, similarities that had not been previously suspected in the actinium–uranium region and similarities that became increasingly striking with increase in atomic number. Indeed, among the heavier species, these were sufficient that the known chemistry of the lanthanides proved invaluable in predicting behaviors and reactions. With the addition of evidence from magnetic and spectroscopic data for the presence of f electrons, Seaborg was prompted to postulate that the elements following actinium are members of a second inner or f-type transition series, a so-called *actinide* series.

The significance of this postulation is indicated by the ease with which it brought order into this developing chemistry and permitted the correlation of both chemical and physical data. Its weakness and major point of criticism are merely that implied similarities to the lanthanides are not always exact. Prominent among observed differences is the tendency of the actinides to show a greater multiplicity of oxidation states with perhaps a greater over-all preference for the tetrapositive state over the tripositive. As was shown for the lanthanides (pp. 17, 19), however, the existence of a particular and common oxidation state of any magnitude is a consequence of an appropriate combination of properties and is in no way as important as similarities and differences in data that reflect electronic arrangements.

For our purposes, it is sufficient to know that the heavy elements do resemble the lanthanides very closely and to explore these similarities in terms of the principles and observations we have developed for the lanthanides. Our exploration can thus be handled more logically on a general basis than as a highly detailed discussion.

Electronic Configurations

The difficulties encountered in assigning ground-state configurations to the lanthanides are even more acute with the actinides. Furthermore, the increasing nuclear instability of the latter with increasing atomic number seriously limits experimental studies. The configurations summarized in Table 5.1 are considered to be the most probable in terms of presently available data. Comparison of these with the corresponding ones for the lanthanides (Table 2.1) shows both a substantial over-all similarity and an enhanced tendency for the lighter members (Ac–Np) to retain d electrons. The latter tendency results both from the even smaller energy separation between the $6d$ and $5f$ orbitals than that already mentioned for the $5d$ and $4f$ orbitals and from the difference in change in binding energy of the most readily removable $6d$ and $5f$ electrons with atomic number, as shown qualitatively in Fig. 5.1. Where the series starts is thus somewhat of an academic question.

The configurations associated with the various oxidation states, as was true with the lanthanides (Table 2.2), show a generally greater regularity. There is a discernible preference for the $5f^0$ and $5f^7$ configurations (compare p. 19). Again, constancy of a given state is less closely related to electronic configuration than to ionization energy, hydration energy, and lattice energy (p. 18), but the more extensive spatial projection of the $5f$ orbitals into the "outer" or valence regions of these atoms reduces the shielding of these electrons, renders them easier to remove, and increases the number of observed oxidation states. The relative stabilities of these states in aqueous solution, where known, are shown by the oxidation potential data in Table 5.2.

TABLE 5.1. Electronic Configurations of the Actinides

Atomic number	Element Name	Symbol	Configuration in oxidation state 0	+3	+4	+5	+6
89	Actinium	Ac	$6d^1 7s^2$	$5f^0$			
90	Thorium	Th	$6d^2 7s^2$	—	$5f^0$		
91	Protactinium	Pa	$5f^2 6d^1 7s^2$	—	$5f^1$	$5f^0$	
92	Uranium	U	$5f^3 6d^1 7s^2$	$5f^3$	$5f^2$	$5f^1$	$5f^0$
93	Neptunium	Np	$5f^4 6d^1 7s^2$	$5f^4$	$5f^3$	$5f^2$	$5f^1$
94	Plutonium	Pu	$5f^5 7s^2$	$5f^5$	$5f^4$	$5f^3$	$5f^2$
95	Americium	Am	$5f^7 7s^2$	$5f^6$	$5f^5$	$5f^4$	$5f^3$
96	Curium	Cm	$5f^7 6d^1 7s^2$	$5f^7$	$5f^6$		
97	Berkelium	Bk	$5f^9 7s^2$	$5f^8$			
98	Californium	Cf	$5f^{10} 7s^2$	$5f^9$			
99	Einsteinium	Es	$5f^{11} 7s^2$	$5f^{10}$			
100	Fermium	Fm	$5f^{12} 7s^2$	$5f^{11}$			
101	Mendelevium*	Md	$5f^{13} 7s^2$	$5f^{12}$			
102	Nobelium*	No	$5f^{14} 7s^2$	$5f^{13}$			
103	Lawrencium	Lw	$5f^{14} 6d^1 7s^2$	$5f^{14}$			

* Name not yet completely accepted.

100

TABLE 5.2. Some Characteristics of Ionic Species

	Oxidation-reduction in acidic media		Crystal radius, Å		Light absorption in aqueous solution		
Symbol	Couple	E°_{298} * v.	+3	+4	Ion	Color	Wave length, Å
Ac	Ac^0-Ac^{3+}	(2.6)	1.11		Ac^{3+}	Colorless	None
Th	Th^0-Th^{4+}	1.90	(1.08)	0.99	Th^{4+}	Colorless	None
Pa	$Pa^0-PaO_2^+$	(1.0)	(1.05)	0.96	Pa^{4+}	Colorless	2240, 2550, 2760
U	U^0-U^{3+}	.80	1.03	0.93	U^{3+}	Reddish	5200, 8800, 9000
	$U^{3+}-U^{4+}$	0.631			U^{4+}	Green	5500, 6500
	$U^{4+}-UO_2^+$	-0.58			UO_2^{2+}	Yellow	4000, 4110, 4250
	$UO_2^+-UO_2^{2+}$	-0.063					
Np	Np^0-Np^{3+}	1.83	1.01	0.92	Np^{3+}	Violet	5520, 6610, 7875
	$Np^{3+}-Np^{4+}$	-0.155			Np^{4+}	Yellow-green	5040, 7430, 8250
	$Np^{4+}-NpO_2^+$	-0.739			NpO_2^{2+}	Pink	4760, 5570
	$NpO_2^+-NpO_2^{2+}$	-1.137					
Pu	Pu^0-Pu^{3+}	2.03	1.00	0.90	Pu^{3+}	Deep blue	5600, 6000, 6030
	$Pu^{3+}-Pu^{4+}$	-0.982			Pu^{4+}	Tan	4700, 6550, 8150
	$Pu^{4+}-PuO_2^+$	-1.172			PuO_2^{2+}	Yellow-orange	8330, 9530, 9830
	$PuO_2^+-PuO_2^{2+}$	-0.913					
Am	Am^0-Am^{3+}	2.32	0.99	0.89	Am^{3+}	Pink	5027, 8200
	$Am^{3+}-AmO_2^+$	-1.74			AmO_2^+	Yellow	5131, 7151
	$AmO_2^+-AmO_2^{2+}$	-1.60			AmO_2^{2+}	Brownish	6660, 9950
Cm	—	—	—	—	Cm^{3+}	Colorless	2368, 2680, 2774

* Estimated values in parentheses.

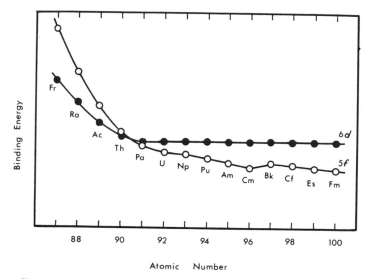

Fig. 5.1. Qualitative comparison of binding energies of 5f and 6d electrons. (Redrawn from Katz, J. J., and Seaborg, G. T., *The Chemistry of the Actinide Elements*, p. 465, Metheun, London, 1957.)

Magnetic and Light Absorption Characteristics

It is apparent from Fig. 5.2 that the magnetic effects resulting from unpaired 5f electrons are closely comparable to those associated with the 4f electrons in the lanthanides (p. 27). It is thus reasonable to conclude that the origins of these effects are similar. It must be pointed out, however, that not all data for the actinides show this parallel and that those used in constructing Fig. 5.2 have been selected rather deliberately. Decrease in the shielding of the 5f electrons makes these electrons more susceptible to enviromental influences than the 4f electrons (p. 28) and thus eliminates the constancy of moment for a given oxidation state that characterizes the lanthanides.

Parallels in the influence of f electrons upon light absorption

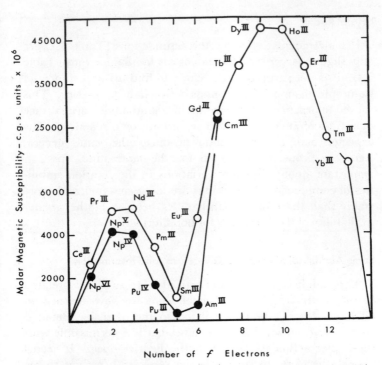

Fig. 5.2. Comparison of magnetic susceptibilities of lanthanide and actinide species. (Redrawn from Katz and Seaborg, *op. cit.*, p. 447.)

are apparent from a comparison of the data on actinide species (Table 5.2) with those for the lanthanides (Table 2.7). Species with the same number of f electrons often have roughly comparable spectra, e.g., Ce^{3+} and Pa^{4+} (f^1), Nd^{3+} and U^{3+} (f^3), Gd^{3+} and Cm^{3+} (f^7). In a number of instances, the absorption peaks of the actinides are even more sharply defined than those of the lanthanides. However, as is true of magnetic moments, light absorption is much more affected by environment than with the lanthanides.

Crystal Radius

In a given oxidation state, the actinide ions (Table 5.2) are only slightly larger than the analogous lanthanide ions (Table 2.4). It is not surprising, therefore, to find many instances of isomorphism among compounds between the two series. This is used to practical advantage when a lanthanide carries trace quantities of an actinide in a separation or a reaction. The expected actinide contraction produces the same general trends in properties as noted for the lanthanides (p. 24). Important among these are variations in the solution stabilities of complex ions. Such ions are more common and more stable than those of the lanthanides because of the· greater availability of the 5*f* orbitals for bond formation.

Some Additional Similarities, Differences, and Information

Although it is true that the actinides are so closely related to the lanthanides that much of what we have learned in Chapters 2–4 can be extrapolated to the 5*f* series, detailed studies have shown this to be somewhat less permissible with the lighter actinides than with the heavier ones. It seems logical, therefore, to subdivide the series rather than to attempt an all-inclusive discussion in presenting our concluding comments. This approach derives support also from the fact that only the elements Ac–U occur in nature in sufficient quantity to permit their recovery in ponderable amounts. Although both neptunium and plutonium (in particular) are undeniably present in uranium minerals as a result of natural fission processes, what we know about the transuranium elements is based entirely upon synthetically produced materials. As a prelude to the summary that follows, comparison of the numerical data in Table 5.3 with comparable data for the lanthanides (Table 3.1) will be useful.

TABLE 5.3. Numerical Constants of the Actinides

Symbol	Atomic weight*	Natural isotopes	Density,† g./cm.³	Melting point, °C.	Boiling point (approx.), °C.
Ac	(227)	227, 228	—	1050	—
Th	232.038	227, 228, 230, 231, 232, 234	11.72	1750	3500–4200
Pa	(231)	231, 234	15.37	—	—
U	238.04	234, 235, 238	19.04	1132	3818
Np	(237)	239	19.5	640	—
Pu	(242)	239	19.82	639.5	3235
Am	(243)	None	11.7	1100	—
Cm	(247)	None	⁻7	—	—
Bk	(247)	None	—	—	—
Cf	(251)	None	—	—	—
Es	(254)	None	—	—	—
Fm	(253)	None	—	—	—
Md	(256)	None	—	—	—
No	(254)	None	—	—	—
Lw	—	None	—	—	—

* Longest-lived isotope in parentheses; others based upon $^{12}C = 12.0000$.
† Of stable modification at room temperature.

The Actinium–Uranium Elements.   The natural abundances of these elements in the igneous rocks of the crust of the earth (Ac, $3 \times 10^{-14}\%$; Th, $1.15 \times 10^{-3}\%$; Pa, $8 \times 10^{-11}\%$; U, $4 \times 10^{-4}\%$) indicate that although thorium and uranium compare in potential availability with such elements as zinc, arsenic, or tungsten, actinium and protactinium are among our scarcest elements. All known isotopes of these elements are radioactive. It is only because the half-lives of their important natural isotopes ($^{232}_{90}Th$, $^{235}_{92}U$, $^{238}_{92}U$) are of the same order of magnitude as the age of the earth (p. 9) that thorium and uranium have persisted to the present. The half-lives of even the most stable actinium ($^{227}_{89}Ac$, 22 years) and protactinium ($^{231}_{91}Pa$, 3.4×10^4 years) isotopes are so short, however, that these elements exist only because they are continuously regenerated as members of the uranium-235 decay series.

The occurrence and recovery of thorium have been discussed (pp. 69, 71). Uranium materials are concentrated from the pitchblendes (U_3O_8, found in Central Africa, Canada, Soviet Russia) and carnotites ($KUO_2VO_4 \cdot 1.5H_2O$, found in the southwestern United States) and separated by solvent extraction or precipitation (commonly as $(NH_4)_2U_2O_7$). Final purification is by solvent extraction. Inasmuch as only minute quantities of actinium or protactinium can be obtained from uranium minerals or process residues, these elements are more conveniently obtained (in gram quantities) as products of the reaction sequences

$$^{226}_{88}Ra(n, \gamma)\,^{227}_{88}Ra \xrightarrow[41.2\ min.]{-\beta^-} \,^{227}_{89}Ac$$

and

$$^{230}_{90}Th(n, \gamma)\,^{231}_{90}Th \xrightarrow[25.6\ hr.]{-\beta^-} \,^{231}_{91}Pa$$

The metals are obtained by the same techniques used for the lanthanides (pp. 41–43). Except that their crystal structures are more complex and that in chemical reactions they yield a greater variety of oxidation states (Tables 5.2 and 5.3), the actinide metals are closely comparable to the lanthanide metals. Actinium is almost indistinguishable from lanthanum in its reactions and those of its ions, and thorium is very similar to cerium (p. 73). Protactinium, however, resembles the lanthanides closely only in its lower and less stable oxidation states. In the common +5 state, its chemistry is not markedly different from that of tantalum. Uranium(III) and uranium(IV) resemble, respectively, the tripositive lanthanides and tetrapositive cerium or thorium, except, of course, in the ease with which they are oxidized. The common uranium(VI) species is the linear uranyl, UO_2^{2+}, ion. This mildly oxidizing and readily complexed species has no parallel except with the comparable transuranium species NpO_2^{2+}, PuO_2^{2+}, AmO_2^{2+}.

Actinium and protactinium are too scarce to be of practical importance. Both thorium and uranium are useful in fission reactors. Nonnuclear applications include thorium in magnesium alloys and in gas-discharge and high-intensity lamps; thorium dioxide in high-emissivity cathodes and refractories; uranium in X-ray and vacuum tubes; and uranium compounds in pigments.

The Transuranium Elements. Typical nuclear reactions for the syntheses of these elements are summarized in Table 5.4.

TABLE 5.4.   Nuclear Syntheses of Transuranium Elements

Symbol	Atomic number	Mass number	Reaction
Np	93	239	$^{238}_{92}\text{U}(n,\gamma)\,^{239}_{92}\text{U} \xrightarrow[\text{23 min.}]{-\beta^-} \,^{239}_{93}\text{Np}$
Pu	94	239	$^{239}_{93}\text{Np} \xrightarrow[\text{2.33 days}]{-\beta^-} \,^{239}_{94}\text{Pu}$
Am	95	241	$^{239}_{94}\text{Pu}(n,\gamma)\,^{240}_{94}\text{Pu}(n,\gamma)\,^{241}_{94}\text{Pu} \xrightarrow[\text{13 yr.}]{-\beta^-} \,^{241}_{95}\text{Am}$
Cm	96	244	$^{241}_{94}\text{Pu}(n,\gamma)\,^{242}_{94}\text{Pu}(n,\gamma)\,^{243}_{94}\text{Pu} \xrightarrow[\text{5 hr.}]{-\beta^-} \,^{243}_{95}\text{Am}$
			$^{243}_{95}\text{Am}(n,\gamma)\,^{244}_{95}\text{Am} \xrightarrow[\text{26 min.}]{-\beta^-} \,^{244}_{96}\text{Cm}$
Bk	97	249	$^{244}_{96}\text{Cm}(n,\gamma)\,^{245}_{96}\text{Cm}(n,\gamma)\,^{246}_{96}\text{Cm}(n,\gamma)\,^{247}_{96}\text{Cm}$
			$^{247}_{96}\text{Cm}(n,\gamma)\,^{248}_{96}\text{Cm}(n,\gamma)\,^{249}_{96}\text{Cm} \xrightarrow[\text{65 min.}]{-\beta^-} \,^{249}_{97}\text{Bk}$
Cf	98	250	$^{249}_{97}\text{Bk}(n,\gamma)\,^{250}_{97}\text{Bk} \xrightarrow[\text{3.13 hr.}]{-\beta^-} \,^{250}_{98}\text{Cf}$
Es	99	253	$^{250}_{98}\text{Cf}(n,\gamma)\,^{251}_{98}\text{Cf}(n,\gamma)\,^{252}_{98}\text{Cf}$
			$^{252}_{98}\text{Cf}(n,\gamma)\,^{253}_{98}\text{Cf} \xrightarrow[\text{20 days}]{-\beta^-} \,^{253}_{99}\text{Es}$
Fm	100	254	$^{253}_{99}\text{Es}(n,\gamma)\,^{254m}_{99}\text{Es} \xrightarrow[\text{36 hr.}]{-\beta^-} \,^{254}_{100}\text{Fm}$
Md	101	256	$^{253}_{99}\text{Es}(\alpha,n)\,^{256}_{101}\text{Md}$
No	102	254	$^{246}_{96}\text{Cm}(^{12}_{6}\text{C},4n)\,^{254}_{102}\text{No}$
Lw	103	257	$^{250}_{98}\text{Cf}(^{11}_{5}\text{B},4n)\,^{257}_{103}\text{Lw}$

As a consequence of its ease of fission and reasonable half-life (24,360 years), plutonium-239 has been prepared in very large quantities. None of the others has been obtained in more than small amounts; indeed, nuclear instability increases so rapidly with increasing nuclear charge that no more than a few atoms of the heaviest elements have been synthesized, and isolation of measurable quantities has been limited to the ·Np-Cm region. As atomic number increases, the stability of the tri-positive state increases, and parallels with the lanthanides become so striking that the known properties of the latter can be used to predict quite exactly the properties of the comparable actinides. This is particularly true of the ion exchange

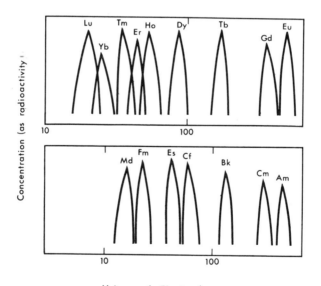

Fig. 5.3. Comparison of ion-exchange behavior of tri-positive lanthanides and actinides with α-hydroxyisobutyrate. (Redrawn from Katz and Seaborg, *op. cit.*, p. 435.)

techniques (pp. 80–88) used to isolate the species from target materials. The nature of this parallelism is shown in Fig. 5.3. Neptunium and plutonium resemble uranium closely both as metals and in their compounds. Divergence to true lanthanide behavior begins in the Am-Cm region. Applications are limited to the nuclear uses of plutonium.

In Conclusion

Thus ends our brief excursion into this fascinating area of chemistry. It is perhaps fitting to conclude by reminding the reader that the assistance in unraveling the chemistry of the actinides provided by the substantial background of information on the lanthanides is only another indication of the wisdom of applying the teachings and experiences of history to the solution of new problems.

Selected Readings

Asprey, L. B., and Cunningham, B. B., "Progress in Inorganic Chemistry," F. A. Cotton, Ed., Vol. 2, pp. 286–302. Interscience Publishers, New York, 1960. (Oxidation states.)

Cunningham, B. B., "XVIIth International Congress of Pure and Applied Chemistry," Vol. I, pp. 64–81, Butterworths, London, 1960. (Comparative chemistry of lanthanides and actinides.)

Cunningham, B. B., "Rare Earth Research," E. V. Kleber, Ed., pp. 127–34, The Macmillan Company, New York, 1961. (Comparative chemistry of lanthanides and actinides.)

Hampel, C. A., Ed., "Rare Metals Handbook," 2nd ed., Reinhold Publishing Corp., New York, 1961. (Plutonium, ch. 18; thorium, ch. 28; uranium, ch. 31.)

Katz, J. J., and Seaborg, G. T., "The Chemistry of the Actinide Elements," Methuen, London, John Wiley & Sons, New York, 1957. (Complete survey.)

Seaborg, G. T., and Katz, J. J., Eds., "The Actinide Elements," McGraw-Hill Book Company, New York, 1954. (Detailed survey.)

Weeks, M. E., "Discovery of the Elements," 6th ed., chs. 29, 31, Journal of Chemical Education, Easton, Pa., 1956. (History.)

INDEX